Inspire

YL

Christmas 2006

THE
PURSUIT OF
HAPP*y*NESS

THE PURSUIT OF HAPPYNESS

CHRIS GARDNER

with

Quincy Troupe

and

Mim Eichler Rivas

Amistad

An Imprint of HarperCollins*Publishers*

Grateful acknowledgment is made to reprint lines from "Mother to Son" from *The Collected Poems of Langston Hughes* by Langston Hughes, copyright © 1994 by The Estate of Langston Hughes. Used by permission of Alfred A. Knopf, a division of Random House, Inc.

HarperCollins books may be purchased for educational, business, or sales promotional use. For information please write: Special Markets Department, HarperCollins Publishers, 10 East 53rd Street, New York, NY 10022.

FIRST EDITION

All photos in the insert courtesy of the author unless otherwise noted.

Designed by Fearn Cutler de Vicq

Printed on acid-free paper

Library of Congress Cataloging-in-Publication Data

Gardner, Chris (Chris P.)
  The pursuit of happyness / Chris Gardner with Quincy Troupe.—1st ed.
    p. cm.
  ISBN 13: 978-0-06-074486-1
  ISBN 10: 0-06-074486-3
  1. Gardner, Chris (Chris P.)   2. Stockbrokers—United States—Biography.
  3. Gardner Rich & Co. I. Title: Pursuit of happiness. II. Troupe, Quincy. III. Title.

HG4928.5.G365 2006
323.6'2092—dc22
  [B]   2005057203

06 07 08 09 10 BG/RRD 10 9 8 7 6 5

For my mother,
Bettye Jean

Well, son, I'll tell you:
Life for me ain't been no crystal stair.

But all the time
I'se been a-climbin' on . . .

—"Mother to Son" by Langston Hughes

Contents

Acknowledgments

My mother always stressed to me that the most important words in the English language are *please* and *thank you*. With that in mind I would like to thank some of the folks that I have been blessed to have in my life and also helped me with the most challenging task of attempting to write this book.

My first thank you is to the team at Gardner Rich & Company (GRC) who allowed me the time, space, and emotional range of motion required to look back while they looked forward. I especially want to thank Collene Carlson, president of GRC, for covering my back and balls for the last twelve years.

I've got to give a shout out to my girl Lynn Redmond at ABC's *20/20*. It was Lynn's passion for a portion of my life's journey that has made so many blessings and opportunities become a reality. I've also got to thank Bob Brown of *20/20* as well. Bob took "getting into his subject's head" a bit further. Bob and I have the same barber!

Quincy Troupe once paid me a backhand compliment by telling me that I was as crazy as his previous subject, Miles Davis. I'll definitely take that as a compliment! It was Quincy who helped me open up all the doors in my mind that I had tried to keep closed.

Mim Eichler Rivas helped me to open up my soul. Quincy put down what happened—Mim put down how what happened *felt*. If there is any sense of feeling, passion, or dreams here, it is all due to Mim.

Also vital to this book was Dawn Davis of Amistad, my brilliant editor, who knows nothing about my garments and cares even less. I knew from the second that we met that she was "the one"—no doubt, never a second thought. When we met, the book she had last published was on its way to winning a Pulitzer Prize. Like I said, no doubt! And thanks to the other hardworking folks at Amistad: Rockelle Henderson, Gilda Squire, Morgan Welebir, and the production and design teams.

I am forever grateful to Will Smith. The boy is the REAL DEAL! It was to Will that I expressed any concerns during the filming of *The Pursuit of Happyness*. I continue to be amazed at his grace, humility, and talent.

The guys from Escape Artists: Todd Black, Jason Blumenthal, and Steve Tisch. Again, I knew from the very beginning that these were the guys to go with. Thank you! Thank you! Thank you!

Mark Clayman, your vision continues to astonish me. None of this could have happened without Mark's vision.

Thanks to Jennifer Gates, my agent at Zachary Schuster Harmsworth Literary Agency, for believing in me, guiding me, and allowing me to be afraid.

Nothing in this life or the next will ever mean as much to me as my two children. With a whole lot of help, they were raised into absolutely fabulous young people: my son, Christopher, and my daughter, Jacintha. My greatest blessings. Thank you for being who you are, even when I wasn't who I should've been.

To H., my love forever. Your support through the process made it all possible. To Madame Baba, my muse, thank you.

Thank you to the family that I was born into, and just as important, thank you to the family that adopted me: my father Bill Lucy; my big brother Reggie Weaver; my badass cousin Charles Ensley; my big sister Anne Davis; my "granddaddy" Rev. Cecil Williams; the godfather, the Original Big Will; my godmother Charlene Mitchell; and Willie L. Brown.

And a most heartfelt thank you to my mentor, Barbara Scott Preiskel.

Author's Note

This is a work of nonfiction. I have rendered the events faithfully and truthfully just as I have recalled them. Some names and descriptions of individuals have been changed in order to respect their privacy. To anyone whose name I did not recall or omitted, I offer sincere apologies. While circumstances and conversations depicted herein come from my keen recollection of them, they are not meant to represent precise time lines of events or exact word-for-word reenactments of my life. They are told in a way that evokes the real feeling and meaning of what was said and my view of what happened to me, in keeping with the true essence of the mood and spirit of those moments that shaped my life.

THE
PURSUIT OF
HAPP*Y*NESS

Go Forward

Whenever I'm asked what exactly it was that helped guide me through my darkest days not only to survive but to move past those circumstances and to ultimately attain a level of success and fulfillment that once sounded impossible, what comes to mind are two events.

One of them took place in the early 1980s, when I was twenty-seven years old, on an unusually hot, sunny day in the Bay Area. In the terminally overcrowded parking lot outside of San Francisco General Hospital, just as I exited the building, a flash of the sun's glare temporarily blocked my vision. As I refocused, what I saw changed the world as I knew it. At any other point in my life it wouldn't have struck me so powerfully, but there was something about that moment in time and the gorgeous, red convertible Ferrari 308 that I saw slowly circling the lot—driven by a guy obviously in search of a parking spot—that compelled me to go and have a life-changing conversation with him.

Some years before, fresh out of the Navy, I had first arrived in San Francisco—lured to the West Coast by a prestigious research job and the opportunity to work for one of the top young heart surgeons in the country. For a kid like me who'd barely stepped foot outside the six-block square of the 'hood in Milwaukee—not counting my three-year stint as a Navy medic in North Carolina—

San Francisco was the be-all and end-all. The city was the Land of Milk and Honey and the Emerald City of Oz rolled into one. Rising up out of the bay into golden glowing mists of possibility, she seduced me from the start, showing off her studded hills and plunging valleys as she laid herself out with arms open. At night the town was an aphrodisiac—with city lights like rare jewels sparkling down from Nob Hill and Pacific Heights, through the better neighborhoods and along the rougher streets of the Mission and the Tenderloin (my new 'hood), spilling out of the towers of the Financial District and reflecting into the bay by Fisherman's Wharf and the Marina.

In the early days, no matter how many times I drove west over the Bay Bridge from Oakland, or north from Daly City heading toward the Golden Gate Bridge, which stretches right up to the horizon before dropping down into Marin County, those views of San Francisco were like falling in love all over again. Even as time went by and I got hip to the weather—the periods of gray foggy skies alternating with days of bone-chilling rain—I'd wake up to one of those glorious, perfect San Francisco days and the beauty wiped away all memory of the gloom. San Francisco remains in my mind to this day the Paris of the Pacific.

Of course, back then, it didn't take long to discover that she was also deceptive, not necessarily easy, sometimes coldhearted, and definitely not cheap. Between steep rents and the chronic car repairs caused by the toll the hills took on transmissions and brakes—not to mention that pile of unpaid parking tickets all too familiar to most San Franciscans—staying afloat could be a challenge. But that wasn't going to mar my belief that I'd make it. Besides, I knew enough about challenge. I knew how to work hard, and in fact, over the next years, challenges helped me to reshape my dreams, to reach further, and to pursue goals with an increased sense of urgency.

In early 1981, when I became a first-time father, overjoyed as I was, that sense of urgency kicked up another notch. As the first months of my son's life flew by, I not only tried to move ahead faster but also began to question the path that I'd chosen, wondering if somehow in all my efforts I wasn't trying to run up the down escalator. Or at least that was my state of mind on that day in the parking lot outside San Francisco General Hospital as I approached the driver of the red Ferrari.

This encounter would crystallize in my memory—almost into a mythological moment that I could return to and visit in the present tense whenever I wanted or needed its message. I see the sports car in front of me just as if it's today, circling in slow motion, with the whirring sound of that unbelievably powerful engine as it idles, waiting and purring like a lion about to pounce. In my mind's ear, I'm hearing the cool calling of a horn blown by Miles Davis, my musical hero—who, back in the day, I was positive I was going to be when I grew up. It's one of those imagined senses in the sound track of our lives that tells us to pay attention.

With the top down and the light glinting fire-engine-metallic-red off the hood, the guy at the wheel is every bit as cool as the jazz musicians I used to idolize. A white guy, dark-haired, clean-shaven, of average height and slight build, he's wearing the sharpest suit, possibly custom-made, out of a beautiful piece of cloth. It's more than just a wonderful garment, it's the whole look—the tasteful tie, the muted shirt, the pocket square, the understated cuff links and watch. Nothing obnoxious, just well put together. No flash, no bullshit. Just sharp.

"Hey, man," I say, approaching the Ferrari and waving at him as I point out where my car is parked, nodding to let him know that I'm coming out. Am I seduced by the Ferrari itself? Yes. I am a red-blooded American male. But it's more than that. In that instant, the car symbolizes all that I lacked while growing up—freedom, escape, options. "You can have my spot," I offer, "but I gotta ask you a couple of questions."

He gets that I'm offering a trade here—my parking place for his information. In my twenty-seven years of life so far, I have learned a little already about the power of information and about the kind of currency that information can become. Now I see an opportunity to get some inside information, I think, and so I draw out my trusty sword—a compulsion for question-asking that has been in my survival kit since childhood.

Seeing that it's not a bad deal for either of us, he shrugs and says, "Fine."

My questions are very simple: "What do you do?" and "How do you do it?"

With a laugh, he answers the first question just as simply, saying, "I'm a stockbroker," but to answer the second question we extend the conversation to a meeting a few weeks later and then a subsequent introduction to the ABCs, of Wall Street, an entirely foreign but mesmerizing venue where I am just crazy enough to think I could do what he and others like him do, if only I can find an opening.

Despite the fact that I had absolutely no experience and no contacts whatsoever, looking to get my big break into the stock market became a major focus over the next several months, but so did other urgent concerns, especially when I suddenly became a single parent amid a series of other unforeseen, tumultuous events.

By this time period, San Francisco's conflicting attitudes toward a growing homeless population were already well known. What officials declared was a new epidemic in homelessness had actually been developing for more than a decade as the result of several factors—including drastic cutbacks to state funding for mental health facilities, limited treatment options for the large number of Vietnam vets suffering from post-traumatic stress syndrome and alcohol and drug addiction, along with the same urban ills plaguing the rest of the country. During the long, cold winter of 1982, as government programs to help the poor were being eliminated, the economy in the Bay Area, as in the rest of the country, was in a downturn. At a time when jobs and affordable housing were becoming harder to find, access to cheap street drugs like angel dust and PCP was starting to get easier.

Though some business leaders complained that the homeless would scare tourists away, if you happened to visit San Francisco in the early 1980s, you were probably unaware of the deepening crisis. You might have heard about what neighborhoods to avoid—areas where you were warned about the winos, junkies, bag ladies, transients, and others who, as they used to say in my part of Milwaukee, "just went crazy." Or maybe you did notice some of the signs—the long food lines, multiplying numbers of panhandlers, the mothers and children on the steps of overcapacity shelters, runaway teenagers, or those sleeping human forms that sometimes looked more like mounds of discarded clothing left in alleys, on park benches, at transit stations, and under the eaves and in the doorways of buildings. Maybe your visit to San Francisco reminded you of similar problems in your hometown, or maybe even alerted you to the increasing percentage of the working poor who'd entered the ranks of the homeless—gainfully employed but overburdened individuals and families forced to choose between paying rent and buying food, medicine, clothing, or other basic necessities. You may have paused to wonder what kinds of lives and dreams and stories had been lived before, and perhaps to consider how easy it would be for anyone to fall through the cracks of whatever support had once existed, or to face a sudden crisis of any proportion and simply stumble into the hole of homelessness.

Chances are, however, no matter how observant you might have been, you wouldn't have noticed me. Or if you did happen to spot me, usually moving at a fast clip as I pushed a lightweight, rickety blue stroller that had become my only wheels and that carried my most precious cargo in the universe—my nineteen-month-old son, Chris Jr., a beautiful, growing, active, alert, talkative, *hungry* toddler—it's unlikely you would have suspected that my baby and I were homeless. Dressed in one of my two business suits, the other in the garment bag that was slung over my shoulder, along with the duffel bag that was filled with all our other earthly possessions (including various articles of clothing, toiletries, and the few books I couldn't live without), as I tried to hold an umbrella in one hand, a briefcase in another, and balance the world's largest box of Pampers under my armpit, still while maneuvering the stroller, we probably looked more like we were going off on a long weekend somewhere. Some of the places where we slept suggested as much—on the Bay Area Rapid Transit subway trains, or in waiting areas at either the Oakland or San Francisco airport. Then again, the more hidden places where we stayed could have given away my situation—at the office, where I'd work late so we could stretch out on the floor under my desk after hours; or, as on occasion we found ourselves, in the public bathroom of an Oakland BART station.

That small, cell-like, windowless tiled box—big enough for us, our stuff, and a toilet and a sink where I could get us washed as best I could—represented both my worst nightmare of being confined, locked up, and excluded and, at the same time, a true godsend of protection where I could lock the door and keep the wolves out. It was what it was—a way station between where I'd come from and where I was going, my version of a pit stop on the underground railroad, '80s style.

As long as I kept my mental focus on destinations that were ahead, destinations that I had the audacity to dream might hold a red Ferrari of my own, I protected myself from despair. The future was uncertain, absolutely, and there were many hurdles, twists, and turns to come, but as long as I kept moving forward, one foot in front of the other, the voices of fear and shame, the messages from those who wanted me to believe that I wasn't good enough, would be stilled.

Go forward. That became my mantra, inspired by the Reverend

Cecil Williams, one of the most enlightened men to ever walk this earth, a friend and mentor whose goodness blessed me in ways I can never sufficiently recount. At Glide Memorial Methodist Church in the Tenderloin—where the Reverend Williams fed, housed, and repaired souls (eventually accommodating thousands of homeless in what became the first homeless hotel in the country)—he was already an icon. Then and later, you couldn't live in the Bay Area without knowing Cecil Williams and getting a sense of his message. Walk that walk, he preached. On any Sunday, his sermon might address a number of subjects, but that theme was always in there, in addition to the rest. Walk that walk and go forward all the time. Don't just talk that talk, walk it and go forward. Also, the walk didn't have to be long strides; baby steps counted too. Go forward.

The phrases repeated in my brain until they were a wordless skat, like the three-beat staccato sound as we rode the train over the BART rails, or like the *clack-clack-clack* syncopation of the stroller wheels with percussion added from the occasional *creaks* and *squeals* and *groans* they made going over curbs, up and down San Francisco's famed steep hills, and around corners.

In years to come, baby carriages would go way high-tech with double and triple wheels on each side and all aerodynamic, streamlined, and leather-cushioned, plus extra compartments for storing stuff and roofs to add on to make them like little inhabitable igloos. But the rickety blue stroller I had, as we forged into the winter of 1982, had none of that. What it did have—during what I'm sure had to be the wettest, coldest winter on record in San Francisco—was a sort of pup tent over Chris Jr. that I made of free plastic sheeting from the dry cleaners.

As much as I kept going forward because I believed a better future lay ahead, and as much as I was sure that the encounter outside San Francisco General Hospital had steered me to that future, the real driving force came from that other pivotal event in my life—which had taken place back in Milwaukee in March 1970, on a day not long after my sixteenth birthday.

Unlike many experiences in childhood that tended to blur in my memory into a series of images that flickered dimly like grainy, old-fashioned moving pictures, this event—which must have taken up little more than a split second of time—became a vivid reality that I could conjure in my senses whenever I wanted, in perfectly preserved detail.

This period was one of the most volatile of my youth, beyond the public turbulence of the era—the Vietnam War, the civil rights movement, echoes of assassinations and riots, and the cultural influences of music, hippies, black power, and political activism, all of which helped to shape my view of myself, my country, and the world.

During my childhood and adolescence, my family—consisting of my three sisters and me, our mother, who was present in my early life only sporadically, and our stepfather—had lived in a series of houses, walk-ups, and flats, punctuated by intermittent separations and stays with a series of relatives, all within a four-block area. Finally, we had moved into a small house in a neighborhood considered to be somewhat upwardly mobile. It may have only been so in comparison to where we'd been living before, but this house was nonetheless "movin' on up"—à la the Jefferson family, who still had another five years to go to get their own TV show.

The TV on this particular day was, in fact, the focus of my attention, and key to my mood of happy expectation, not only because I was getting ready to watch the last of the two games played in the NCAA's Final Four, but because I had the living room all to myself. This meant that I could hoot and holler all I wanted, and that I could talk out loud to myself if I so pleased, and answer myself right back. (My mother had this habit too. When others asked what she was doing, she'd always say, "Talking to someone with good sense.")

Another cause for feeling good that day was that my mother

happened to be the only other person at home. Even if she wasn't sitting down beside me to watch the game but was somewhere nearby—busy ironing clothes in the adjacent dining room, as it so happened—it was as if the house was breathing a sigh of relief for just the two of us to be there, something that almost never occurred, especially without my stepfather's menacing presence.

March Madness, which came every year at the end of the college basketball season, was always thrilling for me, and an excellent distraction from heavier thoughts I was having about the tightrope I was walking from the end of adolescence into manhood. The tournament was always full of surprises, Cinderella stories, and human drama, starting with the nation's sixty-four top teams in thirty-two matchups as they rapidly whittled down to the Sweet Sixteen, then the Elite Eight, and ended up with the two games of the Final Four before the winners played for the championship title. All eyes this year were on how UCLA would fare in its first season without seven-footer Lew Alcindor (soon to become Kareem Abdul-Jabbar) after he had led them to three consecutive titles. The team that seemed destined to make sure UCLA didn't go home with the championship this year was Jacksonville University, a heretofore unknown college program that boasted not one but two stars, Artis Gilmore and Pembrook Burrows III, both over seven feet tall. It was unusual enough at this time for players to hit the seven-foot mark, let alone to have two of them on the same team.

Known as the original Twin Towers, or sometimes the Towers of Power, Gilmore and Burrows had helped Jacksonville obliterate their opposition and had brought them to the Final Four to face St. Bonaventure. As time for the tip-off neared, the excitement was only heightened by the announcers' predictions about the careers and riches awaiting the two giants in the NBA or the ABA.

As it happened, Jacksonville would win the game and then lose the championship to UCLA after all. And Artis Gilmore would go on to success in the NBA while Pembrook Burrows would be drafted by Seattle before turning to a career as a Florida Highway Patrol officer.

None of that is of any consequence as I'm sitting there, so engrossed in anticipation of the tip-off and so very caught up in the announcers' hype of both the athletic ability and fortune awaiting Gilmore and Burrows that I say out loud to no one, "Wow, one day those guys are gonna make a million dollars!"

Moms, standing at the ironing board just behind me in the next room, says very clearly, as though she has been sitting next to me the whole time, "Son, if you want to, one day *you* could make a million dollars."

Stunned, I allow her pronouncement to seep in, without responding. No response is necessary, as Bettye Jean Triplett née Gardner has gone on record with a statement of fact, not to be questioned, or responded to. It is as factual as if one would say on Friday that "tomorrow is Saturday."

It was biblical, one of the ten commandments handed down from God to Momma: "If you want to, one day you could make a million dollars."

All in an instant my world turned inside out. In 1970 the only way a kid from the ghetto like me had a chance to go make a million dollars was if he could sing, dance, run, jump, catch balls, or deal drugs. I could not sing. I am still the only black man in America that cannot dance or play ball. And it was my Momma who'd set me straight about becoming Miles Davis.

"Chris," she had said after hearing me say how I was going to be him one too many times, "you can't be Miles Davis because he already got that job." I had understood from then on that my job was to be Chris Gardner—whatever that was going to entail.

Now she had told me, and I was sixteen years old and I believed her, that my job could be to make a million dollars—*if* I wanted to. The amount of the money wasn't what mattered when Moms said it; the operative part of her message was that if I wanted to do something, whatever it was, I could.

I not only believed her then, at age sixteen, but I continued to believe that statement in all the days that followed, including that fateful day in San Francisco when I got the first inkling of a future in Wall Street, and in those moments pushing up the hills in the downpour with my son looking up at me from his stroller through rain-splattered dry-cleaning plastic, and in the desolate hours when the only place of refuge was in a BART station bathroom.

It was only later in my adulthood, after those days of wandering in the desert of homelessness, believing in the promised land my mother had told me about and then finding it, and only after generating many millions of dollars, that I understood why these two events were both so essential to my eventual success. The encounter with the driver of the red Ferrari showed me the way to discovering *what* the arena was in which I could apply myself and also to learning *how* to do that. But it was my mother's earlier pronouncement that had planted the belief in me that I *could* attain whatever goals I set for myself.

Only after looking as deeply as I could into my mother's life was I able to fully understand why she said those words to me at the time that she did. By recognizing the disappointments that happened in her life before and after I came along, I was able to see that, though too many of her dreams had been crushed, by daring me to dream she was being given another chance.

To fully answer the question of what it was that guided me through and became the secret to the success that followed, I had to go back to my own childhood and take the journey back to where my mother came from—in order to understand at last how that fire to dream got lit in me.

My story is hers.

PART ONE

CHAPTER I

Candy

I n my memory's sketch of early childhood, drawn by an artist of the impressionist school, there is one image that stands out above the rest—which when called forth is preceded by the mouth-watering aroma of pancake syrup warming in a skillet and the crackling, bubbling sounds of the syrup transforming magically into homemade pull candy. Then *she* comes into view, the real, real pretty woman who stands at the stove, making this magic just for me.

Or at least, that's how it feels to a boy of three years old. There is another wonderful smell that accompanies her presence as she turns, smiling right in my direction, as she steps closer to where I stand in the middle of the kitchen—waiting eagerly next to my sister, seven-year-old Ophelia, and two of the other children, Rufus and Pookie, who live in this house. As she slips the cooling candy off the wooden spoon, pulling and breaking it into pieces that she brings and places in my outstretched hand, as she watches me happily gobbling up the tasty sweetness, her wonderful fragrance is there again. Not perfume or anything floral or spicy—it's just a clean, warm, *good* smell that wraps around me like a Superman cape, making me feel strong, special, and loved—even if I don't have words for those concepts yet.

Though I don't know who she is, I sense a familiarity about her, not only because she has come before and made candy in this same fashion, but also because of how she looks at me—like she's talking to me from her eyes, saying, *You remember me, don't you?*

At this point in childhood, and for most of the first five years of my life, the map of my world was broken strictly into two territories—the familiar and the unknown. The happy, safe zone of the familiar was very small, often a shifting dot on the map, while the unknown was vast, terrifying, and constant.

What I did know by the age of three or four was that Ophelia was my older sister and best friend, and also that we were treated with kindness by Mr. and Mrs. Robinson, the adults whose house we lived in. What I didn't know was that the Robinsons' house was a foster home, or what that meant. Our situation—where our real parents were and why we didn't live with them, or why we sometimes did live with uncles and aunts and cousins—was as mysterious as the situations of the other foster children living at the Robinsons'.

What mattered most was that I had a sister who looked out for me, and I had Rufus and Pookie and the other boys to follow outside for fun and mischief. All that was familiar, the backyard and the rest of the block, was safe turf where we could run and play games like tag, kick-the-can, and hide-and-seek, even after dark. That is, except, for the house two doors down from the Robinsons.

Every time we passed it I had to almost look the other way, just knowing the old white woman who lived there might suddenly appear and put an evil curse on me—because, according to Ophelia and everyone else in the neighborhood, the old woman was a witch.

When Ophelia and I passed by the house together once and I confessed that I was scared of the witch, my sister said, "I ain't scared," and to prove it she walked right into the front yard and grabbed a handful of cherries off the woman's cherry tree.

Ophelia ate those cherries with a smile. But within the week I was in the Robinsons' house when here came Ophelia, racing up the steps and stumbling inside, panting and holding her seven-year-old chest, describing how the witch had caught her stealing cherries and grabbed her arm, cackling, "I'm gonna get you!"

Scared to death as she was now, Ophelia soon decided that since she had escaped an untimely death once, she might as well go back to stealing cherries. Even so, she made me promise to avoid the strange woman's house. "Now, remember," Ophelia warned, "when you walk by, if you see her on the porch, don't you look at her and never say nuthin' to her, even if she calls you by name."

I didn't have to promise because I knew that nothing and no one could ever make me do that. But I was still haunted by nightmares so real that I could have sworn I actually snuck into her house and found myself in the middle of a dark, creepy room where I was surrounded by an army of cats, rearing up on their back legs, baring their claws and fangs. The nightmares were so intense that for the longest time I had an irrational fear and dislike of cats. At the same time, I was not entirely convinced that this old woman was in fact a witch. Maybe she was just different. Since I'd never seen any white people other than her, I figured they might all be like that.

Then again, because my big sister was my only resource for explaining all that was unknown, I believed her and accepted her explanations. But as I pieced together fragments of information about our family over the years, mainly from Ophelia and also from some of our uncles and aunts, I found the answers much harder to grasp.

How the real pretty woman who came to make the candy fit into the puzzle, I was never told, but something old and wise inside me knew that she was important. Maybe it was how she seemed to pay special attention to me, even though she was just as nice to Ophelia and the other kids, or maybe it was how she and I seemed to have a secret way of talking without words. In our unspoken conversation, I understood her to be saying that seeing me happy made her even happier, and so somewhere in my cells, that became my first job in life—to make her feel as good as she made me feel. Intuitively, I also understood who she was, in spite of never being told, and there is a moment of recognition that comes during one of her visits—as I watch her at the stove and make observations that will be reinforced in years to come.

More than pretty, she is beautiful, a stop-you-in-your-tracks-turn-around-and-look-twice beautiful. Not tall at five-four, but with a stature of nobility that makes her appear much taller, she is light brown–skinned but not too light—almost the color of the rich maple syrup she stirs and heats into candy. She has supernaturally strong fingernails—capable of breaking an apple in half, bare-handed, something that few women or men can do and something that impresses me for life. She has a stylish way of dressing—the color burgundy and paisley print dresses stand out—with a scarf or shawl thrown over her shoulder to give her a feminine, flowing look. The brightness of color and the flowing layers of fabric give her an appearance I would later describe as Afro-centric.

But the features that most capture her beauty are her expressive eyes and her amazing smile. Then and later, I liken that smile to opening a refrigerator at night. You open up that door—smile—and the light fills up the room. Even on those nights ahead when the refrigerator contains nothing but a lightbulb and ice water, her smile and the memory of her smile are all the comforts I need.

When the recognition occurs exactly, I don't recall, except that it takes place somewhere in my fourth year, maybe after she hands me a piece of candy, in an instant when at last I can respond to that look she has been giving me and reassure her with my own look— *Of course I remember you, you're my momma!*

———

Ours was a family of secrets. Over the years, I heard only parts of my mother's saga, told to me by a variety of sources, so that the understanding that eventually emerged was of a kind of Cinderella story—without the fairy godmother and the part at the end where she marries the prince and they all live happily ever after. The oldest and only daughter of the four surviving children born to parents Archie and Ophelia Gardner, Bettye Jean came into this world in 1928, in Little Rock, Arkansas, but was raised in Depression-era, dirt-poor, rural Louisiana—somewhere near the town of Rayville, population five hundred. With the trials of poverty and racism, life wasn't easy for the Gardners. Bettye and her brother Archie—who cried grown-man tears when he recalled what it was like walking the long, dusty country roads to school in the thirties and forties in Rayville—had to keep their heads up as white children rode by in horse-drawn wagons or on horseback, looking down at the two of them, pointing, calling them "niggers," and spitting on them.

Yet, in spite of hard times and hateful ignorance, Bettye's childhood was relatively stable and very loving. Adored by her three younger brothers—Archie Jr., Willie, and Henry—she was, in fact, a golden girl of promise, a star student who finished third in her class when she graduated from Rayville Colored High School in 1946. But her dreams quickly unraveled the moment it was time to go off to college and pursue her calling as an educator, starting with the devastating sudden death of her mother. Like Cinderella, while she was still in mourning, almost overnight her father remarried, leaving Bettye to cope with a domineering stepmother—who went by the ironic nickname of Little Mama—and a new set of competitive stepsiblings. Just at a time when Bettye Jean was depending on the financial support from her father to go to college, Little Mama saw to it that the money went to her own daughter, Eddie Lee—who had graduated in the same class as Bettye but wasn't among the top students.

Rather than giving up, even though her heart was broken by her father's refusal to help, Bettye found work as a substitute teacher while she put herself through beauty school. But once again, when she needed financial assistance from her father to pay for her state licensing fees, he said no.

With all the talent, brilliance, and beauty that had been naturally bestowed on Bettye Jean Gardner, she had apparently drawn an unlucky card when it came to men—most of whom seemed destined to disappoint her, starting with her own daddy. There was Samuel Salter, a married schoolteacher who professed his love for her and his plan to leave his wife, but who must have changed his mind when she became pregnant. True to form, her daddy and Little Mama were no help. They let it be known that she had embarrassed them enough by being single at age twenty-two, but for her to be an old maid *and* an unwed mother was too much shame for them to bear. On these grounds, they put her out.

Thus began my mother's four-year trek to Milwaukee, where all three of her brothers had settled. Along the way she gave birth to my sister—named Ophelia for her beloved mother—before crossing paths with a tall, dark, handsome stranger during a trip back to Louisiana. His name was Thomas Turner, a married man who swept Bettye Jean off her feet either romantically or by force. The result was me, Christopher Paul Gardner, born in Milwaukee, Wisconsin, on February 9, 1954—the same year, auspiciously, that school segregation was ruled in violation of the Fourteenth Amendment by the U.S. Supreme Court.

In keeping with other family mysteries, my father was a figment of the vast unknown throughout my childhood. His name was mentioned only once or twice. It probably would have bothered me much more if I weren't so occupied trying to get to the bottom of other more pressing questions, especially the how-when-where-why my smart, strong, beautiful mother ever became entangled with Freddie Triplett.

Tall and dark, but not exactly handsome—at times he bore a strong resemblance to Sonny Liston—Freddie had the demeanor of some ill-begotten cross between a pit bull and Godzilla. At six-two, 280 pounds, he did have a stature and brawn that some women found attractive. Whatever it was that first caught her attention must have been a redeeming side of him that later vanished. Or maybe, as I'd wonder in my youthful imagination, my mother was tricked by a magic spell into thinking that he was one of those frog princes. After all, the other men who looked good had not turned out to be dependable; maybe she thought Freddie was the opposite—a man who looked dangerous but was kind and tender underneath his disguise. If that was the case, and she believed in the fairy tale that her kiss would turn the frog into a prince, she was sadly mistaken. In fact, he turned out to be many times more dangerous than he looked, especially after that first kiss, and after he decided she was his.

No one ever laid out the sequence of events that led to my mother being prosecuted and imprisoned for alleged welfare fraud. It started out with an anonymous tip, apparently, that somehow she was a danger to society because she was earning money at a job—to feed and care for her two children (Ophelia and me) and a third on the way (my sister Sharon)—and was receiving assistance at the same time. That anonymous tip had come from Freddie, a man willing to do or say anything to have her locked up for three years because she had committed the crime of trying to leave his sorry ass.

It was because of Freddie's actions in having her sent away that Ophelia and I spent those three years either in foster care or with extended family members. Yet we never knew why or when changes in our living situation would take place.

Just as no one told me that it was my mother who came to make candy and visit us at the foster home under special, supervised leave from prison, no explanation accompanied our move when Ophelia and I went to stay with my Uncle Archie and his wife Clara, or TT as we all called her. Way back in Louisiana, the entire Gardner family must have signed an oath of secrecy because serious questions about the past were almost always shrugged off, a policy my mother may have instituted out of her dislike for discussing anything unpleasant.

Later on in my adolescence there was one occasion when I pressed her about just who my father was and why he wasn't in my life. Moms gave me one of her searing looks, the kind that got me to be quiet real fast.

"But . . ." I tried to protest.

She shook her head no, unwilling to open up.

"Why?"

"Well, because the past is the past," Moms said firmly. Seeing my frustration, she sighed but still insisted, "Ain't nothing you can do about it." She put a stop to my questions, wistfully remarking, "Things happen." And that was all there was to it.

Even as my questions continued, while waiting for clarification to arrive of its own accord, I went back to my job of trying to be as happy as possible—not a difficult assignment at first.

————

The land of the familiar where I grew up in one of the poorer areas of the north side of Milwaukee was a world that I eventually viewed as a black *Happy Days*. Just like on that TV show that was set in the 1950s—in the same time period in which my neighborhood seemed to be frozen even in later decades—there were local hangouts, places where different age groups gathered to socialize, well-known quirky merchants, and an abundance of great characters. While on the TV show the only black color you ever saw was Fonzie's leather jacket, in my neighborhood, for nearly the first dozen years of my life, the only white people I ever saw were on television and in police cars.

Some of the greatest characters in our *Happy Days* version were my own family members, starting with my three stubborn uncles.

After both Willie and Henry got out of the Army, having traveled to many distant shores, the two returned to Louisiana long enough to join with Uncle Archie as each came to the simultaneous decision to get as far away from southern bigotry as he possibly could. Their plan was to go to Canada, but when their car broke down in Milwaukee, so the story goes, they laid anchor and went no farther.

The hardworking Gardner brothers didn't have too much trouble making Milwaukee home. To them, the fertile, versatile city that had been plunked down at the meeting place of the Milwaukee River and Lake Michigan—which provided rich soil for farming and ample waterways for trade and industry—was their land of milk and honey, of golden opportunity. To put up with the extremes in the seasons, the brutal winters and scorching summers, you had to have an innate toughness and the kind of deeply practical, hustling ability that my relatives and many of the other minorities and immigrants brought with them to Wisconsin from other places. Those traits must have existed as well as in the descendents of the true Milwaukeeans—members of tribes like the Winnebago and Potawatomi. There was another local personality trait not exclusive to the new arrivals of blacks, Jews, Italians, and eastern Europeans or the families of the first wave of settlers from Germany, Ireland, and Scandinavia, or the area's Native Americans, and that was an almost crazy optimism.

All that ambitious, pragmatic dreaming sometimes resulted in overachievement. It wasn't enough to just have one brand of beer, Milwaukee had to have several. The region couldn't just be famous for its dairies, it had to have the best cheese in the world. There wasn't just one major industry but several—from the brickyards, tanneries, breweries, shipyards, and meatpacking businesses to the dominating steel factories like Inland Steel and A. O. Smith and the automotive giant American Motors (deceased as of the late 1980s).

It was mainly the steel mills and foundries and carmakers that brought so many blacks from states like Louisiana, Alabama, Mississippi, Georgia, and all points south of the Mason-Dixon north to Milwaukee, Detroit, Chicago, and Cleveland. These blue-collar jobs were far and away preferable to a life sharecropping in the sweltering heat way down south in Dixie, in places where less than a century earlier many of our people had been enslaved. Seemed like almost everyone had family members that brought with them their country ways and who tended to stick together. Sam Salter— Ophelia's father—ended up with his family in Milwaukee, as well as other friends from Louisiana. The Tripletts, some of the nicest, kindest folks you could meet—with the exception of Freddie, the bad seed—had come from Mississippi.

As hard as everyone worked all week, at least in my neighborhood, over the weekend they played and prayed even harder. No such thing as casual drinking in our part of Milwaukee. From Friday evening when the whistle blew at Inland Steel—where all three of my uncles worked, Archie and Willie until they retired from there and Henry until his dying day, which came much too early—the party began and lasted until Sunday morning, when it was time to go to church and pray for forgiveness.

Between the ages of four and five, at which point I was living with Uncle Archie and Aunt TT, I'd come to appreciate the familiar rhythm of the working week. My uncle and his wife maintained an easygoing, peaceful atmosphere without too many rules. A devout Christian, TT made sure we got that old-time religion in us. Every Sunday, all day, we spent at the Tabernacle Baptist Church, and in summers we attended Bible school daily, plus we accompanied her to any and all special midweek meetings and were present for the funerals of every member of the church who ever died, whether we knew them or not. Most of this I didn't mind so much, considering all the entertainment value as I watched the various characters from the neighborhood I'd seen sinning all week now change their clothes and themselves. I loved the singing and shouting, the feeling of heat and passion, and especially the connection to community that I experienced at a time when I didn't know exactly who or where my mother was.

TT never tried to be a substitute for Momma, but she provided love and comfort all the same. Nobody could cook like Bettye Jean, but my aunt did make an unforgettable hot-water cornbread that a growing kid like me couldn't devour fast enough. Nor could I devour fast enough the books that TT seemed to have limitless funds to buy for me. My mother later reinforced the importance of reading, raising me with her own credo to spend as much time at our public library as possible. What she'd say to show me how powerful a building full of books could be was, "The most dangerous place in the world is a public library." That was, of course, only if you could read, because, Momma explained, if you could read, that meant you could go in there and figure anything out. But if you couldn't read, well. . . .

It was TT, however, who first instilled in me the love of reading books and storytelling. Though I didn't read yet, after TT read books to me, by looking at the illustrations afterward, I could partly remember the words and stories, and I felt as if I was reading already. There were books of Greek and Roman mythology, children's classic fairy tales, adventure stories, and my early favorite genre—tales of King Arthur and the Knights of the Round Table. The story of the Sword in the Stone made a lasting impression on me, setting up the idea that someday, somehow, I would find the destiny that awaited me.

Books allowed me not only to travel in my imagination but to look through windows into the world of the unknown and not feel afraid. That was until TT brought me a book I had been dying to have, *The Boys' Book of Snakes*. A big light green book, the color of a garden snake, it captivated me for days on end as I studied every minute detail of the snake world—from the friendly-sounding milk snakes and coral snakes to the deadly rattlers, cobras, and pythons. During waking hours I was fascinated, but at night, especially during one particular snake-infested nightmare in which my bed was full of writhing, hissing poisonous snakes, I regretted ever seeing those pictures.

Apparently so did TT and Uncle Archie, who woke up in the middle of the night to find me wedged in between them in the bed. "What in the . . ." Uncle Archie started up, but no amount of placating or chiding could get me to my own bed. In the end, they both went back to sleep, letting me feel safe and not making me feel too embarrassed—until later when I was a big, strong guy and they teased me about it mercilessly.

The other window into the world of the unknown was the black-and-white TV set, and the finest vision I ever saw on it was of Sugar Ray Robinson standing next to a Cadillac.

"Now I seen all," Uncle Archie exclaimed, his hand on my shoulder, pointing at the TV screen. "Sugar Ray Robinson got himself a *pink* Cadillac!"

With black-and-white TV, we wouldn't have known it was pink if the announcer hadn't said so, but it was no less amazing.

Friday fight nights sponsored by Gillette Blue Blades was our time, me and Uncle Archie, to sit down together—without TT and Ophelia—and enjoy every minute, from our conversations beforehand where he'd tell me everything he knew about boxing history, and the moment we'd hear that suspenseful intro music leading into the announcer's booming "Gillette presents!" to the match itself.

Uncle Archie had a contagious aura of calm that he maintained even during the excitement of the fights or when crises came up. A man in his late twenties at the time, he never had a son, and I didn't have a father, so that drew us closer. Besides his hardworking ethic on the job, Archie used his quiet, strong intelligence to rise up through the ranks of his union at Inland Steel, setting an example for me about tenacity and focus. A very handsome guy who was the male version of Moms in looks—nut brown in color, slender, and on the short side but appearing taller than he was—Archie was an incredibly sharp dresser, something that influenced my later sense of style and the clothes habit I acquired long before I could afford it. Never overdressed, he was immaculate in his grooming, with his short haircut and neat trim mustache and clothes that weren't showy but always impeccable. Always.

In Uncle Archie's lore, no one could touch Joe Louis, the Brown Bomber, the fighter he grew up following on the radio—hearing, feeling, smelling, and seeing every move, jab, swing, punch, and step, all on a nonvisual medium. As a result, Uncle Archie could narrate those fights for me as well as any announcer of his time. Now we were watching history unfold together, with Sugar Ray Robinson still going strong, including his fight with Jake LaMotta, which I'd never forget. Sugar Ray and the other boxers were larger than life, superheroes who could do and have it all, including a pink Cadillac. What that said to a poor kid from the ghetto like me was everything, a very early precursor to the red Ferrari. But Sugar Ray Robinson and his Caddy were on television. I had something closer at hand to show me the beautiful world beyond the ghetto: the Spiegel catalog.

Through those dream pages, Ophelia and I lived vicarious lives as we played a game we made up with the household's catalog. We called it "this-page-that-page," and it was played simply by flipping randomly to a page and then claiming all the treasures pictured on it as mine or hers. "Look at all my stuff," I'd say after flipping to my page. "Look at my furniture—all these clothes are mine!" and Ophelia would follow, flipping to her page, singing, "Look at my stuff, my nice stove and my jewelry!" The Spiegel catalog must have been three hundred pages or more, so we never tired of this-page-that-page.

In the dead of winter one year, we changed the game in recognition of Christmas. When it was Ophelia's turn, she flipped to a page and smiled her big-sister smile, announcing that this page was for me, pointing to all the stuff she was giving me for Christmas. "I'm giving you this page. All this is yours."

Then it was my turn. I flipped to a page and exclaimed, "I'm giving you this page for Christmas. This is all yours!" I wasn't sure what made me happier, getting a page all for me or having one to give.

In those hours spent playing this-page-that-page, there was no discussion about who Momma was, where she went, or when she was coming back. But there was a feeling of anticipation I recognized. We were biding time, waiting for something or someone to come for us. For that reason, it wasn't a shock or even a memorable instance when, at last, I learned that Momma was leaving wherever she'd been—prison, I now know—and that she was coming to get me and Ophelia and our baby sister Sharon, who suddenly appeared on the scene.

Though Momma's Cinderella story hadn't worked out like in the storybook, I had the briefly held idea that a fairy tale was about to happen in being reunited with my mother. All the happy memories of the beautiful woman who made me candy filled me with wondrous expectation, and for one brilliant flash of time the reality of our being together made me happier than anything I could have dreamt. But those feelings were rapidly overshadowed from almost the first moment that Freddie Triplett bulldozed his way into my life. You would think that I would have had a honeymoon phase with the man who had become Momma's husband and our stepfather, but he was my enemy from the second I laid eyes on him.

While I had no inkling of the violence he was going to cause in our lives, I must have sensed that he was mean and seemed to take pleasure in hurting my feelings. My hunch was confirmed when he launched the line he loved to throw at me every chance he got, which killed me every time he said it, stirring up the sediment of anger and resentment that would later erupt. Unprovoked, out of nowhere, he turned to me that first time I can recall seeing him and proclaimed in no uncertain terms, eyes blazing and voice blasting, "I ain't your goddamn daddy!"

CHAPTER 2

The No-Daddy Blues

"C hris! Chris, wake up!" lisps the three-year-old voice of my sister Sharon, her little hand tugging on my shoulder.

Without opening my eyes, I force myself to remember where I am. It's very late on Halloween night, and I'm in my bed that occupies most of the small room in the back house where we're living now—behind the "Big House" on Eighth and Wright that is owned by Freddie's sister Bessie. As soon as these facts register, I ease back down into sleep, wanting to rest just a little longer. The irony is that while sleep sometimes brings nightmares, it's the reality of my waking hours that can cause me the greater fear.

From the time that Momma came to get us, first taking me, Ophelia, and Sharon—who had been born in the women's correctional facility during that time my mother was away—to live with her and Freddie, life had changed drastically and mostly for the worse. The world of the unknown that overwhelmed me when we stayed with Uncle Archie and TT seemed wonderful by comparison to everything that took place in the territory of the familiar over which Freddie Triplett ruled. Moms gave us all the love, protection, and approval that she could, but often that seemed to make him more brutal than he already was.

My instincts told me that the logical thing to do was to find some kind of way to get Freddie to like me. But no matter what I

did, his response was to beat me down, often literally. Ophelia and
I almost never got whippings when we lived with Uncle Archie
and TT, but with Freddie we all got whupped all the time, usually
for no good reason other than he was an illiterate, belligerent, abusive, and complete drunk.

Initially, I thought Freddie might be proud of my academic success. At five, six, and seven years old, school was a haven for me, a
place where I seemed to thrive at learning and in social interac-
tions. My early exposure to books paid off, and with Momma's
continuing encouragement, I quickly mastered reading. One of my
favorite teachers, Mrs. Broderick, reinforced my love of books by
frequently asking me to read aloud—longer than any of my classmates. Since we didn't have a television at this time, reading became all the more meaningful at home, especially because Momma
loved to sit down after her long day of working as a domestic to
hear what I had read or learned that day.

My mother still clung to the hope that she would one day obtain the necessary schooling and licensing to teach in the state of
Wisconsin. Until that time, she devoted herself to doing what
she had to do to take care of her four children—Ophelia, myself,
Sharon, and the youngest, my baby sister Kim, who arrived in this
time period. While Momma didn't complain about her days spent
cleaning rich (white) people's houses, she didn't talk about her
work either, instead living vicariously through reports of what my
teachers had taught that day or by looking with me at some of the
picture storybooks that I brought home. *The Red Balloon* was one
book that I could read over and over, sitting next to Momma and
showing her the photographic illustrations of a magical city where
a little boy and his red balloon went flying, exploring the rooftops.
Momma's eyes lit up with a beautiful serenity, as if she was somewhere up in the clouds, maybe dreaming of being that balloon
and flying up, up, and away. I never knew that the magical city in
the story was a place called Paris in a country called France.

And I certainly had no idea that I would visit Paris on several occasions.

My accomplishments as an elementary school student obviously made Moms proud. But if I ever fooled myself into thinking this was going to win me points with Freddie, I was sadly mistaken. In fact, Freddie Triplett—who could not read or write to save his life—spent every minute waging a one-man antiliteracy campaign. In his early thirties at this time, Freddie had stopped his schooling in the third grade back in Mississippi and couldn't even dial a telephone until later in his life, and he could barely do it then. This undoubtedly fed a deep-seated insecurity in him that he covered up by declaring that anybody who could read or write was a "slick motherfucker."

Of course, in his logic, this would have included Momma, me, my sisters, or anybody he thought knew something that he didn't, which meant they could take advantage of him. You could see it in the crazed flare of his eyes that he lived in a world full of slick motherfuckers out to get him. Mix that attitude with alcohol and the result was big-time paranoia.

Though I started to figure out some of these dynamics early on, for a while I was actually willing to see past them and to be on my best behavior in the hopes that he'd somehow find a fatherly side of himself with me. That hope was shattered one afternoon during a visit from Sam Salter, Ophelia's daddy.

In an odd matchup, Salter and Freddie turned out to be great friends and drinking buddies. This made no sense, not only because both had kids by Moms, but also because they were so different. Just as he did every time he visited, Salter entered a room with warmth and a southern gentleman's charm. A nicely dressed, articulate high school teacher—who could read and write and talk trash so good everybody thought he was a lawyer, although Freddie never once accused him of being a slick motherfucker—Samuel Salter had nothing in common with Freddie Triplett, who took over any space he entered by siege. Sometimes Freddie cleared a room at gunpoint, waving his shotgun, hollering, "Get the fuck outta my goddamn house!" Other times Freddie cleared the room with a rant, gesticulating angrily with a lit Pall Mall in one hand and his ever-present half-pint of whiskey in the other.

Old Taylor was Freddie's brand of choice, but he also drank Old Granddad and Old Crow, or basically any half-pint of whiskey he could wrap his hands around. He didn't have a hip flask for his whiskey, like some of the more sophisticated black men I saw. Dressed in his workingman's uniform that consisted of jeans or khakis, a wool shirt, a T-shirt underneath, always, and work shoes, Freddie just carried his little half-pint bottle. Everywhere. It was an appendage. How he managed to keep his job at A. O. Smith— eventually retiring from there, pension and all—was another mystery to me. Granted, as a steel man, he was a hard worker. But he was an even harder drinker.

That afternoon when Salter arrived, Ophelia and I ran to greet him, followed immediately by Freddie's arrival in the living room. Whenever he came by, Salter brought a little something for us— usually two dollars for Ophelia, his real blood daughter, and one dollar for me, because he treated me as a pretend son. This day we went through the routine, with Ophelia getting a hug and a kiss and her two dollars before skipping off, waving, "Bye, Daddy!" and then it was my turn.

Salter grinned at my open hand and didn't make me wait, commending me first on my good work at school and then handing me the crisp single dollar bill. Happy feelings swirled up inside, and I couldn't help it as I asked, "Ain't you my daddy too?"

"Yeah," said Salter, nodding his head thoughtfully, "I'm your daddy too. Here—" and he took out another dollar bill that he handed to me, saying, "Now you go and put that in your bank, son."

With a big smile on my face, even though I had no bank, I

started to turn and strut off, one dollar richer, with Ophelia's daddy agreeing to be my daddy too, when I was met by Freddie's scowl as he bellowed, out of nowhere, "Well, I ain't your goddamned daddy, and you ain't getting shit from me!"

Talk about bursting my balloon. For a moment I glanced back at Salter, who shot Freddie a strange look that went right over my head and Freddie's as well. Probably Salter meant something along the lines of what I was feeling—that Freddie had no call to say anything, number one 'cause I was talking to Salter at the time, and number two 'cause it was cruel and unusual punishment. Freddie had just made his point one too many times, on top of his incessant commentary about the size of my ears.

Even when I was standing nearby, whenever anybody asked about where I was, he answered with a roar, "I don't know where that big-eared motherfucker is."

Then, as if he did not care, he'd turn and look at me with a grin—like it made him a bigger man for stomping on me and my self-esteem—while I stood there and felt my naturally dark shade of skin burn red with hurt and embarrassment.

Another time I was in the bathroom when I heard someone asking for me and had to hear Freddie snarl, "I don't know where that big-eared motherfucker is," behind my back. It was bad enough when he said it in front of me, especially since he enjoyed watching me try to mask my seven-year-old pain, but it was almost worse hearing him say it when he really didn't know where I was. Besides, when I looked at my ears in the bathroom mirror to see how big they were, I realized they were sort of big, which made his comments sting all the more. It didn't matter that I would grow into them one day.

Between Freddie's remarks and some of the kids in the neighborhood and at school calling me "Dumbo"—the flying elephant from the Disney cartoon movie—a toll was being taken on my self-esteem, compounded by the gaping hole left by having no daddy. Everybody else knew who their daddy was. Ophelia's daddy was Salter, Sharon and Kim had Freddie, my friends all had daddies. That needless comment from Freddie that afternoon when Salter gave me the one dollar made it clear to my young sensibilities, finally, that he was never going to warm to me. The question for me then became—what could I do about it?

My long-term plan had already been formulated, starting with the solemn promise I made to myself that when I grew up and had a son of my own, he would always know who I was and I would never disappear from his life. But the short-term plan was much harder to figure out. How could I fend off the powerlessness not only of having no daddy and of being labeled "you big-eared motherfucker" but, much more damaging to my psyche, the powerlessness that came from the fear that never seemed to let up at home.

It was fear of what Freddie might do and what he'd already done. Big-time fear. Fear that I'd come home to find my mother murdered. Fear that my sisters and I would be murdered. Fear that the next time Freddie came home drunk, pulled out his shotgun, and woke all of us at the end of the barrel, shouting, "Everybody get the fuck outta my goddamned house!" he'd make good on his promise to kill us all. It had gotten to the point by this time that Moms slept on the living room couch with her shoes on—in case she had to run, carrying the baby and dragging the rest of us out of the house fast. Fear that the next time Freddie beat Momma up within an inch of her life he would go that inch too far. Fear that I'd have to watch that beating or watch Freddie beat Ophelia or take the beating myself and not be able to do anything to stop it. What could I do that the police couldn't or wouldn't, as many times as they'd show up and either do nothing or take Freddie away and send him home after he sobered up?

The questions of what was I going to do and how was I going to do it loomed large. They followed me at school, snuck into my waking and sleeping thoughts, and stirred up the nightmares that had troubled me most of my young life, nightmares that went back to foster care when there was a supposed witch down the street. Some of the dreams I was having were so terrifying, I was too paralyzed to wake, believing in my sleep that if I could knock something over, a bedside lamp, for example, it would rouse some- one in the house to come to my rescue and help me escape what- ever terror was in that dream at the time.

"Chris!" Sharon's voice pierces my semiconscious state once more.

Now I open my eyes, sitting bolt upright, taking a fast inven- tory. Before I went to sleep, nothing eventful had happened, other than some Halloween trick-or-treating, after which Ophelia went to a party with her friends—where she is, apparently, at the pres- ent. Otherwise, it had been a fairly quiet night in the back house that we rent from my entrepreneurial aunt, Miss Bessie, the first in our extended family to own a home—which houses her beauty salon business, Bessie's Hair Factory, in the basement.

Crying, Sharon pulls at my sleeve, telling me, "Momma's on the floor."

Not knowing what I'm going to find, I throw off the covers, grab my robe, and hurry down the hall into the front room. There, lying face down on the floor, is Momma, unconscious, a two-by- four stuck in the back of her head and a pool of blood spreading underneath and around her. Sharon's cries begin to escalate as she stares down at our mother alongside me. "Wake up, wake up!" she screams. "Wake up!"

Fighting the paralysis of shock, I feel some other mechanism take over, and my immediate reaction is to assess what has taken place, like a crime-scene analyst.

First I observe that Momma was trying to get out of the house and move toward the door when Freddie attacked her with the two-by-four, bashing it into the back of her skull with such a force that the wood splintered into her skin, sticking into her, spewing blood not just underneath her but everywhere in the room.

Next, feeling the waves of terror that Momma is dead or about to die, I turn to see Baby on the telephone calling the ambulance. Freddie's baby sister, affectionately known as Baby, reassures me that the paramedics are on their way and goes to calm Sharon.

Amid all my senses trying to compute the mess of blood, fear, my sister's sobbing, and Baby's insistence that Momma is going to the hospital and she is going to be all right, and more blood, the volcanic question of *What can I do?* erupts in me. The answer: clean the stove! I have to do something, anything. I need a job, a duty to perform. So I race to the kitchen and begin to scrub our old-fashioned cookstove that seems like it's been used since the time of the Pilgrims and is caked with a grime of an unknown lineage. Using a scrap of a dishrag, Brillo, and soap and water, I commence to clean and scour with all my being, at the same time that I commence to pray. My prayer is even more elaborate than *Oh, God, please don't let Momma die*. It's that, but it's also *God, please don't let anyone come in here and see this place all dirty like this*.

The idea that the white paramedics and policemen will see the blood everywhere and then the dirty stove as well is too shameful to bear. So my job is to clean it up, to prove that decent people live here, not savages, with the exception of Freddie, who has drawn blood, once again, from a woman.

When the ambulance came, the attendants moved in quickly, spoke to Baby and Bessie, not to me of course, put Momma on a stretcher, with the two-by-four removed, took her out to the ambulance, and drove off.

Even then I continued to clean, the only task I could find to create order in the chaos. The world became very small for me that night. A part of me shut down in a way that froze me emotionally but was also necessary for my survival.

My efforts didn't save Momma. Apparently what saved her was

her thickheadedness. Literally. Thanks to the strength and resilience of her skull, Freddie's attempt to kill her had failed. She returned the next day, bandaged, battered, but conscious enough to promise he was never going to be allowed to return. With a resolve I hadn't heard before, she looked us all in the eyes and swore, "Well, he ain't coming back in here no more."

We might have gone an entire week without him, but before I could relax he had returned after all. I knew this roller coaster. We'd been on it since I could remember. Every time he came back, apologetic, contrite, he'd start off being real nice. But he was as predictable as rain. Nobody knew when he'd go off, but at some point everybody knew he would. Again, and again, and again.

Why Moms fell for it each time was confusing, without question. By the same token, I understood that we were sometimes in the most dangerous straits when we were trying to get away.

While I had no control over the short term, I expanded my long-term plan. Not only was I going to make sure my children had a daddy, I was never going to be Freddie Triplett. I was never going to terrorize, threaten, harm, or abuse a woman or a child, and I was never going to drink so hard that I couldn't account for my actions. This plan evolved over time as I studied at the virtual college of how to grow up and not be Freddie. For now, I could only hate him. It was an emotional truth that lived under my skin, close to the bone.

Small flickers of rebellion had begun to flare. As an antidote to my feeling of powerlessness, I did little things just to see if I could mess with Freddie. For instance, I knew that he couldn't read and was threatened by anyone who could—which gave me an opening.

Sometimes I'd start reading aloud, for no reason other than sending him a message—*I may have big ears, but I can read. Real good. You can beat us down, but you can't read.* Other times I was even more calculating, holding my book and pointing to a word as I asked

Momma, very loud to make sure Freddie heard, "What does this word mean?" Or another variation: "What does this spell?" Or, at my most devilish, I might, out of the blue, ask her how to spell a particular word.

Momma had only to give me a gentle look, telling me just with the expression in her eyes—*Son, you know very well what the answer is*. It was our unspoken conspiracy, our private agreement that he wasn't going to break us. Then, out loud, she'd say, "I don't know," and the two of us would smile at each other with our eyes.

Finally, in the dead of night that same winter after the two-by-four incident, Moms enlisted me and the rest of us in a full-scale rebellion. After Freddie unleashed on her, for the umpteenth time, and left the house to go drink in one of several local watering holes in the neighborhood, Momma got up from the floor, put ice on her swelling face, and began packing, urging us to help.

"We have to move," she said simply as Ophelia and I helped pack, throwing our clothes and stuff into bags, gathering up whatever we could because we knew, without being told, that time was of the essence. Instead of going to stay with relatives, we were moving to a place that Momma had rented on Sixth Street, just two blocks over from the back house on Eighth and Wright. After we piled everything into a shopping cart that we wheeled together over to the new place, all four of us in tow, I watched her face fall as she frantically rummaged in her pockets and purse. Looking up at the second-floor apartment, she shook her head mournfully, saying, "The key . . . I don't have the key." She looked shell-shocked, completely defeated.

Studying the building, I pointed to a pole, telling Momma, "I can climb up there, jump down on the porch, come through the window, and then open the door from inside." Being a scrappy, skinny kid at the time—used to climbing up tall trees for the fun of it—I not only thought I could do it, it was imperative that I succeed at opening up that door to our new life, free of Freddie. It was having a job to do, something concrete, and it was also a battle between him and me. I had to win. As proposed, I executed my plan—scaling the pole to the roof, jumping down from the roof to the porch, thankfully raising the window on the porch level, and sliding inside. From there, I opened the apartment door and flew downstairs, where the relieved look on my mother's face was all I needed to see. As we all settled in that night, I couldn't have felt more proud of myself.

Over the next few days Moms caught me looking worried and knew that I was scared Freddie would show up and try to conquer our new land.

"He ain't coming back," she reassured me in words. "No more. He ain't never coming back."

One evening I was summoned to the living room in the new place by the sound of a man's voice that seemed to be threatening. The conversation was about money or rent. Instead of belonging to Freddie, the voice turned out to be that of a white man I'd never seen before. A nondescript fellow in layers of winter clothes appropriate for the season, he was speaking in a disrespectful way that caused my mother to tremble.

Almost by reflex, I ran to the kitchen and returned with a butcher knife, pointing it at the white man. "You can't talk to my momma like that," I interrupted.

My mother threw me a look that spoke volumes, warning me to amend my tone and my words, to be polite.

I sent her a look right back, telling her that I would obey her. Turning back to the man, knife still in hand, I spoke again, this time saying, "You can't talk to my momma like that, *Mister*."

He backed down, soon leaving us alone. It was, unfortunately, not the last time I heard that dismissive, superior tone being used toward my mother, my siblings, and myself. Throughout my life I would battle that same reflex to want to strike back when certain individuals of a different race or class spoke to me in that way.

The more immediate consequence was that Freddie came back. The roller coaster crested the top and plunged down again. Each time I hated him that much more. Barely gone more than a week, we packed up and returned to the back house, with Freddie giving us a respite of no less than a week without violence. Disappointment, and not understanding why, ate at me. Because I didn't know that Momma had been in prison before, I couldn't yet grasp that she was mostly afraid that Freddie would send her back again. Only later would I fully understand that she had little financial independence, certainly not enough to raise four kids, and no means of escape, but I could already sense that she was stuck between the proverbial rock and a hard place.

This made my need to find that remedy to fix our situation that much more urgent. The answer came one Sunday afternoon, while watching Freddie eat a plate of Momma's cooking—in this case, her unrivaled neck bones. As a rule, watching Freddie eat was as close as a city boy like me ever got to a pig trough. But on this occasion it only took this once to watch him suck, break, and knock neck bones on the kitchen table to experience permanent revulsion. Lacking any sense of embarrassment, Freddie not only embraced the porcine essence of himself while eating but combined that with the apparent ability to fart, belch, and sneeze all at once. Who was this Sonny Liston–looking and –acting, Pall Mall–smoking, whiskey-drinking, gun-crazed giant pig man? Where was the humanity in a man who didn't seem to give a damn what anyone else thought of him and never missed an opportunity to batter, insult, embarrass, or humiliate any of us, especially me? Was it because I was the only male in the house, because I could read, because I was my mother's only son, or a combination of all of those things and others known only to himself?

The answers to those questions were long in coming, if ever. But finally, I had an answer to what my short-term plan of action should be. I wasn't even eight years old when it hit me like a strike of lightning, that Sunday afternoon, watching him suck on those bones as I thought to myself: *I'm gonna kill this motherfucker.*

————

In contrast to the danger that lurked at home, outside on the streets of Milwaukee's north side—with all the fun and drama of our black *Happy Days* setting—I got to experience elements of a relatively safe and normal childhood. Safety came in part from knowing the lay of the land and also from having a sense of its boundaries. On the north border, running east-west, was W. Capitol Drive, above which the upwardly mobile bourgeois Negroes lived—where kids' daddies worked as professionals, some of them doctors and lawyers, others teachers, insurance men, or government workers. There in the center of the north side was our lower-income yet still industrious community—mostly working-class steel and automotive workers stuck in between the land of movin' on up (where we all secretly aspired to live one day, though we pretended we didn't want to be with all the nose-in-the-air folks) and the bridge to the white world at the south side, which was never to be crossed, went the unwritten law of the racial divide. One of the main arteries, running north-south, was Third Street, which was lined with some of the nicer stores like Gimbels, the Boston Store, and Brill's, as well as the Discount Center, right at Third and North, my favorite spot for buying clothes on a budget.

A couple blocks away from where we lived at Eighth and Wright was the lively intersection of Ninth and Meineke, near where I attended Lee Street Elementary School—coincidentally a school attended by Oprah Winfrey's sister Pat when they lived in Wisconsin—across from which was Sy's store. A big, balding Jewish guy, Sy was one of those few splashes of white in our community—even though I didn't know until later that being Jewish was different from being White Anglo-Saxon Protestant—and he was well liked for extending short lines of credit to regular customers like us. We also felt comfortable with the two black men who helped run the business for Sy and later bought the store from him. Henry and his son—aptly nicknamed Bulldog on account of that's what he looked like—were great characters and contributed to the inviting atmosphere.

Sy made and sold an array of incredible-tasting food, including the best sausage I ever ate in my life, and also offered an eclectic selection of home and personal items. Whenever Momma called for "Chrissy Paul . . ." it was her vocal signal that she was going to ask me to run an errand for her to pick something up at Sy's, anything from a can of Sweet Garrett, the snuff she loved to dip, or Day's Work, a popular brand of chewing tobacco, to some obscure personal item that I'd never heard of before. Whatever Kotex were, I had no idea. Much as I wanted to please my mother and return with what she needed, I almost always came back with the wrong item, especially when she asked, "Chrissy Paul, go run down to Sy's and get me some taupe stockings." I came back with any color but taupe. Eventually she started writing notes to Sy rather than have me try to figure it out.

Two blocks north from there, at Ninth and Clarke, was another landmark of the neighborhood that we familiarly referred to as the "nigga store"—not in any pejorative sense but because the owners, unlike most of the white-owned businesses, were black. Any money in my pocket, I was out the door to Ninth and Clarke to pick up a dollar's worth of candy and a bag or two of Okey Doke cheese popcorn.

The challenge for me, starting at the age of seven or earlier, was figuring out how to get that money in my pocket. Most of the older kids and all the adults I saw seemed to have similar concerns. Everybody, on some level, was looking for their particular hustle, their angle to get over. My cousin Terry, Bessie's thirteen-year-old son, was a ringleader of a group of cats I followed around some-

times—they provided me with the fundamentals of being an en-
trepreneur, 1960s ghetto style.

Opportunity came knocking when the City of Milwaukee began building a stretch of Interstate 43 right down the middle of our
neighborhood between Seventh and Eighth Streets. Since all the
residential and business properties on Seventh Street were being
evacuated and prepared for demolition, Terry and his cohorts figured they'd try their hands at junking.

Eager to join in, even though I had no idea what junking was,
I tagged along and helped the older boys literally tear apart places
that had been condemned, looking for materials—fixtures, lead,
copper wire, window weights, old clothes, rags, even paper. This
wasn't stealing—or so Terry would have argued—because we
were really just helping the city to tear down condemned houses.
And instead of the demo guys having to cart the stuff off, we
helped by piling up shopping carts and rolling them all the way
to the east side of Milwaukee, just short of where you crossed the
river before hitting the lake. This was where Mr. Katz, a Jewish
entrepreneur who bought this stuff by the pound, ran his junking
business.

Wanting to increase our profit margin, we tried to be slick a few
times, but we were no match for Mr. Katz—he had invented this
game. Our silly ploy was to try to weight down our load—before
he put our junk up on his scales—by wetting the rags and hiding
them under milk cartons buried at the bottom of our heaps.

Mr. Katz knew all the tricks, backward and forward. He knew,
almost instinctually, when the weight was too heavy for what he
was seeing, as he immediately began to yell in Yiddish and start
digging for the wet rags. It never worked. Nonetheless, we didn't
fare too badly in the junking business with Mr. Katz as our regular
buyer. That is to say, Terry and his friends didn't do too badly. My
take of five or ten dollars was much less than each of their shares.
Still, I was more than happy to spend my money on a few little

things I wanted, without having to ask Momma for money for the movies or candy. It also introduced me to the main operating principle of any marketplace: supply and demand. The demand was obviously somebody out there who paid Mr. Katz for the junk we supplied. Not such a shabby deal.

Some of cousin Terry's other hustles weren't necessarily on the up and up, like the time he showed up in our backyard with cases of cigarette cartons and all of a sudden all the kids from the neighborhood, myself included, were back there smoking, with a vaguely suspicious-sounding story about these cases having fallen off a truck or some such thing. They were actually somehow stolen from a local tavern by Terry. It didn't matter to me. We were so cool, I thought. Even better, we didn't get caught.

But we usually did. In fact, part of the reason that we were given a lot of free rein to come and go as we pleased was that our friends' parents were keeping an eye out on all of us. This was made quite plain to me once when I went over to see the Ball brothers, Arthur and Willie. With this group of friends, football later became our thing, and once I started to get bigger and taller, I assumed the role of quarterback. Our games were all about passing, running, and scoring, which resulted in so many touchdowns that final scores would end up being something like 114 to 98, more like basketball scores. The Ball brothers were the best blockers any after-school team could want, on their way to becoming the biggest cats you ever saw in your life. Two of the nicest, most gentle guys I knew, they were the size of professional football linemen by the time they hit adolescence. Early on, one of the first times I went to their house happened to be a particularly hot summer day, and when I arrived it was apparent that the screen in the door to the Ball house had been knocked out and the door was just a wooden frame. So, rather than mentioning the obvious, I just walked right through the wood frame and into the house.

All at once, Mrs. Ball, their mother, came into view and shook her finger at me. "Boy, you better get back outta here and open that door! Where's yo' manners?!"

I stood there for a second, not understanding. The screen was knocked out, so the door was already open, wasn't it?

Mrs. Ball didn't see it that way. As I pivoted around to obey her, she added, "You weren't raised like that! I know your mother. Now, open that door like you got some sense. G'on back out there and open the door, you hear me?"

A heavyset woman, a little older than Moms, Mrs. Ball made it clear that this was her house and she was in charge.

Still saying nothing, I didn't know how I was supposed to go back out through a door that was already opened. Did I exit by stepping out as I had entered, or did I push open the frame of the door? With her standing there, hands on hips, eagle-eyed watching me, I opened the wood frame of the door, went back out, and closed it.

Now she said, "Come on in."

The moment I did, Mrs. Ball smiled and added, "How you doing, Chrissy?"

Not everybody's family enforced the importance of manners in this way, but there were unwritten community rules for keeping kids out of trouble. In many households at the time, there was a distinction between abuse and being punished forcefully for something you did wrong. Rods were definitely not spared. Since everybody's mommas and daddies all knew each other, it was perfectly acceptable for somebody else's parent to give you a whuppin' if you stepped out of line. Then they'd call your momma and you'd get it from her when you got home. Then you'd have to wait for your old man to come home, and he would just mop up the floor with you again, giving you a whuppin' worse than any of the others.

Our household was slightly different. Freddie was excessive enough with beating us on a regular basis, whether we were being punished or not, so Momma chose not to whip us. As a true teacher, she was able to give us the real lessons we needed to learn without force; instead, her well-chosen words, the sharp tone of her voice, and the look in her eyes said all we needed to hear.

There were very occasional exceptions, like the one time I got it for stealing a nickel bag of Okey Doke cheese popcorn from the "nigga store." The African American woman who owned the store not only knew my momma, she announced—when she caught me trying to be slick and walk out the door all seven-year-old innocent and grabbed me by the collar—but also knew where Momma was employed. For my trying to shoplift a nickel bag of popcorn, both the police and Momma received phone calls. And after my mother had to come and collect me at the store before escorting me home, I got my butt whipped with all the ferocity of a woman hell-bent on making sure I would never steal again.

Being creative about it, Momma whipped me with the coiled-up, thick, old-fashioned telephone cord that caused the bell on the phone to ring each time she struck me. *Bing! Bing! Bing!* Besides the physical agony of it—harsh enough to make me wonder if she was going to kill me—the psychological piece of it was the fact that for weeks after that, every time the phone rang, I had flashbacks. As the last beating she ever gave me, it certainly prevented me from even thinking about stealing anything for a very long time—at least until I was a teenager.

Maybe part of my mother's fury was making sure that while I might enjoy tagging along with my cousin Terry, she didn't want me following in his footsteps. The reality was that we all sensed Terry was on his way to trouble, one of those kids born to be a hoodlum.

"Hey, Chrissy," Terry was always calling across our backyard, inviting me up to the Big House, as he did one morning when a bunch of us—his sisters and mine—followed his lead by turning the large staircase into a Disneyland ride. This was a change of pace from the competition to see who could claim to be the most interesting character from different movies. My pick from *The Magnificent Seven* was the character Chris, played by Yul Brynner, a really cool-looking cat in that movie. Even though my name was a match, I'd been overruled by the older guys who got first picks. Movies had a powerful influence on me, like books, letting me look through windows into other worlds. Nothing shaped my view of life more than *The Wizard of Oz*, my favorite movie from childhood. One day I planned on living in Kansas where nothing bad ever happened except for a very occasional tornado.

In the meantime, I got to have some good old-fashioned playtime at Terry's instigation. We spent most of that day while the adults were out by sliding down the stairs in cardboard boxes that went zooming down the steps and colliding into bumpers we made from the couch cushions. When we exhausted the fun from that, Terry proposed, "Hey, Chrissy, let's do a pillow fight. Boys against girls!"

"Yeah!" I was all for it. It was him and me versus two of my sisters and three of my girl cousins.

Before long the pillow fight got out of hand, mainly because Terry decided to put a sizable piece of lead in his pillowcase. The next thing we knew he had smacked his sister Elaine in the head with his lead pillow, followed by shrieks, screams, and blood everywhere.

Everyone scattered as one of the older girls went to find Paul Crawford. This was Terry's father, a man who was always referred to by both names. Although he wasn't married to Ms. Bessie, Paul Crawford—a carpenter, handyman, and hustler—was very much present in the Big House, not only as our resident sheriff but as the provider of limitless supplies of one-hundred-pound bags of potatoes. We might have been money-poor but we weren't ever going to starve.

Paul Crawford was somebody else's daddy that I would have been proud to call my father, if that had been the case. He had a style, a hustling, tough guy, workingman's pizzazz, just in the way he was never seen without his fully loaded tool belt slung low, his workman's cap with an authoritative tilt, and, never without an unlit cigar hanging from his lower lip. The only time I ever saw Paul Crawford light it was the day he confronted his son about the serious injury inflicted on Elaine.

Once she was bandaged and taken to the emergency room, Paul Crawford summoned all of us to the living room in the Big House, where the furniture had been pushed to one side. In an eerily close reenactment of *High Plains Drifter*, a film I saw many years later, Paul Crawford slowly took off his tool belt, pacing the floor and looking into our eyes, waiting for one of us to spill the beans on Terry. We all claimed not to know who was responsible, including Terry.

"Well," said Paul Crawford, striking terror in our souls, "somebody g'on tell me something," and he now pulled out his pants belt, pausing dramatically to light his cigar.

The only difference between this cigar lighting and Clint Eastwood's version was that in the movie he wore a cowboy hat; in Paul Crawford's version he wore his worker's hat. Instead of being a gunslinger, he was a belt slinger as it came alive in his hands, like an angry, out-of-control snake. Though his main focus was Terry, we all caught ricochet blows as Paul Crawford taught each of us the meaning of "putting the fear o' God in yo' black ass."

That was the end of our indoor ghetto Disneyland, cigarettes, and pillow fights.

Looking for less controversial pursuits sometime later when the weather had turned beautiful and sunny, Terry and I thought no one would mind if we built ourselves a little clubhouse in the yard out back with some of the loose lumber lying around.

Unbeknownst to us, Freddie did mind and had supposedly been hollering, "Stop making all that goddamned noise!" because he was trying to sleep. With Terry hammering on the outside and me inside the clubhouse hammering, we couldn't hear anything. Then I became aware that Terry had stopped hammering. Suddenly, the clubhouse begins to disintegrate around me with a giant reverberating sound going *Whop! Whop! Whop!* and the sun reflecting off the shiny metal blade of Freddie's long-handled ax.

All I know is that the clubhouse is being chopped down with me in it, and Terry has split. Not only does Freddie not give a damn that I'm inside, he seems uninterested in the fact that splintering wood has slashed into one of my legs, which is now bleeding a small river onto our structure-turned-woodpile as I shriek from pain. Freddie is impervious, like a human buzz saw, demonically possessed with turning our annoying noisy project and me into mulch.

Amid the *whop!*s and my shrieks and blood and wood splinters flying everywhere, Momma's voice enters the cacophony as she screams at Freddie, "Stop! Stop it!"

With a grunt, he brings his destruction to a grinding halt, defending himself by declaring, "I told him to stop making all that goddamn noise."

Leave it to Freddie to destroy anybody else's good time. Momma comforted me, making sure to clean out the gash on my leg and put a bandage on it. When it started to scab over, the irritation was so bad that I picked at it and the scab was soon infected. Momma applied another bandage that happened to fall off one day when she was at work.

After washing it off again, I looked for a big bandage to put over it and found what looked like a soft, fluffy, clean white bandage in that package from Sy's store. I placed it carefully over the scabbing area by tying it around my leg. Then, pretty proud of my precocious medical abilities, I thought I'd take a stroll through the neighborhood and show off my cool-looking bandage.

Who should I run into on the street but my cousin Terry? I strutted up, only to watch his horrified face looking me up and down.

"What is that on your leg, Chrissy?" he exclaimed. Before I could answer, he went on, "What you doing wearing a Kotex? You crazy?"

For the life of me, I didn't know why he was so angry and embarrassed.

Terry wagged his finger at me. "Don't you ever let me catch you wearing a woman's Kotex! Take it off! Right now! And don't you ever let me see you wearing those things again!"

Although the scar caused by the ax incident never went away, I did outgrow the delayed humiliation that hit me when I found out why Kotex weren't supposed to be used as bandages.

It was yet one more reminder of how much I hated Freddie, how badly I wanted him gone from our lives. But coming up with a way to get rid of him felt like one of those impossible quests given to young inexperienced knights to go off and slay unslayable, fire-breathing dragons.

How could I do it? With a gun? The prospect was terrifying. For Freddie, with his hunting and fishing country upbringing, gunplay was a natural prevalent thing, something he'd been doing all his life. It was also a form of addiction, like drinking, the only way he knew how to express himself when things didn't go his way, to placate that inner rage, to settle differences when kicking somebody's ass didn't do the job.

At age eight, my track record with a loaded weapon was dismal. A couple of years before, one of my friends and I had been playing in an alley near the Thunderbird Inn and found a .22 in an abandoned stove. Without knowing if it was real, we decided to test it out by aiming at somebody—a true nightmare scenario. We missed, miraculously, but the girl we aimed the gun toward could have been killed. When Freddie got that phone call, which may have come from Momma for all I know, he barreled for me. I knew what I'd done was terrible, stupid, and wrong, but I didn't want to get whupped, so I raced into my bedroom, slid under the bed, and held my breath. Before I had a moment to exhale, Freddie had lifted up the entire bed, exposing me there, shaking like prey. The belt lashing was bad, but the sense that he was omnipotent was worse.

Besides, even if I'd had a gun and could use it, that wouldn't necessarily do the job. In fact, there was one night when news arrived that he'd been in a drunken bar fight and his best friend, Simon Grant, had shot Freddie in the stomach. *Glory Hallelujah, praise the Lord!* But Freddie's huge belly acted like a bulletproof vest. He bled profusely, but after they removed the bullet and kept him in the hospital overnight for observation, he went right on in to work the next day.

Not knowing what tactic would serve me in the quest I had absolutely resigned myself to undertaking, every violent episode was further proof that I had no choice but to do away with him. That was very much in my mind one night when he was obviously preparing to beat Momma again and I ran to call the cops.

Right near Sy's at the intersection of Ninth and Meineke was a bar called the Casbah. Sure that somebody would loan me ten cents to make a call on the pay phone outside the bar, I approached the first guy I saw—a cat who looked like a postcard version of a 1962 north-side Milwaukee player, with a snap brim hat, sharkskin suit, and pin knot tie.

"Mister, look," I say, dashing toward him, out of breath, "can you please give me a dime? I gotta call the police, 'cause my stepfather's about to beat up my mother."

This cat, he doesn't blink an eye, saying only, "You can't hustle me, nigger."

Now I want to kill this motherfucker in addition to Freddie.

After I find someone willing to trust me that my mother's life really is in danger, I get through to the police, and two police officers, both white, are sent to the house.

When they arrive, Freddie is sitting on the couch, and they're obviously surprised to see a man of his size. After they exchange nervous glances at each other, one of them clears his throat, asking, "Mr. Triplett, can we use your phone? We need to call the wagon."

One of the few times Freddie exhibits anything close to a sense of humor he leans in to them and replies, "Hell, naw, you can't use my goddamn phone to call the police to bring a wagon to take me to jail. Fuck you!"

It was ludicrous. They eventually coaxed him to go with them down to the station. Once he was gone, I asked Momma why they had tried to use our phone to call the police if they *were* the police and *were* already at our house. She said, "Well, maybe they thought they needed a couple of *big* police officers to get him out of here."

This was as maddening as the day that Momma ran to hide at Odom's corner store on Tenth and Wright. The owner, Mr. Odom, was the daddy of a school friend of mine, and he didn't try to stop my mother from lying down behind the counter.

Waving his shotgun, Freddie stalked her into the store, demanding that Mr. Odom tell him, "Where is that bitch?"

Mr. Odom shrugged. "Well, she's not in here, Freddie, and you got to get out of my store with that shotgun. You hear me?"

Mr. Odom suffered no fools. Knowing this, Freddie, like all bullies, was actually a coward when confronted by someone who refused to be bullied. Without so much as an argument, Freddie turned around and left, continuing up the block, holding his shotgun in broad daylight, looking for Momma.

She was able to lay low until later that evening, when he apparently cooled down. For the next two days or so, Freddie's internal barometric pressure seemed to indicate that storms weren't imminent, as if the valve had temporarily released some steam. But the signs were sometimes misleading, so we all walked on eggshells, all of us—me, Momma, twelve-year-old Ophelia, four-year-old Sharon, and two-year-old Kim—all the time.

While I knew that we all feared and pretty much loathed Freddie, the question of how my mother really felt about our increasingly intolerable situation was left as unanswered as the question about who and where my real daddy was. That is, until I happened to stumble over one of the only clues to her inner world that I would ever have.

Around this time, Moms actually made one of the only references to the man who fathered me. Freddie had, once again, reminded me that he wasn't my goddamn daddy. Trying to console me, she mentioned offhandedly that I did have a daddy down in Louisiana, who had once sent me a letter with five dollars or so enclosed. I had never seen the letter, the money, or his name. Momma pointed out that she was always giving me money, as much as she could, which was true. But that didn't explain why she thought my seeing my real father's letter would cause me more heartache than not knowing anything about him.

That may have been on my mind when I was surprised to find myself home alone in the back house one late afternoon and decided to go rummaging in drawers, looking for that letter perhaps, and others. What I found instead was a letter written in Momma's careful, simple script, which had no salutation, even though it was obviously being sent to a trusted friend. It seemed to slip right into my hands when I reached into her bedside drawer to pick up Momma's little worn Bible she kept in there.

It was evident to me that even though Freddie couldn't read any of it, Momma was aware that if he just saw the letter, he would view it as an act of treason. For that reason, she probably had to write it in stealth and then keep it tucked secretly into her Bible, where he wasn't likely to find it.

There was much in the letter about things that were going on between her and the old man that I knew nothing about, and didn't understand, including a business proposition he had going in Detroit that never got off the ground. The contents were overwhelming, staggering, especially the sheer panic in the words at the very start of the letter: *Help, I fear for my life.*

Of course, I knew that snooping around wasn't right. But still, it took my reading of that letter to know the truth about what she was feeling and to know that she was trying to get help. For the next few days I watched her, making sure she didn't suspect that I'd found that letter. Without realizing it, I had already developed the family skill of being able to keep a few secrets myself.

As a result, when at long last I came up with a viable method of killing Freddie and began to concoct the lethal potion that he was going to mistake for alcohol, nobody had a clue about what I was doing. My first feat was to slip off with *his* cup, his stainless steel drinking cup, the only one he drank from and treated as lovingly as a silver goblet embedded with jewels. Next, without any watch-ful eyes, I poured a little liquid bleach in, some rubbing alcohol, with healthy doses of all the cleaning agents and medicines that had poison warnings on them, and finally mixed it all together by adding near-boiling water. All bubbling and foaming, it was better than anything any Dr. Frankenstein could cook up in a movie, but the horrific stench was a problem. How was I going to get Freddie to drink it now?

One possibility was to leave it in the bathroom and just hope that he would take a sip out of curiosity. Great idea. Except, when I got in there and heard voices coming near, I got nervous that he'd make me drink it out of curiosity. My next thought was to try to trick him that it was one of those fancy flaming drinks. Ridiculous as that was, I lit a match and tossed it in. *Poof!* A towering blue and orange flame shot up in Freddie's big steel cup! Besides my death potion being a bust, I was now going to burn myself up. The only option I could see was to empty the burning, foaming mess down the toilet. Throwing the top down, I figured that it was over but smoke and flames began to issue forth from under the lid.

"What's that goddamn smell?" came Freddie's voice.

Flushing the toilet—which miraculously made the smell disap-pear and didn't cause an explosion that burned up me or the house—I stepped out of the bathroom, returned Freddie's cup to where I'd found it, and answered, "What smell?"

Depressed that my effort had come to naught, I tried to comfort myself that it was a trial run and my next attempt would be successful. My latest plan was to try to do it in his sleep. Little did I know that my mother, with her gift for secrecy, was being pushed to a similar extreme. One night, after another brutal beating, she said out loud, to no one in particular, "He ain't never coming back." She added that if he did, she would kill him before he could hurt her or us again, stating matter-of-factly, "I'll do it when he's asleep."

If she kept the details of her own fantasies of revenge a secret, there was one thing Bettye Jean Gardner Triplett couldn't keep from me. Toward the end of these three and a half years that had followed since she came to get us from Uncle Archie's house and just before she vanished again—without warning or explanation from others—I discovered that she had the astonishing ability to become almost supernaturally still. Shortly after finding her letter, I was in the living room watching TV in the evening, and she was at the dining table reading the newspaper when Freddie performed his one-man stampede to her side, ranting and raving, trying to agitate and engage her, outdoing all former tirades with language more foul and abusive than I'd ever heard.

On one level this was the most surreal atmosphere of denial, with Freddie acting the part of the ax murderer in the horror movie while Moms and I pretended to play the part of the kid watching TV and the mother reading the newspaper, a normal family at home. The more sound and fury that came from Freddie's raging storm, the more still my mother grew.

I'd never witnessed anything like this in my life before—or since. Her stillness was fueled by a million times the energy that thundered in Freddie. That was the most still I've ever seen anything or anybody be in my life. A table moves more. Momma sat there motionless, eyes on her newspaper, frozen, not even turning a page, as if she had vanished deep within herself to prevent herself from responding—because she knew that if she said anything, if she turned a page, flicked an eyelash, breathed, he would hit her. Her stillness defeated his storm. To my shock, he gave up, blew his wad of rage, and turned to her like he just changed the channel on a TV set and said, "C'mon, let's get it on!"

The ability to become still was born in me that night from watching Moms. It exists in the realm of instinct, when the choice is flight or fight. Stillness was my mother's only defense against a predator, the way prey can avoid the attack of a killer cobra or a shark by being so still as to be invisible. And it may have been in that moment of stillness that she decided the time had come for the prey to find another way to get rid of the predator, to enact her own plan to make sure Freddie wouldn't be coming back. It may have been then that she decided to take the necessary precautions to make sure that she had all of her children out of the house, me included, one night after Freddie had returned home drunk and passed out.

With her children out of harm's way, she followed through on her plan to burn the house down while Freddie slept. Or that was the story I would eventually hear. How he woke up and stopped the fire, I never did learn. But I do know Freddie used her attempt to kill him to support his claim that she had violated her parole from her earlier imprisonment—which he had also instigated. And once again, his actions caused her to be sent back to prison.

The full details were never revealed to me or my sisters. All I got from this time was a mechanism for becoming still when scary forces preyed on me. Fear of losing my life, losing the life of a loved one, or the fear of losing everything I have—those fears followed me for years. Stillness has been my refuge and my defense. Even later, as an adult, I would cope by being still. Very still. It's not something I would always feel good about, but it's where I go whenever there's too much chaos around me, when the world seems like it's crumbling, when I suddenly fear that everything or everyone I cherish is going to be taken from me in the blink of the eye.

I get still.

CHAPTER 3

Where's Momma?

In the blink of an eye, one of my greatest fears came to pass. After a return of only a few years, my mother disappeared almost as suddenly as she had reappeared. Everything in my world suddenly went to white noise—an infinite grainy uncertainty. When I blinked again, I found myself twelve blocks west at my Uncle Willie's house on Nineteenth and Meineke—where I would live for most of the next three years. It was as though the script I was living one day got switched and I had to just jump in the next day with a new script and a whole new cast of characters, without asking any questions.

Unlike the evasive reactions I'd gotten to questions at Uncle Archie's house when I was much younger, or the way that my mother would answer a question generally or partially, whenever I asked questions at Uncle Willie's house, he or his wife Ella Mae gave no response at all, like I was talking a foreign language.

Almost ten months went by—a lifetime to an eight-year-old—before I had even a clue about what had happened to Momma and where she was. Then, on one of the saddest occasions of my childhood—at a funeral, as it happened—I caught sight of her standing at a distance with a prison guard at her side. Until that piece of stark evidence showed up—a major puzzle piece that was only further explained decades later—I didn't know for those months whether or not she was even alive.

To make matters more confusing, it was about this time that Ophelia was sent away. Now the second most important person in my life was missing. Explanations, as always, were vague; but many, many years later I learned that Uncle Willie and Aunt Ella Mae had decided that my twelve-year-old sister would be better off living in a kind of detention home and school for girls who had trouble conforming to rules.

With a full house, counting me and their own three kids, it was understandable that my uncle and, in particular, my aunt saw fit to establish a fairly strict code of conduct. But compared to the easygoing atmosphere that Uncle Archie and TT had maintained, and in contrast to the chaotic drama under Freddie's drunken reign—where us kids could do what we wanted if we stayed out of his way—the new rules presented big-time culture shock. While Ophelia initially did her best to adapt to the rules, I initially rebelled, hating that I suddenly had a bedtime and had to do chores and that there was one way to do them.

Dishes? I had to do them if it was so ordered by Aunt Ella Mae—dark, tall, and big-boned, built like one of the last Amazons—who watched over us hawkishly in her cat-eye glasses. But dishes? This went against my rules. Actually, it was the subject of one of the few arguments I ever had with Ophelia when Momma had left her in charge and my sister had tried to force me to clean the kitchen—including the dishes. The one time in my life that I ever invoked a philosophy of Freddie Triplett, I refused, insisting, "Freddie says that washing dishes is for girls." Ophelia was ready to kick my ass, but I ran away laughing.

There was no running from Aunt Ella Mae. At one point she made me do the dishes for a month because she claimed to have spotted some grease on a glass—after I'd sworn to having washed it. She smirked, saying, "I can see grease, and I don't even have my glasses on." That was only the beginning.

A woman who stood at least six inches taller than Uncle Willie—who was preoccupied with much more pressing worries than the execution of household chores—Aunt Ella Mae, in my estimation, had simply figured out how to give us more work so she could do less. Plus she really took the adage "waste not, want not" to heart. To conserve milk, for example, she had all of us kids take turns eating cereal out of the same bowl, with a fork, one by one. Once I got wise to her system, I volunteered to go last, knowing that when my cereal was eaten I could turn up the bowl and drink the lion's share of the milk.

Maybe Ophelia was already at a breaking point from residual anger over our situation, or from an accumulation of the fear and hurt we all had experienced. Or maybe, because she was strong-minded in her own right, she expressed her defiance by acting out. A good, smart, loving person always, Ophelia didn't do anything specific—to my knowledge—to be sent away, but she must have at least talked back or disobeyed a rule or come home late one too many times. In any case, to blink my eyes yet again and find not just my momma gone but Ophelia too felt like too much heartbreak to bear. Adding insult to injury, Sharon and Kim were staying with family members on Freddie's side, so I was a stranger in a strange land—even if Uncle Willie and Aunt Ella Mae were family.

It was only after Ophelia was no longer in the household that I really appreciated how she had always been there for me, how we were there for each other. We hardly had ever fought, except for maybe once when I performed surgery on her Barbie doll and sort of decapitated it. Maybe this was about jealousy over her having more Christmas presents than me—some years my take was just socks. Or it could have been my displaced anger over Freddie telling me, "You the only one who ain't got no daddy," or it could have been an early exploration of my latent surgical skills. Of course Ophelia was mad at me for destroying her toy. But she soon forgave me. Then there was the time that I spied on her and her friends during a girls' club meeting. When I was detected looking through the peephole, one of her friends took a squeegee doused in soapy water and splashed it right into my eye! That burned like hell, but what really injured my eye was when I ran home and tried to wash the soap out with a rag that had cosmetics in it already. I was mad at Ophelia for not being more concerned—and it did cause permanent trouble for my eye.

For the rest, we had been almost inseparable, best friends. The previous July 4 stood out in my memory. Bessie's kids and some of our older relatives and friends had money to go to Muskogee Beach, the place to go. Because we didn't have that money, our option was to go to Lake Michigan to see the fireworks. To get there, we had to depend on Freddie to drive us there, drop us off, and come back to pick us up.

We arrived in time and enjoyed watching the fireworks with a large, local crowd. That was, until, as though choreographed, the last rocket burst into a thousand glittering chards in the sky and there was a sudden roll of thunder as the rain began to pour down. There was no shelter, and before long we realized that there was no Freddie to pick us up.

After it became really late, the only thing we knew to do was to walk home—like Hansel and Gretel trying to retrace and reverse our footsteps the opposite way he'd driven us. Combating the wet, cold, and hunger and our fear of getting lost, as we walked and walked we talked and talked. Still my main source of information about everything I knew nothing about, Ophelia decided to explain to me why the mail never came on time in our neighborhood.

"Why?" The rain was coming down so hard we had to raise our voices to be heard over it.

" 'Cause," she said, "our mailman's over at Luke's with Freddie." Luke's House of Joy, one of Freddie's favorite watering holes, was right across the street from the Big House at Eighth and Wright. We were pretty sure that's where he was this night, too drunk to remember or care to come pick us up. Ophelia reported that the adults in the neighborhood said that if you wanted to get your mail on time, you'd have to go to Luke's and find the mailman at his regular bar stool, sort through his bag, and take out what belonged to you. If you wanted to get your welfare check, said Ophelia, you'd have to go to Luke's and tell the mailman, "Nigger, you give me my check!"

The rain didn't let up for the whole hour and a half it took to walk home from the lake, but her stories and commentary made the ordeal much more bearable. When we arrived at home, nobody was there, so I managed to break in by squeezing through the milk chute.

That, in a nutshell, was how we survived as a team, cheering each other up, complaining to each other, distracting ourselves from thinking about the troublesome stuff that was too painful to discuss. With Momma gone and without Ophelia close at hand to be my ally, I couldn't imagine anyone filling the void.

But apparently, as the saying goes, nature abhors a vacuum, and by the time I blinked once more, my mother's three brothers had stepped in to occupy that empty place and make sure I wasn't left entirely unattended. They were father figures, teachers, entertainers, and preachers, each in his own way. The perfect antidote to the no-daddy, no-momma, no-sister blues, they collectively helped me to realize, just when I had started to feel sorry for myself, how lucky I was to be a Gardner.

Whenever I went to visit or stay with Uncle Archie, I took away lasting lessons about the value of hard work, goal setting, focus, and self-education. A union man in his blood, Uncle Archie eventually ascended the ladder to become president of his union, all the while reading, studying, and familiarizing himself with issues of concern to the community.

Then there was Uncle Willie, a character of the highest order who could turn a humdrum afternoon into an adventure full of international intrigue and espionage. Ever since he had come back from the Korean War, so I heard, Uncle Willie hadn't been quite right in the head. That was one of the euphemisms used for mental illness, which ran strong in different branches of our extended family, it turned out, as well as in the rest of the 'hood—where, besides not being able to afford help, most folks would go to a snake charmer before they'd seek out psychotherapy.

Calling someone crazy—an equal opportunity euphemism that could have applied to someone like Freddie, who was probably bipolar or borderline schizophrenic, made worse by alcohol—was really another form of denying how troubled someone was, which made the problem, if not okay, then at least typical. No matter how bad it was, you'd hear people say, "Well, the nigger crazy, you know. He just crazy." And no one contemplated therapy. That solution was crazy itself to a lot of people. "Oh, no," they'd say about Freddie. "He'll be all right. He just drunk. Probably he should eat something to coat his stomach against the liquor."

In point of fact, Uncle Willie had been diagnosed with some form of battle fatigue or shell shock that had become progressively worse, though he was harmless. Although I wasn't told about his condition during the time I was living in his home, it seemed he was convinced that he was in the FBI—of which he is still convinced to this day, and no one at the mental health facility where he lives has tried to correct him on that. Neither did I the first time I had direct experience working with him on "assignment," a little later in this era. On that occasion we were driving to do an errand one day in his unassuming green Rambler—one of the classic midsixties models made right there in Milwaukee—I couldn't help observing his cool outfit: a jacket and white shirt, tie with a stickpin in it, and little snap brim straw hat and shades. That became his undercover disguise; it helped him blend in, so he said. Without any reference to his "work," all of a sudden he pulled over, looked straight ahead, and spoke through clenched teeth, like a ventriloquist, so as not to appear to be talking to me.

"Yeah, they're over there checking me out right now," Uncle Willie said. "They're checking me out."

"They are?" I asked excitedly, thinking of Bill Cosby's *I Spy* series and all the latest James Bond stories I'd seen or read. Wow, this was cool!

Just as I turned my head to look over and see who was tailing us, Uncle Willie grabbed the steering wheel, whispering hoarsely, "Don't look! Don't look! They'll know we're on to them!"

Unfortunately, I had already turned and looked, only to discover that nobody was there. In one fell swoop, I realized that this meant many of the grandiose claims he'd made over the years, or that others had heard from him, weren't true. One of those claims that I heard from others, for instance, was that he had some original Picasso paintings stashed in an undisclosed location and that he had willed them to Ophelia. These were glamorous, bold visions, the kind of daydreams that I loved to think about and that I hated to learn were only true in his fantasy world.

Still, he could be very convincing. Not long after I went on assignment with him, one of the Gardner relatives received a call from the Palmer House Hotel—one of Chicago's most luxurious, illustrious hotels, along the lines of the Waldorf Astoria in New York. It seemed that Uncle Willie—who frequented the racetrack—had checked in at the front desk by showing them his winning stubs from the track. With the explanation that he'd pay them the next day once he had time to cash them in, he charmed himself right into the presidential penthouse suite. Once the hotel management figured out that the stubs were worthless—just discarded stubs, not even somebody else's winning tickets—they called the family to come get Uncle Willie rather than have the negative publicity from police involvement.

As one of the family members along for the ride to coax Uncle Willie out of the penthouse, I had the fortune to catch a glimpse of the stuff of which dreams were made. The luxurious lobby of the Palmer House made the pages of the Spiegel catalog seem almost ordinary. And that penthouse suite—with multiple bed-rooms, a bathroom that could house two families, a sitting room here, a living room there, and furnishings made of gold, silk, satin, velvet—was like nothing I'd ever dreamt of, let alone seen. To think that I'd ever stay in such a place was too much to dream, too crazy to want. But as I cajoled Uncle Willie into going home with us, I planted that fantasy inside myself just the same.

Many lifetimes later, after I'd found myself staying in the suites of a few extraordinary hotels, I was invited to the Palmer House Hotel to attend a reception hosted by the president of the National Education Association, one of my largest institutional investment clients. It didn't occur to me until I arrived at the reception, which happened to be in that very same presidential penthouse suite, why it was that I began to have such a powerful déjà vu. At first, I thought better than to confess the reason I was able to direct any-one who asked to the bathroom, the wet bar, or the exit to the patio, but then I did mention it to a couple of older women, who laughed right along with me.

One of them said, "We all have an Uncle Willie in our family." The other woman added, "And some of us have an Aunt Willa-mena too."

At the age of eight I obviously had few insights into the causes of mental illness. So when I started picking up on my family mem-bers not being quite right, it gave me something new to fear. If this crazy thing ran in the family, what did that say about me? What if I had it or was going to get it? The fear may have also been why I stayed away from becoming much of a drinker. I didn't want to lose the little control of my world I had, that modest feeling of be-ing able to respond to rapidly changing surroundings, situations, and circumstances over which I otherwise had no control.

At the same time, Uncle Willie's stories, delusional or not, gave me a worldview that I had never had before, replacing the old fear of the unknown with a desire to see some of the places he talked about. Besides the foreign ports of call he described from his time in the service—in Korea, the Philippines, Italy, and other stops along the way—he also talked about how beautiful and welcoming the women were over there, a subject that was to become an increasing source of fascination for me.

But the person who most opened the door to the world beyond our neighborhood and made me know that I had to go see it one day was my Uncle Henry—who came shining into my life in this era as if he had been sent just for me. We had seen Momma's baby brother only periodically in earlier years since he was stationed abroad at the time. Now that he was retired from the military and working as a steel man alongside my other uncles, he suddenly appeared on the scene—as suddenly as Momma had disappeared.

Whenever Uncle Henry came to look after us at Uncle Willie's house—or better yet, to take me somewhere on an excursion, just the two of us—it was Christmas, my birthday, and every other holiday rolled into one for me. He made me feel as special as Momma had when she visited at the foster home and made candy. Uncle Henry not only made me feel special but allowed me, for the first time ever, to feel love for a man—really to fall in love, in the way that boys fall in love with their fathers and yearn to be like them one day. I knew what that falling-in-love feeling was with the important women in my life, like Momma, with her spreading smile—always reminding me of an opening refrigerator door that the light of hope and comfort spilled from. I knew the love of my sister, how it was without condition or limitation. But until I was eight years old, when Uncle Henry took me under his wing of protection, love, and fun, the dominant messages from a male adult had mainly been "Get outta my goddamn house" and "I ain't your goddamn daddy," barked at me down the barrel of a shotgun.

Uncle Henry and I had an unspoken agreement whenever he came to stay with us—if Uncle Willie and Aunt Ella Mae happened to be going away for the weekend or out for the night—that I would go up to bed with the younger kids and sneak back down later. By the time I came tiptoeing downstairs, there was always a party going on, with Henry Gardner at the center. About five-ten—although, like Momma, he looked much taller—Uncle Henry was a pretty boy, single and loved by the ladies, with a lean physique and an athletic, tigerlike way of moving. In his hip goatee, he would scan a room, not missing a beat, knowing the ladies weren't missing him. Never once did I see him looking anything but perfectly attired, every crease, every cuff pressed to perfection.

At one of these parties, not long after I'd come back downstairs and was checking out Henry's different friends, watching the various guests—some playing cards, others in conversation, a few dancing—something remarkable happened. When I arrived, there was one distinct groove going on—with soul music, blues, and standards coming off the record player as singers like Sam Cooke, Jackie Wilson, and Sarah Vaughn stirred up the festive atmosphere. Between the music, laughter, chatter, and smoke, it was hot and happening, boisterous and loud. Then, all at once, the mood changed when a record was put on that I had never heard. Everything stopped: the laughter, the chatter, even the smoke. The record was Miles Davis playing "Round Midnight." Later I would appreciate the mastery of his trumpet playing, the haunting tone that crept under my skin, and the incredible complexities of tempo and melody. But what got me that night was the power of Miles Davis to alter the mood in the room like that. It was still a party, but much more intimate, more cool, more fluid. It even seemed that I moved differently with Miles on the record player. My decision to study trumpet didn't happen that night, but I did contemplate for the first time ever how powerful it would feel to be able to change the mood, to make strangers feel something transformational that way. The music bug done bit.

From then on, Uncle Henry and I had Miles Davis in common.

The music and the time spent listening together formed a shelter in the storm so that all my angst was forgotten, if only for a while. On those many occasions when he let me stay up late and we'd listen to every Miles Davis recording he could get his hands on, he'd tell me about his overseas adventures in the Philippines, Korea, and Japan. "Come here," he beckoned to me in the middle of talking one night, and led me to the bookshelf, pulling out the encyclopedia Uncle Willie and Aunt Ella Mae had in their home.

He pointed out the facts and cultural descriptions of these different places, recommending that I always take advantage of resources like the encyclopedia. He made a point of emphasizing that the world was full of many different types of people with attitudes, customs, beliefs, and colors different from ours. Then there was the smile that lit up his face when he described the women over there. He might as well have been spinning the globe for me and egging me out the door, saying, "Here it is, Chris, the world is your oyster. It's up to you to find the pearls."

Nothing Uncle Henry said or did indicated that our time together would be limited for any reason, but looking back, I would later wonder if he knew on some level that he wasn't going to be around forever and was trying to pass on everything he had seen and learned in a short amount of time. In any case, his message wasn't explicit, but the theme was always clear: live large.

That message wasn't meant in any kind of negative or selfish way. To me, it meant to dare to dream, to commit to living on my own terms, to pursue my vision—one that others didn't have to see, just me.

One of our earliest outings together had been to the Mississippi River, where Uncle Henry taught me to swim and where he'd take me boating whenever good weather came around. There was one day on the river that I remember as the essence of happiness, one of those perfect summer days that stretch on forever. Not a cloud in the sky, there was just the sound and smell of the gas engine, the two of us: Uncle Henry in the back gunning the Evinrude engine, steering us across the river, and me up front with my legs dangling over the side, kicking up the water and throwing spray back into my face. Sensations of well-being ran through my senses: the ups and downs of the small craft skimming over the mellow rolling of waves; the feel and sound of the waves slapping on the bottom of the boat; the spray of mist around me, lovingly touching my face and skin.

That was probably the most dangerous position possible in which to ride inside of a small boat, but that was part of what made it the most daring, spectacular fun I'd ever had. Decades hence I would recall that glorious day while watching *Titanic* and seeing Leonardo DiCaprio shout, "I'm king of the world!" That was the exact feeling that came over me on the Mississippi with Uncle Henry, a feeling of being completely alive. Uncle Henry had a look of satisfaction as he saw me happy, as if he had done well to set me on a path that he might not always be around to guide me along. Or so I later interpreted our most memorable time spent together.

One night at the end of that first summer I'd stayed with Uncle Willie and Aunt Ella Mae, I had gone to bed but was still awake when I heard my aunt cry out, "Oh, no!" followed by muffled crying from her and my uncle. I sat up in bed in a panic, not only because I had never heard grown-ups cry before, but also because I knew. It was Uncle Henry. No question. The pain was so pronounced it reverberated all the way up to the attic where I slept at the time. I prayed more genuinely than ever before: *Dear God, please don't let it be my Uncle Henry.* I didn't sleep, I prayed and prayed, feeling more powerless than ever to alter whatever it was.

The next morning, at breakfast, my Aunt Ella Mae, her eyes puffy under her cat-eye glasses, said in a somber, strained voice, "Henry had an accident. Yesterday. He drowned."

Reeling from the shock and sorrow that he was gone and the

disbelief that he could have had an accident, because he knew everything and was careful and because he couldn't be gone, he couldn't, I barely pieced together the details. Aunt Ella Mae was really talking to me, since the younger kids wouldn't understand, but I was numb, devastated. In that place of stillness where I went to brace myself against hurt, I pushed away the haze and tried to understand the chronology of what happened. Uncle Henry apparently had gone out to fish from a small island, and the boat had come off its mooring and drifted away from shore. When he attempted to swim out to the boat and bring it back in to redock it, the undercurrent was too strong and took him down.

How many times Uncle Henry had warned me about the undercurrent, how you could never tell just by looking at the surface, I couldn't count. It didn't make sense. Nothing made sense. My heart wanted to explode into a million pieces, but something inside wouldn't let me. It was that feeling of not allowing myself to cry, because I was sure that if I started I'd never stop. So I took all that emotion, that weight of the world hanging over me in the shape of a massive question mark, and dragged it deep down below, into a dangerous undercurrent of my own.

After attending so many funerals with TT, I thought that I'd know what to expect from Uncle Henry's funeral. But of course I was very young then, and we didn't really know any of the people from church who died. I was unprepared for the finality of his loss, as if I'd been waiting to hear that it was a mistake or even a trick so he could take off and have a foreign adventure without having to say good-bye. More than that, I was completely unprepared to see Momma there, the first time I'd seen her in almost a year.

Every time I tried to move toward her, various relatives blocked my path. We couldn't hug. She couldn't tell me where she was staying, what had happened, when and if she was coming back. The atmosphere was surreal enough with all the weeping and wailing, but to see Momma, real and in front of me, yet beyond my reach, was enough to put me in a grave next to Uncle Henry. Maybe because she knew it would have hurt too much, she didn't even make eye contact or try to speak to me. My only consoling thought was that she was glancing over when I wasn't looking. I wanted Momma to see that I was starting to get tall, that I was composed, strong, being a mostly good kid. Every time I looked over at her, hoping for some sign that she had seen me, all I saw was the pain of losing her baby brother and not being able to talk to her children. She kept her gaze down at the earth where they put Uncle Henry's casket.

When it hit me that the woman standing next to my mother was a female prison guard—the only white person at the funeral, dressed in a navy-colored uniform—it came down like a thunderbolt where she had gone. But as one monumental question was answered, a whole batch of confusing new ones were born. Why was she in prison? When was she coming back? Was she coming back?

Only much later would I piece together that this was her second imprisonment. But even that day my gut told me that Freddie was responsible. Though he was the one who should have done time for his abuse, Freddie told the authorities that she had attempted to burn the house down with him in it, thereby breaking her parole. Not surprisingly, he did it without an ounce of concern for what it would do to us kids.

I was also reunited with Ophelia. Seeing her, Sharon, and Kim at the funeral was awkward, with our "don't ask, don't tell" family tradition. The warring configuration of emotions inside of me was so overwhelming that I reverted to the need for something to do, some plan of action to stick my focus on. For one thing, despite the fact that I hadn't seen much of Freddie since Momma had been gone, I resolved to resume the job of putting him out of our misery, a determination I'd only temporarily shelved when my poison potion exploded on me. And another thing, I decided, for however long my mother was going to be away, I was going to have as much of my childhood as I could muster. I was going to hang out with my group of friends, "my boys," get into a little trouble—instigate some of it too—go riding on our homemade skate trucks put together from wood and old skate wheels, and maybe figure out how to earn some chore money to buy myself a bike. Then me and my boys were going to cruise around town, out to the lake if we felt like it, or pedal all the way uphill to the highest point in our part of Milwaukee, near the water reservoir, and look out beyond, feeling like kings of the world. And then, living large, we were going to take that plunge down Snake Hill, the biggest rush of our lives, taking our feet off the pedals so we could go even faster, pushing the limits of danger and excitement and just letting it rip.

What I also decided at Uncle Henry's funeral was that I wouldn't cry. That was my signal to Momma that I was hanging tough and that she didn't need to worry about me.

For the next two years I did the best I could not to break down. My resolve was severely challenged one afternoon when I stopped by Baby's house, where my younger sisters were staying. One of the only redeeming aspects of having the scourge of Freddie in our lives was how good his sisters Baby and Bessie were to us. Baby saw how her brother rode me and tried to compensate, saying nice things whenever she could, and she would even kick a few dollars in my direction here and there.

"You hungry, Chris?" she greeted me that day, knowing the answer before I grinningly nodded yes and starting to take out some sandwich fixings. As she did, Baby remembered the laundry she was doing downstairs and asked if I'd go load the clothes in the dryer.

Without hesitation, I head down to the basement and begin to pull the wet clothes out of the washer when a smell surrounds me. It's the wonderful smell that first came into my senses when I lived in foster care. Not a specific perfume, nothing rich or heavy, just a clean, warm, *good* smell that wraps around me like a Superman cape, making me feel special, strong, safe, loved, and *her.*

Standing there loading the dryer, not sure why my mother's presence is so vivid in my senses, I don't yet know that Baby happens to be storing some of Momma's clothes and things for her down here in the basement. I don't yet know that in a few weeks to come there will be one more blink, and that the channel will change, Momma will come home, and we'll all be reunited, living just as before.

Just like the scripts being switched back, we'll pick up where we left off—practically midsentence. Without explanation, and with Freddie.

All I know in the emptiness of Baby's basement is that I'm about to cry until I can't cry anymore, as the dam gets ready to bust from ten years' worth of pent-up question marks and a Mississippi River's worth of unshed tears.

But first, as her beautiful smell blankets me even more, just to be sure, I turn around and ask out loud, "Momma?"

CHAPTER 4

Bitches Brew
(side a)

C hrissy Paul!" came to be a constant refrain, sung out in the Big House on Eighth and Wright, where we next lived temporarily with Bessie, not just by my mother, now free, to let me know she wanted me to run an errand, but by my sisters and girl cousins too.

Between the ages of ten and fourteen, without asking for it, I received intensive on-the-job training for a career as a professional gofer. But it was not what I had in mind in preparation for my illustrious future as Miles Davis, a goal I had obsessed over since hearing his music for the first time that evening with Uncle Henry.

Yet I was so grateful to Moms for listening to me go on and on about how desperate I was to learn to play, for finding and purchasing a secondhand trumpet for me, and for seeing that I had lessons too, that I couldn't say no to whatever it was she sent me out to get. Some of the errands I didn't mind at all, including the different stops I'd make on those days when we had to pay a few dollars on our grocery-store bills. A typical run might start with Moms saying, "Chrissy Paul, go on over to Baby's and pick up a package."

I knew that meant we were getting a small loan to pay down another loan, even though the details were never discussed. It was all very discreet, as if to discuss how tight money was at home would be in poor taste. When I arrived at Baby's, she too didn't refer to the contents of the small folded package she handed to me, but of course I knew there were two or three dollar bills balled up inside. As the courier in these transactions, I may not have been privy to the exact numbers involved, but the process deepened my appreciation for my mother's ability to make ends meet—sometimes in order for us to eat that night.

This entire money thing was to become a subject of necessary interest, since I had no daddy to bankroll my wants and needs—like a certain style I wanted in my threads, which I learned to afford by economizing and stretching what cash I could earn doing odd extra jobs, and later, when having a car of my own would become a preoccupation. In the meantime, these money runs provided me with an introduction to a host of financial principles, like assets versus deficits, loans and interest, and how to get more value for less money.

Besides errands to Sy's and other local grocers, from time to time I'd stop to make payments at Uncle Ben's Store on Ninth and Meineke. A black-owned store, Uncle Ben's had a meat case where Moms occasionally had me get a dollar's worth of cold cuts—fifty cents' worth of salami and fifty cents' worth of cheese, dinner for a family of seven if you counted her, Freddie, me, Sharon, Kim, Ophelia, and our latest addition to the family, DeShanna, who was Ophelia's baby girl, born while my sister was in the detention home.

Unless I was literally starving to death, I refused to eat anything that came out of Uncle Ben's meat case. Nothing against Ben, but he had a cat he'd let snack on his deli meats. The sight of that cat sniffing and pawing the cold cuts horrified me from a scientific, medical standpoint. I might have only been twelve years old and was by no means an expert, but logic told me that a cat that just finished digging in kitty litter shouldn't be crawling over salami we were going to eat. But I kept my misgivings to myself.

One of the errands that I had least enjoyed was during the time when we were all getting settled back in together and DeShanna was still being kept in foster care, until Ophelia was able to get a job and bring her home to live with us. My assignment was to pick up DeShanna from the foster home, ten blocks away, and bring her to visit Ophelia at our house, and then return the toddler to the foster home.

Poor DeShanna didn't know me, and she barely knew Ophelia, so whenever she saw me coming, it was a gut-wrenching scene for all of us. The foster lady who was keeping DeShanna didn't make it any easier. As soon as the baby started to cry and throw a fit, screaming, falling on the floor, pounding her fists, and kicking her legs in the air, the foster mother started to cry too—giving me the evil eye, as if I had caused all this turmoil. Pretty soon I was ready to cry myself, because I had no say in the matter. She wasn't my baby, and I was just doing my job. The expression "Don't shoot the messenger" would resonate from this experience on.

When we finally got out the door, DeShanna cried all up and down the neighborhood as I tried to walk her to our place, causing me to have to pick her up and carry her. Every trip she seemed to scream louder, and she also got heavier. At that point, I'd have to put her down and coax her into walking. DeShanna made her displeasure known by screaming more and refusing to hold on to my fingers, like toddlers usually do. That meant I had to hold her hand, which gave her another reason to scream and try to pull away. People stopped and stared, saying nothing, but obviously thinking, *What is he doing to that child? What's wrong with that baby?*

The return trip after DeShanna visited Ophelia wasn't bad, especially as the two began to bond and the visit seemed to calm my niece down. But getting there the next time was just as horrific. We were all happy when social services finally allowed DeShanna to come live with Ophelia and the rest of us. Not surprisingly, the circumstances of how my sister had gotten pregnant weren't discussed. Didn't ask, and nobody told. But when I thought about DeShanna's situation, not having a daddy in her life, it was another reminder to myself that I wasn't going to bring sons and daughters into this world without having a presence in their lives.

———

"Chrissy Paul . . . !" rang through the house one day from three separate voices, almost like choir practice. Moms came first, continuing, "Go on down to the 'nigga' store and pick me up some Kotex."

Ophelia and my cousin Linda chimed in that they wanted Kotex too. This was the gofer job I most hated. Why couldn't they share the same package? Because Moms wanted the light red package, Ophelia the sky blue, and Linda the lavender. How could the same brand of sanitary napkin have so many variations? My cousin Terry had been through this plenty with his three sisters and walked by smirking. Whenever they asked him to go, he'd gleefully remark, "Send Chris!"

Later, Ophelia at least felt sorry for me and started handing me a note and a brown paper bag for this errand, but it was too late. On my way home that particular day, I had my arms full with three different boxes of Kotex—which wouldn't fit in a store bag—when I heard a taunting voice behind me calling, "Hey, Pussy Man! Pussy Man!"

What was I going to do? Drop the sanitary napkins and go kick someone's ass? Or ignore them and suffer how fast this would get around school and the neighborhood? In my mind I could already see the mailman and Freddie—the Big Wheel was what everybody called him, fearing and almost admiring him—the two of them hanging on the bar at Luke's House of Joy telling everybody about the Pussy Man without no goddamn daddy. How was I going to live that down?

Still, I chose not to take the bait and kept on trudging back to all those waiting female family members who were having their cycles at the same time, not appreciating that my sensitivity to women could be an asset one day. Even though I was pissed off at whoever called me that, my MO with my peers by now was to take the path of least resistance whenever possible. It was bad enough to have to be in battle mode all the time at home, so at school and around the neighborhood I preferred using diplomacy.

Unfortunately, because I was on my way to being a big kid, always a head or more taller than anyone in my group of friends, whenever we went somewhere and got into an argument, it was inevitable that I was going to fight. That was street logic. Other kids would jump on me first to psyche out my friends, the tactic being that if you could beat me up, my buddies would fall in line. Tired of the routine, more than once I thought, *Man, I got to get me some big friends.* But before long I learned how to use my size and my intensity, with a look or a remark, to avoid a confrontation. There had to be serious provocation to make me hit someone.

One of my friends, Norman, discovered what serious provocation for me was when a group of us were walking back to Tenth and Wright one afternoon, informally playing "the dozens."

Norman had heard about what had happened a week earlier when Moms ran into a store to hide from Freddie—who'd chased her in there at gunpoint. This was not an incident that I'd witnessed, but I was still in a rage over accounts I'd heard about how Freddie had terrorized everyone in the store, pointing the shotgun at them and demanding to know, "Where is she?" and how when she snuck out and managed to get into a taxi, the cab driver wouldn't budge, even with my mother begging, "Take off, take off!"

I was sick when I heard how Freddie had run up, dragged Moms out of the taxi, and beat her bloody right there in the street with folks running out of shops and standing on stoops watching— doing nothing, saying nothing. Talk about insult to injury. No one could explain to me how the police and people of our neighborhood couldn't or wouldn't intervene. Even my uncles fell short in not standing up to Freddie. It wasn't fear, because any one of them could hold their own in a street fight; it was more about not getting in Momma's business. That didn't fly with me. Unbeknownst to me at the time, many communities were starting to break the silence about domestic violence, but whatever resources were available, we just didn't know about them. What I saw were too many people turning to look the other way, which I found—and still find—unconscionable.

Not that I needed any more incitement to kill Freddie Triplett, but when Norman decided to do his imitation of my mother running from my stepfather, it increased my sense of urgency tenfold.

"Hey, Chris!" Norman says, walking along, pretending to be Moms cowering. "Remember?" And then he does Freddie pointing his shotgun and says, " 'Where is she? Where is she?' Remember?"

Like a volcano, shocking even myself, I erupted on Norman, pummeling him with my fists and kicking him down the block, giving him the whipping I wish I could've put on Freddie.

From then on nobody ever had the nerve to bring up my momma, dozens or not. The exception to that was a relative of Freddie's, who was already in his twenties at this time and later started coming around too often for my liking, acting like he was entitled to boss Moms around and disrespect her any way he pleased. Once when I was in my teens, after she told him to lay off, he blasted her, saying, "You know you ain't talking to me because I'll knock your goddamn brains out."

As much as I wanted to do exactly to this creep what I had in mind for Freddie, I had to sit there and restrain myself. But I never forgot it. Though he didn't amount to much, I didn't become any more forgiving in the years that followed, and almost four decades later, when a family member invited him to a Thanksgiving dinner in Chicago—at my home, which I owned, to eat food that I bought—I couldn't eat. I couldn't sit in his presence because I didn't trust myself to not jump him and beat him within an inch of his miserable life. He was already missing a kidney, which meant that I could probably have killed him with one kidney punch. There was no forgetting what he had said to Momma and no forgiving. That was what being deeply provoked was to me.

But in other cases with my friends, when it came to someone having a laugh at my expense, I developed a fairly thick skin. Bottom line, I wanted to be liked, not so much to be popular with everyone—including my teachers and principals—but to be special, to have my own identity, to be cool.

To that end, the year before, I'd gotten it into my head that it would be the height of coolness to bring the glass eyeball belonging to one of Freddie's sisters to show-and-tell in my fifth-grade class. More and more, it seemed that whenever an idea got into my head, I had an ability to *focus* on it exclusively. This was the greatest double-edged sword I'd ever have to learn to wield. Whatever it was that drove me to pester Sis—as we called Freddie's sister—to let me take her glass eyeball to school, I couldn't say. But I was relentless.

In her early fifties, graying, Sis lived in her housecoat with her pint of whiskey in one of her housecoat pockets and a pack of Lucky Strikes in the other. Even outside the house, she rarely wore any other sort of attire, and never did I see her in dressy clothes. In 1965 in northeast Milwaukee, women did have a thing for housecoats: they'd put one over anything and wear it around town like it was a mink coat. Another member of the extended family, Miss Alberta, a great big, round, fat woman, had a habit of wearing five layers of clothes around underneath her housecoat, just another curious sight in our black *Happy Days* neighborhood. Sis wasn't far behind her.

Each time I went to beg, "Sis, can I take your glass eye to school for show-and-tell?" I got the same response.

Taking a swig of whiskey, each time her answer was, "No, moth-erfucker. Take my goddamn eye? No! Hell, no!"

Finally, I developed an alternative plan of action. Since I knew where she kept her glass eye—in a jar with some liquid to keep it wet at night when she slept—my plot was to stop by in the morn-ing, borrow it while she was asleep, then return it at lunchtime just before her usual rising hour.

All went beautifully that morning, and when I arrived at school, I could hardly wait until my turn at show-and-tell. Nobody had ever brought in a glass eyeball. Sitting in my seat just before it was my turn, I couldn't mask the smile stretching across my face be-cause this was going to be my day to shine.

All of a sudden, an ungodly screeching came ricocheting down the hallway, at first unintelligible but soon coherent enough for all of us to hear: "Chris! Chris! Give me back my eye. Give me my eye. I'm g'on whup your ass. Give me back my goddamn eye!"

In unison, every single classmate spun around and gawked at me.

Another torrent of screeching followed, clearly threatening: "Boy, give me my goddamn eye. I want my eye. I'm g'on whup your ass, you little thievin' motherfucker!"

With that, Sis threw open my classroom door and stood there out of breath, hair all scraggly and matted, in her slippers and rag-gedy housecoat, shaking with fury, glaring at everybody with her one good eye and her empty socket as she roared, "Give me back my goddamn eye!" Slack-jawed, the teacher and my classmates stared at me in bewilderment, not knowing who she was or any-thing about an eye. A complete fiasco.

Embarrassment weighed on me like cement shoes as I had to go up to Sis, in front of everyone, reach into my pocket, and pull out her eyeball. She squinted her good eye at what looked like a marble in my open palm and snatched it from me, plopped it right back into the socket in front of the class, turned around, and exited, cussing me out all the way back down the hall.

I thought my teacher was going to faint. One little girl did throw up. Apparently neither of them had ever seen the likes of Sis or the insertion of a glass eye.

The repercussions at home weren't terrible. Freddie was predictable, barking, "Chris, don't you be taking Sis's eye again, you hear me? 'Cause if you do, I'm g'on beat yo ass and you won't be able to sit down for a week!" That didn't bother me much because he'd use any excuse to beat my ass.

It was at school where I felt the pain. For a long while I was the laughingstock of Lee Elementary, and kids were talking about Sis and her glass eye for weeks. But of course, I lived to tell. Other than that debacle, I usually did well in school—as long as I was interested and challenged. Besides my increasingly voracious appetite for books, which now took me down the library aisles to find classics by the likes of Charles Dickens and Mark Twain, and a budding interest in history, I found math fun and kind of satisfying, with problems to be solved like games that yielded answers to questions that were either right or wrong, yes or no.

Not like the questions that dominated at home.

——

During the few years after Moms came back from prison, I tried to get a read on what they had done to her, how she had changed, or not, and what was in her heart. Freddie, the old man, was a prison for all of us, a ball and chain. He was an addiction, I supposed, the reason that no matter how many times she escaped or pushed him out the door, promising, "He ain't never coming back," he always did. After a while, I wondered if she was really *afraid* of Freddie anymore. I wondered if she stayed as a reminder to him that no matter what dreams he took away from her, he couldn't break her; even if he got her sent to prison twice, he couldn't defeat Bettye Jean. In fact, if she ever felt low, if she ever got down, Moms refused to reveal it.

Rarely did she express impatience or frustration with me, even when I deserved it. But the couple of instances when she did, in her inimitable style of brutal understatement, she made her point better than with any ass whupping.

There was the time when she came home and presented me with a new pair of pants she'd bought from somewhere like Gimbels. When I looked at them and spotted the eight-dollar price tag, without thinking, and instead of being honored and grateful she'd spent that money on me, I said, almost as if to myself, "Man, for eight dollars, at the Discount Center, I could've got some shoes, pants, and a shirt *and* had money left over to go to the movies too."

Momma gave me a hard look that cut me to the quick, then snatched back the pants and said, "Boy, you too big a scrub to wear some eight-dollar pants!"

Too late for an apology, I felt as terrible as I should have, knowing that was the last I'd see of those pants. That day made me work even harder to watch my mouth. Not to excuse myself, but the tendency to use words in mean, hurtful ways, without thinking, was an ugly characteristic that I had picked up from Freddie. Actually, my three sisters and I all developed the ability to be verbally abusive in extreme situations. Even now I have to make a conscious effort, not always successfully, to keep my mouth in check.

In her way, Moms showed me how powerful both words and silence can be. After the telephone cord whuppin' she gave me for stealing a bag of popcorn much earlier, the next time I tried to be slick and steal something, she only needed to give me a disappointed look to invoke the pain of the cord.

At thirteen years old, hormones churning, big kid that I'm becoming, wanting to be cool and look good, I go out and decide to shoplift a pair of pants from the Discount Center, thinking I'm real slick. The stupidity of it is that getting caught never registers while my brain's concentrating only on the opportunity to slip on those pants underneath my own and fool myself that no one's going to suspect a schoolboy like me, my stack of books under my arms and all.

As I head out the door, reality sets in with a tap on my shoulder from a store manager. Now I am a criminal, schoolbooks and all. Bracing myself for a stern lecture and a warning, I get walloped by something much worse: the arrival of two white cops who push and shove me out to their patrol car and take me down to the station. Once more, I prepare for the painful phone call home and the subsequent arrival of my upset mother and crazy, drunk stepfather. Instead, I stand by as the desk officer makes the phone call and listen as he reaches the old man while, obviously, the plan changes. As he delivers the news to Freddie that I'm being held at the station until someone comes to get me, the cop starts laughing hilariously, then hangs up the phone and drags me off to a holding cell.

He explains that Freddie won't come get me. The quote from Freddie was: "Come get him? Naw, leave his ass in there. Fuck him!"

Muttering to myself under my breath, I take a book from the top of my stack and start to read, hoping that Melville and *Moby-Dick* and the escape through reading will calm me down.

This also causes the white cops to laugh their asses off. One of them asks, "You're not reading that shit, are you? 'Cause if you're so smart, what the fuck are you doing in jail?"

The other cop repeats Freddie's words, "His old man says, 'Leave his ass in there. Fuck him!'"

When Moms and Freddie do come to get me, neither one has to say a word, because they can see from my shame that I've gotten a crash course in what it feels like to be in a jam with the police, to be confined and locked up—none of which I've ever experienced. For a flash, the gloating look on Freddie's face makes me angry enough to forget I was the wrongdoer in this situation. Momma's disappointed expression corrects that misapprehension in a heartbeat.

Of course, there was nothing I wanted more in the universe than to make my mother proud of me. So naturally, on those few occasions when I let her down, it hurt me forever.

My trumpet playing, I hoped, could be something to make Moms proud. I practiced tenaciously, for both the youth concerts I was starting to do and Roosevelt Junior High School's band. One evening before dinner, instead of asking me to run over and pick up some essentials—my job, after all—Moms heard me practicing and decided she would go, as long as I'd keep an eye on the beans she had on the stove.

"Great!" I responded, glad that I didn't have to run out but could stay in my room and continue memorizing "Song for My Father" by Horace Silver—my solo at an upcoming concert. With my gift for extreme focus, I was so locked into practicing, I forgot all about the beans until a scorched smell came wafting into my room. When I ran to the kitchen and took a look, the beans were burned pretty badly.

Somehow I thought that it would make my mother less mad if I was practicing yet still aware there was a problem when she came home, as if I'd been checking on them all along. "Moms," I called from my bedroom when she came in the front door, "you better check the beans, I think they burned up."

The sound of the lid of the pot being removed and then re-placed loudly echoed down the hallway. My stomach clenched. Momma worked her magic from day to day to stretch our re-sources and feed us all, and I had to let the beans burn up. Even though she probably wanted to kill me, Moms mustered the great-est control, walked slowly down the hall, and stood in the doorway of my room, saying quietly, "Chris, you know most of the argu-ments and fights Freddie and I get in are over you, and you can't even watch a pot of beans."

Her one statement spoke ten volumes, every inference cutting me to the bone. The harshest truth was that I had been selfish, caught up in myself and my trumpet practice. The other truth was that she would do anything for me, even incite his wrath if it meant taking my side. Was it true that I was the main reason they fought? If it was, that was crazy, as crazy as Freddie was. The thought just kicked up the flame underneath the burner of my hatred for him, scorching and burning me up like those beans.

Moms, having said her piece, let it go. She turned and went back to the kitchen, opened up a can of tomato sauce, and added some seasoning, salvaging the burned beans and turning them into a hearty pot of good beans that we had for dinner that night.

Yet for all that I knew about her, she was a mystery. Only a couple of times did I catch a glimmer of what she experienced in her inner world. One of those times was in passing, really, one night when Freddie was out and I'd finished my homework and the two of us saw that a Bette Davis movie was coming on television. Moms loved Bette Davis, I always assumed because of their names being almost identical. No, my mother said, all bluesy and philosophical, the reason she liked Bette Davis movies was because she was so strong and convincing. "And she plays them parts so good," Moms admitted, "you just have to get mad at her."

What else made my Momma happy? Probably it was when she felt that she was being who she was meant to be—a teacher. In her own way, to me and my sisters, she was our professor, our Socrates. It had to make her happy to see that she was getting through to us, seeing me respond to her repeated insistence that without the ability to read and write, I would be nothing more than a slave. When I left for the public library over on Seventh and North Avenue with only one book or question that I wanted to answer, but then got caught up exploring the card catalog and discovering book after book, reading all day long—that made Moms happy. Books made her happy. She loved reading, and she loved *Reader's Digest*. She got me hooked on it too. We both read it cover to cover and then discussed the issue together. Maybe the happiest I ever saw her was the day I found a poem in an old issue of *Reader's Digest* at the library and copied it down to read to her. Poetry hadn't done much for me, but there was something that grabbed me about the music and feelings in a poem by Elizabeth Barrett Browning. Momma listened quietly at first, becoming very still—as only she could do—when I read the first few lines: *How do I love thee? Let me count the ways. I love thee to the depth and breadth and height my soul can reach . . .*

By the time I finished reading "How Do I Love Thee," my mother had tears overflowing from her eyes. She said that was her favorite poem and my discovering it made her happy.

———

Nineteen sixty-eight was the year of the Great Awakening for me. It set off a Big Bang in the universe of my being, exploding with the atomic energy of my own coming of age and the monumental changes taking place all around me. This period marked the dawning of my consciousness as a person of color, following on the heels of my discovery, lo and behold, that the world was not all black. Five years earlier, the adult reaction to the assassination of President Kennedy had been a hint about what it meant to be a minority and to lose a champion. But it was a year after that when I and some of my classmates were bused to a white school on the east side of Milwaukee that I saw with my own eyes what Moms experienced every day when she left the neighborhood to go to work. It wasn't just that with the few exceptions of janitors and a sprinkling of black kids, everyone was white, which was the polar opposite of the ghetto, where everyone was black except for a shopkeeper here and a policemen there. It was also feeling what it was to have my color as my identity, to be looked down on, to be regarded as less than, to feel shame, or to be invisible, a non-entity other than a dark-skinned black boy. But the real shock was when four little

girls were bombed to death down in Birmingham, Alabama—
because they were black.

Seeing Momma crying as she watched the TV coverage made
the lightbulb go on. They could have been my sisters. And in fact,
I now saw, in my connection to the black community at large, that
they were indeed my sisters. With new outrage and fervor to protest all past, present, and future wrongs done to my people, I experienced a new sense of connection as I began to follow what was
happening in the world outside Milwaukee. In 1965 the Watts riots
in Los Angeles took place, the same year Dr. Martin Luther King
led civil rights marches down in Selma, Alabama, and Malcolm X
was killed in Harlem. The following year, when a coalition of Milwaukee minority groups and activists came together—organized
by Father James Groppi, a Catholic priest—I took to the streets to
march, along with two of my good friends, Garvin, a trumpet
player in the school band with me, and Ken, or "Zulu," as we called
him. A true character, Zulu was not a good-looking cat by any
stroke, but he had brilliant acting talent and could have gone far
putting it to use. Later on, he actually got on a kick that he was
going to be in the movies and convinced me that I could be an
actor too.

Testing out the possibility, I ran it by Moms over breakfast, stating matter-of-factly in between bites, "Yeah, I'm gonna be an actor
when I finish school."

My mother nodded patiently and asked rhetorically, "Okay,
Chris, go get the newspaper and you tell me—how many jobs they
got in there for actors?"

But that wasn't enough to make me reject the idea, and I continued to drop comments about how I had the stature and voice
and composure to be a fine actor.

That was until I asked Moms for five dollars for something—
yet again.

Eyes down on her newspaper, not even lifting them, instead of making a dig that maybe I could go out and hustle up more hours doing odd jobs after school, she said with trademark subtle sarcasm, "Well, why don't you just *act* like you got five dollars?"

How do you act like you've got five dollars? I got the point.

With that, I got over that fleeting ambition and rededicated myself to the trumpet. Zulu was the one who really should have stuck with it. He had a gift for marching and singing "We Shall Overcome" with the intensity and power of a movement leader, at the same time that he used every opportunity to pinch white women's booties. When they turned around to see who'd done it, Zulu plastered his face with the most noble of expressions and kept on singing.

Garvin and I were amazed. "If he did that to a black woman," said Garvin when we saw Zulu pinching several booties during a big march we did, "she'd turn around and slap his face."

"Yeah," I whispered back, "and tell his momma too."

St. Boniface Catholic Church, Father Groppi's home base, offered a haven away from the minefields in the Triplett household, and besides marching for important concerns like open housing and desegregation of clubs that still barred blacks, Jews, and Catholics, the organizers fed us—everything from doughnuts and sandwiches to a variety of homemade ethnic food. Fulfilling many needs, our young activism was often as fun as it was meaningful. To have such a powerful boost to my self-image—especially at a time when my preoccupation with the opposite sex was all-consuming—was a true blessing.

My self-esteem had suffered not only from Freddie's near-daily attacks but from the higher status my community seemed to give lighter-skinned blacks. For years I had hated Smokey Robinson for being the epitome of the kind of guy that every girl I knew wanted. Slender, light-skinned, green-eyed, with his wavy "good" hair and lilting voice, he had no idea how he ruined life for tall, muscular, dark-skinned, "nappy"-haired baritone guys like me. Even to this day, I swear, if he came in the room I'd have to challenge him to a damn duel for pain and suffering—including the time a girl I liked turned her nose up and told me, "You just a big black ugmo."

Mercifully, it soon turned out that Smokey wasn't the only singer happening. Yes, Smokey could sing, and he was an amazing songwriter and performer, but so were a lot of darker-skinned black guys. When James Brown, Godfather of Soul, came along and proclaimed, "Say it loud, I'm black and I'm proud," that was the Holy Grail for a kid as black as me.

Before long, processes that never worked for me and hideous-smelling conks that only burned my scalp were out while Afros and naturals were in, along with dashikis and beads. Man, I took to that look so fast, I must have been the first and youngest black hippie in America. The dashiki thing didn't work in the 'hood in Milwaukee, but eventually I blended the Black & Proud look with hippie garb from secondhand garments bought at the Good Will and the Salvation Army to have the best beads, best bell-bottomed hip-pants, and best tie-dyes around, topped off by a big Afro. Smokey Robinson could kiss my ass.

James Brown was my man. When my boy Garvin and I started hanging out at St. Boniface and got into marching, we made it a policy to make sure everyone we knew shopped only where they accepted the Black & Brown Stamps that James Brown was promoting to help impoverished inner cities across the country. These were something like S&H Green Stamps. Our efforts seemed to go well until we filled up two shopping carts at the A&P in a white neighborhood and waited until we were in the checkout line before I asked the cashier, "Do you have Black & Brown Stamps? 'Cause if you ain't got no Black & Brown Stamps, we can't do no business here. We can't shop here." Black power, thirteen-year-old style.

So fast it made our heads spin, the police arrived on the scene and stood like backup singers behind the manager, who looked coldly into our faces and said, "You two put everything back, we'll just forget about it. But if you don't put it all back where it came from, you're both going to jail." As he turned to walk away and we sheepishly went to return each item to the shelves, most of the store personnel laughed themselves silly.

Nonetheless, we were proud of our efforts as we headed back to St. Boniface for a meeting and a march with the NAACP Youth Council, only to learn that the offices of the NAACP's Milwaukee chapter had been bombed. That instantly intensified the seriousness of what we were doing.

On July 30, 1967, on the heels of major riots in Detroit, Newark, Harlem, and D.C., a riot broke out in Milwaukee after word spread that police brutality had been used to stop a fight in a black nightspot. Though I was out there taking part in spirit, I was dismayed to see stores like Sy's looted. But that didn't stop me from rushing over to Third Street in the hopes of getting to the Discount Center before its contents were emptied. Unfortunately, by the time I got there nothing was left in my size and all I could grab were some clothes I could never wear. Fortunately, I wasn't dragged off to jail again with the almost two thousand other folks who were arrested—including my cousin Terry after he was caught actually trying on shoes and checking them out in front of a shoe mirror. The riot was significant enough that the National Guard was called in and a three-day curfew was imposed. Among the one hundred or so injuries, three people were killed that night.

Amid this turmoil, Vietnam was raging, and young, poor Americans, black and white, were being sent off to fight and, in escalating numbers, coming home in coffins, addicted, or shell-shocked. Muhammad Ali had been my hero as a boxer even before he changed his name from Cassius Clay, back when he was a newcomer and turned the boxing world on its head by beating Sonny Liston. But when he refused to go fight in the war because, as he said, "I ain't got no quarrel with the Vietcong"—who had never, he

went on, "called me 'nigger' or lynched me"—Ali became a different kind of lifelong hero to me, almost a symbolic father figure.

The defining moment in the evolution of my consciousness in
this era—and for millions of Americans from all backgrounds—
took place on the night of April 4, 1968. After returning to St.
Boniface from an open housing march, I and my sidekicks Garvin
and Zulu sit down hungrily in the meeting room to plates full of
doughnuts, cold cuts, and chips when a suit-and-tie-type brother
from the NAACP runs into our midst, wailing and choking, "Dr.
King's been shot!"

Pandemonium ensues. Everyone's yelling, wanting to know
what's happened. Someone's turning on a radio, another person
runs to check the TV news, we're hearing snatches of reports about
Memphis, Tennessee, the sanitation workers' strike Dr. King went
to support, how he was shot on the balcony of his motel. Then
suddenly a voice screams above the others: "He's dead! They murdered Dr. King!"

Now comes a silence. Shock. Disbelief. Lifetimes pass in these
seconds. Then a wave of sorrow and rage explodes in the room,
rocketing through me, carrying all of us outside into the street, as
we begin to throw whatever we can get our hands on. Madness.
Terror. Anger. The power underneath these emotions feels like the
night of the riots multiplied to the nth degree, even though the
fiery talk of storming into all-white neighborhoods to wreak havoc
soon passes.

With the assassination of Robert Kennedy only a few months
later, 1968 brought to a thunderous peak everything that had
been happening in civil rights, protests over Vietnam, women's
liberation, the sexual revolution, as well as what was going on in
music and culture at large. Some of our idealism had been struck
down at the same time that the momentum of power to the people was unstoppable. The promise of we shall overcome and we
are going to the mountaintop hadn't been broken, but the strug-

gle was going to be much longer and more arduous than we first believed.

Books, as always, fulfilled my need to find power through knowledge. Over the next few years I journeyed through black history by reading whatever I could get my hands on. Moms would never discourage me from reading any book, although she was slightly alarmed when I came home with *Die, Nigger, Die* by H. Rap Brown and *Soul on Ice* by Eldridge Cleaver.

She was down with the antiwar movement and had no problem with the sweatshirts we wore and sold that had black-pride slogans on them like "Soul Brother" and "Black Power" and "Keep the Faith" and the generic "Sock It to Me." Moms even wore her "Soul Sister" sweatshirt while she was washing my clothes. But just to make sure I didn't get too radicalized or militant, periodically she would warn me, "Boy, if you gonna be another Rap Brown, you got to get out of here."

When I kept on reading, not because I was overly radical but because I wanted to know what something said before I rejected it, she'd ask, a little nervously, "You don't believe in all that stuff, do you?"

Of course, I reassured her, I didn't believe in it all and wasn't going to become militant.

Moms also knew that there were many other influences calling to me, none more powerfully than music. Only later did I truly appreciate how incredible it was to come of age in the heyday of every significant phenomenon that the late sixties produced, with everyone saying something that mattered: from James Brown and Bob Dylan to the Beatles, the Rolling Stones, Marvin Gaye, Stevie Wonder, the Temptations, Jimi Hendrix, Sly Stone, and, of course, Miles Davis—who capped off the 1960s with his groundbreaking *Bitches Brew*. Considered by some the greatest musical masterpiece of the twentieth century, it was almost as transformational as the invention of jazz itself. For me, it was as if Miles had poured everything that was happening historically, politically, socially, racially, and musically into a cauldron—mixing it all up with every emotional high and low, every hope and fear, every pleasure, sorrow, anger, and ecstasy—and created this big-time fusion.

That fusion also felt like a musical expression for what was going on in my personal life during my teen years—a simmering brew of new preoccupations and old ones. On the new frontier, right along with puberty, had come the most unbelievably constant interest in girls and sex. I loved everything about both. For several years now everything about the feminine species had turned me on. Everything, apparently, turned me on. All of a sudden, the wind would blow and my dick got hard. It had started earlier and without warning. Riding the bus, the jostling got my dick hard. Nobody explained to me that this was normal or that sometimes when your dick got so hard you thought it might break off or something, it was both normal to feel that way and not likely to happen.

On the one hand, having the ability to feel so potentially powerful was miraculous. Like you woke up one day and owned a high-powered expensive sports car you didn't even ask for. On the other hand, being a kid with churning hormones and limited opportunities to do anything about it was like owning a high-powered expensive sports car and not having your damn license yet! I had a couple of opportunities to go for a test drive, but until I had a regular girlfriend, I was left to do things like I did when I was a little kid staying at Uncle Willie's and I tried to get the attention of a neighbor girl by standing up on a milk crate under her bedroom window and breaking my kneecap in the process. So much for my attempts at serenading.

The most confusing thing to me was getting hard at inappropriate moments, like when the little old lady who paid me to shovel snow off her driveway and do odd jobs around her house needed me to help her get up from the couch. "Just help me, Chris," she asked. "Hold me until I get steady on my feet?"

"Yes, ma'am," I replied and carefully helped her up to a standing position, and as I leaned in to hold up a frail seventy-year-old spinster with failing eyesight, my dick got hard. That was more horrifying than any of the scary movies that my buddy Garvin and I spent all our money going to see up at the Oasis Theater on Twenty-seventh and Center. Knowing that it was nothing more than a ripple of human body heat and not anything about me being attracted to a senior citizen, I was still freaked out enough to curtail my part-time employment with her.

The only person in whom I might have confided these latest confusions was Ophelia, but she and DeShanna had since moved out of the house. That was rough on me as well as my younger sisters. Though we were half-siblings, none of us had been raised that way. They were my three sisters, and I was their only brother, plain and simple. That was in part because of how Moms insisted it was going to be, and also because we were all a team: us versus Freddie. Later, my baby sister Kim even used Gardner as her last name, putting it on every piece of identification she owned, even though she was born a Triplett. Kim and Sharon probably felt like me in wishing that Sam Salter could have been their daddy too. An equal opportunity abuser, Freddie didn't spare them much because he was their father.

What I did confide in Ophelia whenever I saw her was my ongoing preoccupation with putting an end to his brutality and him, even if it meant going to jail. Since Freddie was the reason she'd moved out—he'd actually campaigned to get her to do so— she understood my motivation. First of all, whenever she was going out on dates, Freddie showed up just in time to make sure the guy was disgusted—talking about the date's raggedy or uppity clothes, and farting, burping, slurping, scratching, whatever else he could do to make Ophelia want to slip through a hole in the floor. Anybody who came to pick her up, from then on, just honked, and she'd blow out of the house and keep on rolling.

Then he started going after her for not doing things right around the house. When one particular confrontation escalated and he warned her not to talk back or he'd kick her ass, Ophelia tried to walk away, but he blocked her path and bellowed, "Either I'm gonna kick your ass or you get your ass outta here. One of the two of them things gonna happen! You choose!"

The final straw came the next week when he began stalking into the bedroom that Ophelia and DeShanna shared with Sharon and Kim, my sisters sleeping three in the bed and the baby in a crib.

One night Ophelia felt so threatened by the volume of his voice and was so afraid that he'd hurt DeShanna, she picked up a large-sized protractor I usually used for my geometry homework and used the pointed end to let Freddie know, "You come in here and hit me, I'm gonna kill you."

Two days later my big sister and my niece left for good and went to live with our cousin Elaine over on Eighth Street—two houses away from Sam Salter. Ophelia saw her daddy every day, knew his wife and their kids, and whenever she needed anything and asked him for help, Salter gave it to her—though he did always say that it was his last two dollars.

Whenever possible I'd go visit Ophelia, sharing some of my concerns and secrets with her. But not all of them.

Bitches Brew
(side b)

What you doin'?'" I ask Garvin on a Friday night as he and I, along with our friend Fat Sam, a guitar player, on our way downtown to the movies, pass by The Auditorium and Garun makes a beeline for the entrance door.

It's springtime, decent weather, not long after my thirteenth birthday as it happens, on one of the last days of the Home and Garden Show, a big annual convention, and he suggests we see if we can sneak in and check out the exhibits. As soon as we pull open the doors, a tide of people comes pouring out, allowing us to slip inside without paying.

Fat Sam says, "Let's just lay low for a minute," and I suggest we head up the stairs to the stands and lie down between the bleacher levels.

Before long the place has emptied, and we're in semidarkness, with exit signs providing a subtle glow, holding our breath as a guard with a flashlight makes his last rounds. Finally the coast is clear, and we hit our first stop: a bakery display, complete with wedding cakes, jelly rolls, pastries, and fresh breads, all tasting as fantastically delicious as the display we destroy looks. Stuffed to the gills, with our pockets filled for later, we start throwing powdered sugar doughnuts at each other and laugh uproariously with our faces covered in white sugary fluff.

At the next display, Garvin calls excitedly for us to come see what he's just found. Fat Sam and I join him and our jaws drop. In an ultracool display is everything that three budding musicians could want for making their own music and then some: amplifiers, stereos, transistor radios, microphones, reel-to-reel tape decks. To take anything is a crime, we know. But we're basically drunk on sugar, and our musical recording aspirations suddenly supersede our better judgment. Talk about kids in a candy store! After emptying our pockets of pastries to fit in radios and tape reels, we load up the larger items, stacking and rolling them any way we can. Sam goes for a set of Vox amplifiers on wheels while I claim a state-of-the-art reel-to-reel tape recorder, among other things. This is like playing a variation of this-page-that-page, only with real stuff.

Getting all this home is a major ordeal, less so for Fat Sam because he lives closest by in the projects, but no easy feat for me and Garvin. We weave through the alleys over to the north side, avoiding being spotted by the police. Every time I start to have second thoughts, Garvin urges me on, saying, "Man, we just made a good rip and we just got a little ways to go."

At the second-floor apartment where my family's living now, everybody's home, but I have no key. To sneak in, I have to use a ladder that I'd previously adapted from an iron fence in order to bring up the stolen goods and stash them in my small room in the back, where nobody ever comes in. Exhausted but triumphant, I relax, dreams billowing around me of recording my first jazz album and also making some money off the extra electronics that I don't need. Now my focus capabilities start to kick into overdrive. Who's going to buy the stolen merchandise?

The following afternoon, with everybody in my household out, I'm busy sweeping the stairs in the front hall of the building—one of the latest part-time gigs, that I did for five dollars, paid for by the super—and a group of neighbors who are new to the building return from their outing. For a flash, my instincts remind me that I don't know anything about these people. They're a very loud, argumentative household and appear not to be a family but just a group of adults sharing the rent maybe. Playing cool, watching them head up the stairs, I notice an additional threesome of guys with them who don't live in the building. They seem on the shady side, not the kind of cats to report a kid for selling hot electronics. Listening to my instincts, I lift my head up from my sweeping and say to the one who looks like the leader of the pack, "Hey, man, y'all want to buy some tape recorders? Want to buy some radios?"

Glancing at the other two, he shrugs. "Yeah, let's see what you got."

Cool. I'm Mr. Hustler now, a natural. The three follow me to our place and down the hall to my room, where I show them my stash. As they're picking up the stuff, looking it over, talking like it's not that interesting a deal, my instincts are starting to sound big-time alarms, telling me these dudes are bad news and that I've made a grave error in judgment. Edging into the hallway toward the closet where Freddie keeps his shotgun, I feel tremors of fear rippling through me as I try to keep my wits together. Just as I enter the closet and go to reach for the gun, the main guy grabs ahold of my arm, jerks me out of the closet, and the three jump on me, pushing me down, not hurting me but restraining me long enough to gather up all the stuff and get out—which does hurt.

Now furious at them as well as myself, I fret and fume, well aware that I can't call the police, and I certainly can't tell the old man. As if I've got any recourse, I sit and seethe, trying to do a crime sketch of each of them in my head. At least I'll tell Garvin and Fat Sam to keep an eye out for these motherfuckers, who are all in their late twenties and early thirties. The main guy is average size, nondescript, while the second is maybe tall and lanky, also leaving little impression. But the third man—who looked like he held back when the other two were jumping me—was distinctive in the way he walked with a pronounced limp, a cripple maybe, or gimpy, the result of a deformity rather than an accident.

Without any recourse, and with no sense of lessons learned, I feel like shit yet have no alternative but to return to sweeping the stairs. As is my habit, I shift focus and try to forget my failed stint as Mr. Hustler.

"Hey," a low voice calls to me after twenty minutes or so have passed. I look up and see the cat with the limp, standing there holding a grocery bag. He explains, "Listen, man, I brought you some of your stuff back. And I brought you some money."

Cool. That takes the edge off. We return to the apartment, and I do a quick inventory of what he's brought back. About a third of the goods are there, obviously his share, but the reel-to-reel tape deck is still gone. He hands me ten bucks, and as I go to put the money in my pocket, instead of moving toward the door to leave, he takes a step toward me and says, "I done you a favor, now I want you to do me a favor."

"Oh, yeah," I say, "what is it?"

"I want to play with your dick."

"Naw, man," I protest, thinking I still have the right to decline and a chance to maneuver him toward the door. Another error in judgment.

The next slice of time, maybe ten, fifteen minutes, or shorter, do not take place in normal speed: parts of it stretch out in tortuously slow motion and other parts are heart-stoppingly fast. But even if I can't track time, I remember every detail of what happens, from the second he pulls a knife to my throat, forces me on my back, pulls down my pants, puts his dick between my legs, to registering the confused horror of my dick getting hard from the stimulation, to the true horror of him hoisting me into position so he can fuck me in the ass, right on the living room floor. Every grunt, every breath. His smell overwhelms. Funky. Rancid even, inhuman. White hot pain. Cold hard linoleum.

He finishes. Says, "Fine." Pulls me up by my shirt. Then pushes me into the hall, through the bathroom door, forces me face down onto the tile of the bathroom floor. Fucks me in the ass. Again. My brain understands he has raped me twice, but my emotions refuse to compute, all messed up over the fear that he's going to kill me after he's done. It's what he says next that starts my rage.

"Damn," he says, "I didn't even come."

In the terrible moment of fear in which I think he is going to make me do something else, he stands up, puts the knife away, as though he realizes other folks might show up soon, buttons up his pants, limps down the hall, and leaves. The smell lingers. Feeling sick, feeling dirty, permanently dirty, I start turning the analytical gears of my brain, trying to strategize what to do. What to do. No one can know. Not Freddie, the Big Wheel, who'll spread the story from Luke's bar across the city. Not Moms, who'll want to know how I got the stuff and how he got into the apartment in the first place. No police. No one. Instead, I'll take the mental record, spool it up on a tape reel, and stick it away, contained, not forgotten, but not to live in my consciousness every day.

A desolate quiet descends on the apartment as feelings of total powerlessness and hurt wash over me. The no-daddy blues plays in my imagination, taunting me that if I'd had a daddy, he wouldn't have left me unprotected—either from my own juvenile mistakes or from the street predators. To drown out those sounds, I walk into my room and take my trumpet out of its case and begin to practice, playing without passion, by rote, knowing as I do that now there are two motherfuckers in this world that I got to kill.

———

Was there anything positive that could be said about Freddie Triplett? He was, after all, my mother's husband, for better and for worse. What part of our day-to-day lives would count as better?

Often I was hard-pressed to come up with anything, other than that the members of his immediate and extended family were wonderful. There was his sister Miss Bessie, always industrious, owner of the Big House and Bessie's Hair Factory, generous to relatives all up and down our various family trees. There was his sister Baby, always taking Momma's side over her own brother, even warning me to be careful when I started talking—probably too much—about how I was planning on killing Freddie.

Baby didn't try to talk me out of my plans, she just wanted me to do it right. She said, "Chris, if he find out that you trying to think of how to kill him, he g'on git that gun out and he g'on kill you first. You hear me? Believe me, so you remember that!"

She was right. The plan became not to plan but to seize a moment, as though by accident, so as not to give myself away to him or anyone else. My friends and I had been going downtown to watch the amateur wrestling matches, and even if a lot of that stuff was for show—as I'd learned, much to my disappointment—I had mentally practiced putting Freddie in any number of bone-crushing moves. It would have to happen fast, and I couldn't just maim him. Utter annihilation was the only way to go.

Shortly after Baby's warning, a golden opportunity for him to suffer a freak accidental death was given to me when Freddie and I went to move a refrigerator into her house. Barking orders, Freddie told me to go in front and pull the dolly up, while he took the position below, pushing the dolly and the refrigerator up the stairs. In perfect timing, I missed a step, on purpose, and let the refrigerator go. A priceless look of confusion and horror came over his face, and like a work of art, the next thing I knew Freddie had a refrigerator on his chest and they were both tumbling down the steps. All he said was, "Goddamn!" as it came down on him. "Accidentally." He slid down, veering backward, breathing his last breaths, and just before it crushed him to death, he braced himself, puffed out his chest, regained his footing, and bench-pressed all those hundreds of pounds of metal right back into place and up the steps.

He *was* Godzilla. Giving me the evil eye, he surely had no idea that accident had been deliberate. Otherwise, he would have crushed *me* with the refrigerator. Only Baby, seeing my disappointed face when we rolled the dolly inside, figured out what had really happened on the steps.

Besides Baby and Freddie's other sisters, I was also fond of a friend of his who became my adopted uncle, a man everybody called Doodabug—a nickname that may have been some form of "Do the bug" or may not have been. Folks said he was so ugly, it looked like God just hit him in the face with a shovel. He was short, skinny, completely toothless, and drunk all day long, but everybody loved him just the same, even if he wasn't a blood relation to any of us. Once a player with the sharpest clothes, women, cars, and money, he fell into a hole of joblessness and alcohol and never got out. While he provided another lesson to me about the perils of being a drunk, he also became a living example of the old adage "where there's a will, there's a way." Don't ask me how he did it, but when Uncle Doodabug decided he was going to bestow on me a very special gift that nobody else had ever given me, he stayed true to his word and presented me with my first pair of silk drawers and a matching black silk T-shirt. I wore them until there wasn't anything left but the waistband.

Uncle Doodabug brought out the best in Freddie. In fact, at Luke's House of Joy, which Freddie ran like he owned it, because he was that mean, anybody who gave Uncle Doodabug a hard time would hear from Freddie: "You fuck with Doodabug and you'll have to deal with me."

But Freddie's protective nature wore off during one excursion when Uncle Doodabug fell asleep with a cigarette hanging out of his mouth in the backseat of Freddie's pride and joy—his 1964 powder blue Cadillac Coupe de Ville. With its darker blue vinyl top, dark blue interior, and fishtails, supposedly just like one that Elvis owned, that Caddy, the Elvis-mobile was the old man's sacred space, and nobody dared so much as drip sweat on the seats. Nobody except Uncle Doodabug, who fell asleep and didn't notice the smell of anything burning until Freddie—behind the driver's wheel—and I, in the front passenger seat, figured out that the burning smell was coming from the backseat floor upholstery. All of a sudden, Uncle Doodabug and the backseat were engulfed in flames. Freddie put the fire out with my orange soda, cussing at the top of his lungs, "Get outta my goddamn car, Doodabug, you drunken motherfucker! Get outta my goddamn car!"

No one was hurt luckily, although I couldn't help fantasizing about a scenario in which Uncle Doodabug and I survived the fiery inferno that took Freddie's life.

Otherwise, Doodabug brought out Freddie's softer side. Whatever it was that had gone so vicious in Freddie, the only other time he seemed docile was when he was out in the middle of the river in any kind of boat with his best fishing gear and a half-pint of Old Taylor. In fact, if you could have kept Freddie out fishing or hunting, he might have been all right. A Mississippi country boy, he probably should've never come to the city. In the outdoors, the farther from the city the better, he was in his element. Sometimes I went out fishing with Freddie and other family members on both the Gardner and Triplett sides, and sometimes just with Freddie. In the groups, I was in heaven, listening to the men tell their fish tales up at the bait shop, seeing places way out in the boonies of Wisconsin and Minnesota, loving the summer days and nights, learning the art, science, and luck of success as a fisherman, wiping sweat off my forehead on a hot, hot day, and trying to find the sweet spot where a light breeze would cool me right off.

Alone with Freddie, I had to be more alert. It could have been that as I got bigger and posed more of a threat to him, he was trying a tactic of making me his underling, bringing me out on these fishing trips to possibly groom me to be a black Huckleberry Finn or something. Not that I trusted or liked him, but I actually enjoyed fishing and did feel somewhat safer when he didn't have any guns with him.

On the water, Freddie drank but didn't get crazy. There were even fleeting moments of camaraderie when we cooked up our catch in a skillet over a fire on the bank and ate it right there. And there were moments, out on the river in the boat, waiting for the fish to bite, just me and him, when the sky was clear and the sun not yet too high, that I could feel a sense of peace in him.

But by the time we returned home, he was back to his old self, beating Moms, me, and my sisters, going for his shotgun, waking us all up in the middle of the night to get out of his "goddamn house." Needless to say, I made sure to avoid hunting trips with him, though to his credit, he put a lot of food on the table. Freddie liked to call himself the "Great White Hunter of the Ghetto" because he could catch, trap, or kill anything he came across out in the woods. This was no exaggeration, except for the white part. He brought home all kinds of animals: raccoons, squirrels, rabbits, possums, turtles, geese, ducks, and a variety of winged creatures. Much to his regret, he never shot a deer, although he did bring one home strapped to the hood of his Elvis-mobile, like killing Bambi was something to show off. Not even local drunks asked, "Where did you shoot it?" because it was clear it hadn't been shot but run over.

Whether we fished together or he brought home a sack full of rabbits and squirrels or whatever, my primary job in our household was now no longer head gofer but Freddie's apprentice in gutting, scaling, skinning, declawing, cleaning, and deboning his kill. Not surprisingly, this involved knives. Sharp knives.

When it came to fish, I was amazed by the consistency in the anatomy: their bladder, stomach, heart, lungs, and gills. I didn't mind skinning, gutting, and cleaning the fish because the better I did my job, the more delicious it was going to taste when Moms battered and fried it all up and we ate her cooking with white bread and hot sauce. But I learned to hate gutting and cleaning the other animals. At first, it was interesting to be given on-the-job anatomy lessons. For someone who couldn't read or write, Freddie was a whiz at demonstrating how to identify the stomach, gall bladder, liver, and vital organs of several species. Even though Moms could cook anything that Freddie brought home—fried with rice and gravy, it was filet mignon to me, perfect with cornbread, greens, and maybe some yams on the side—cleaning and skinning anything with fur or feathers became a horrific undertaking after a while. Freddie's various hunting and fishing hauls were strewn throughout the little house at 3951 North Fourteenth Street, where we were living by the time I started high school. Our good fortune to have made it up to Capitol Drive to the better neighborhood, no longer in the ghetto, was due mainly to Uncle Archie, who owned the house we were renting. Fish showed up in the bathtub, possums in the freezer, and you never knew what else you were going to find.

That was the deal with the old man. You never knew if the outdoorsman or the psychopath was going to come to dinner. Every time I'd think he was mellowing, I'd come home and find a crime scene, police carting him away yet again. Everyone in the family was alarmed by Freddie's widening collection of handguns. Momma's stepsister Dicey Bell—who now lived in Chicago—was especially concerned. (Seemed like all those southern aunts and girl cousins had two names like Bettye Jean, Dicey Bell, Lillie Mae, and Eddie Lee.) The older relatives made sure their younger kids, particularly females, weren't left alone with Freddie.

On one occasion Moms and I were alone at home, and we knew we were in grave danger, with Freddie returning at any time. The moment he entered the house, without Moms saying a word, I knew by her look that she was telling me, *Go call the police.* That panic, that fear as I ran convinced me without a doubt that by the time I made it to the pay phone a block away she would already be dead. Racing back to the house, I imagined a bloody sight waiting for me, and my dread ballooned higher into a gigantic tower. It was a sensation that Spike Lee later captured in his film shots; moving the camera instead of the actor, he conveyed exactly how the wiring in our brains goes askew during a crisis. As the house came into sight that time, I saw that the police had just taken a loaded .38 pistol away from Freddie and were driving him away in their car. At least for a night.

By 1970, at age sixteen, a junior already, I honestly didn't think that I could survive the roller coaster anymore. Moms saw it happening and just urged me to hold on, pointing out that I had already skipped a grade and had only one more school year before graduating. By this point, playing music, having girlfriends, and hanging out with my buddies all provided outlets but school was no longer the haven it had once been. Besides the academics no longer being of interest, my anti-establishment attitude set me at great odds with the repressive, racially charged atmosphere.

A major confrontation arose in my sophomore year when the coach of the football team refused to play me as quarterback. An outrage. I had always played quarterback on every football team I'd been on, starting back when we were playing street football and going throughout my junior high seasons. Everybody knew Chris could throw the ball. That was my rep and my future, or so I imagined, since Moms had convinced me I wasn't going to be Miles Davis because he already had that job. After all, at sixteen, Miles had left home and was doing sessions with Charlie Parker and Dizzy Gillespie in New York City. I was in a hot band, but suddenly didn't see myself coming out anytime soon with my own *Bitches Brew*. Football might not have been a career, but I was damned good and the best candidate for quarterback.

The football coach of the recently integrated high school didn't share my vision. He took one look at me, saw a big black kid already six-one, not too far from my top height of six-three, and decided that I was an offensive tackle. Me block? Play on the line? Nothing against the offensive linemen, who are important to any quarterback, but that star role was the job I wanted. Besides the precision of my arm, I had the smarts, strategy, and leadership qualities to win football games and had been burning them up in practice. Sticking to principle, though I agreed to play on the line, I continued to raise the issue with the coach until our discussions became so testy, it was clear he wanted to throw me off the team. But unless he came up with a reason for doing so, he would look like a racist if he did.

The reason, announced to me in his office, was the discovery of contraband in my locker. With a shrug, he told me that I was being cut because, "you are a bad element for what we're trying to do here at this school."

The contraband? Books. To be more precise: *Die, Nigger, Die, Soul on Ice*, and *The Autobiography of Malcolm X*.

Thus ended any taste I had for athletics. That, combined with my continuing activism, my new observations about the gaps between the haves and the have-nots, black and white, and the stories I began to hear from the brothers returning from Vietnam fueled a desire to rebel against the status quo even more. Rather than becoming militant, I rebelled by making my own personal statement—my Afro, tie-dyes, and beads—and by putting my energies into the band that I was in.

The Realistic Band happened to be a James Brown–style band, with strains of Sly Stone and Buddy Miles that I was pushing. Of course, I was totally down with Mr. Brown, and for years, whenever he was in town, I was there, taking in everything that he and his band did to create that unbelievable energy.

At each concert I'd start all the way back up in the bleachers of the Milwaukee County Stadium of sixteen thousand fans, and by the time James hit the stage I was in the front row. A mainly all-black audience, they went crazy, sheer pandemonium, before he even opened his mouth, and then every song he did was a show-stopper, a religious experience. Something about how he did *Please, Please, Please,* just the guttural, pleading, soulful, slowed-down funk of it, was mind-blowing. That shit hit it, every time.

At one memorable concert a sister jumped onstage during that song and tore off the hot pink sequined cape he was wearing and threw it into the audience. The next thing we knew we had a feeding frenzy, everybody ripping and tearing up James Brown's cape. My piece, no bigger than a washcloth, became my most prized possession at the time. Moms, who loved her some James Brown too, was excited for me when I came home with my pink scrap of immortality.

To duplicate the James Brown sound—with its own rhythm and pulse that was off the charts—was an impossible goal. But we weren't bad. Our lead singer, Big Ed, a cat in his twenties and older than most of us, had started the band and then gone over to Nam while we kept the ball rolling. When he returned, he picked up the microphone where he had left off. For Milwaukee, he put on a good show, screaming and falling out, dressing up flashy, albeit somewhat strangely, in pants that were too short on his six-six frame and silk waistcoats that fit oddly. In my heart of hearts, I knew that music wasn't going to be my ticket to fame and fortune—one of several realizations that soon motivated me to find a job after school and on weekends.

The other concern was that, after he came home from Nam, Big Ed became increasingly volatile. Garvin and I stopped by to see him at his house one day to go over our playlist for that evening, with the TV showing news behind us, and as we made small talk, out of nowhere, Big Ed pulled out a .45, aimed it at the TV screen, right over my head, and pulled the trigger. *Ka-boom!* The TV just blew up! Just disintegrated! Not missing a beat, he put the gun away, some kind of sleight of hand, and kept on talking like nothing had happened. "Chris, what we playing tonight?"

Garvin and I got out of there as fast as we could. "Damn," I said, "all he had to do was change the channel!"

Turned out that he had shot up some other TVs, and his own mother had to hide her television set whenever he went to see her.

Weed took his edge off. A few nights later Garvin and I were sitting in a parked car with Big Ed as he smoked a joint. When a police car pulled up behind us, Big Ed managed to throw out what was left of the joint before the two police officers approached.

We were ordered out of the car, and the two searched the smoky interior. Finding nothing, one of them said, "You must have been smoking marijuana in there because I smell it. I'm going to have to take you down and arrest you."

Big Ed said, "Take the smell to court, man. We ain't got nothing here."

For a tense moment, the cop looked shocked, like he couldn't believe what he had just heard. But it worked. He let us off with a warning.

My respect for Big Ed increased dramatically. For a cat who flipped out over the news and shot up TVs, he sure knew how to keep his cool in that situation.

The marijuana of the late sixties and seventies was nothing like the psycho-pot of later decades. For me, even though I had my fun drinking cheap wine in this era, smoking weed was preferable. Then again, I never wanted to get too high because I needed to be able to handle whatever insanity Freddie might pull at home.

Out with the boys after a gig in the same time period as our encounter with the cops, I smoked some crazy Thai-stick and went home paranoid as all hell, with a monster case of the munchies. Looking for something to eat, I tiptoed downstairs to the basement refrigerator and the moment I opened the door heard this *honk-honk-honk* poultry sound. Whirling around, I found myself face-to-face with a live goose. In our basement! Either I was way too stoned or Freddie had transformed the basement into an animal preserve.

In fact, Freddie had brought that live goose home for Sunday dinner the following night. This is his explanation when I wake up the next day. The three of us—Freddie, me, and the ill-fated goose—go together out into the backyard to the chopping block.

Freddie, whiskey thick on his breath at midday, hands me the ax. He smiles like the devil, as if to say that either I'm going to be initiated into chopping a live goose's head off, which I don't want to do, or, as the thought enters my head, I am going to be given my best shot to do what I've been trying to do for years.

When I hesitate at taking the ax, he says, "I'll do it then, god-damnit. You hold the goose."

Dizzy with opportunity, I realize that he is giving me this choice: to hold the goose while he chops its head off with the axe, or to chop off its head while he holds it. With the image of this drunken motherfucker chopping my fingers off, I opt for swinging the ax.

Blade suspended in air, I look down at the goose and what comes to mind is an image of a cowering, vulnerable, powerless female, not unlike Moms when Freddie towers over her. I look over at him and see where on his anatomy to bring down the ax blade. My most prominent thought is a geometric calculation: do I have the absolute correct angle to enable me to generate sufficient force and velocity to kill Freddie with one stroke? There is to be no chop-chop-chop. I have *one shot, one swing*. I inhale, living a lifetime in my deliberation, thinking of the story I'll tell to explain the accident, reliving my previous failures, and not wanting to fail again. With a big inhale, I exhale and bring the ax down with all my might, decapitating mother goose.

Damn. After all that time, I finally had my real chance and couldn't do it. The only feeling I had in the aftermath was hard-core deprivation. As if a prize had just been dangled in front of me and I couldn't grasp it.

Freddie said, "Hey, good job. Now you just got to one, pluck him, two, boil him, and three, gut him."

Though it took me some years to realize how killing the old man would have ruined my life, I was deflated. Without anywhere to put my feelings of anger toward Freddie, I transferred them over to the savings account of the other guy I was still looking to kill—an opportunity that arrived shortly after the goose incident.

Sooner or later I had assumed that I'd cross his path. When I did, it was his limp and his smell that caught my attention, both unmistakable. The fear came back to me when I saw him. Not a fear he could do anything to me, but fear that maybe he might get away. Even more, with the rage bottled up for three years, it was fear about what I was going to do to him. After he passed me on the street, he turned and went into a tavern. I waited for over an hour, holding a cinder block.

Each time the tavern door opened, out would spill a mix of music, laughter, smoke, and the combination smells of beer and different kinds of booze, old tavern smells and human body smells. Each time, someone else came out. Maybe he had escaped. Maybe he had snuck out in the shadows. But then, at last, the door opened and the smells and sounds poured out one more time, and he came out alone, turning down toward where I was waiting. I needed him to see me; I needed to see the recognition in his eyes. When I came toward him, I saw not only recognition but fear, maybe the only time in my life that I caused fear to come into someone else's eyes.

"Oh, shit," he said, not even finishing the statement before I crowned him with the cinder block, bearing down with all my strength on the top of his head.

At first, he didn't fall, but he faltered. After more pounding, he finally crumpled to the sidewalk, and I threw the brick down, left it right there, and walked away. Didn't look back, didn't run. Right or wrong, I silently said the last words that I'd ever think about him—*Got your motherfucking ass.*

What became of him, I never knew. But I did know this: he had one gigantic headache and he would never forget me. For me, there was no need to keep the image in memory. I tossed it out that night on the street, like him, like the cinder block.

The score had been settled, the case was closed.

———

My destiny was probably carved on the Mississippi River when I was eight years old, riding in the motorboat with Uncle Henry, hearing stories about him going overseas and meeting women, seeing the world. Between him and Uncle Willie, it was only a matter of time before those stories caught up with me and sent me down to the recruiting offices.

There wasn't much holding me in Milwaukee. After that spring of 1970, while watching the March Madness NCAA finals when Moms gave me the greatest gift her wisdom could offer by saying, "Son, if you want to, one day you could make a million dollars," I knew that wherever my path lay, I was going to have to leave my home turf and go find it.

Sometimes in years to come I'd realize that I must have been born at the perfect time—to be able to witness everything that happened in every decade from the fifties on. Lucky for me that the mandatory draft was being phased out around the time I came of age. If I had been born a year or two earlier, I would've been drafted, and I probably would have been there in Vietnam too. It was also amazing to be growing up right in the middle of a sexual revolution at a time when the stereotypes of color were changing and black was especially beautiful. All of my early romantic relationships left me with positive feelings about what had gone on emotionally and physically.

My first serious girlfriend had been Jeanetta, the sweetest, prettiest girl in all of north Milwaukee. It didn't even occur to me how crazy I was about her until Momma said something to me after I came in late for the umpteenth time. "Boy, I used to be able to set my watch by you."

Jeanetta and I were unsophisticated in our lovemaking but no less passionate. Even after we broke up, every now and then we'd sneak down to her basement and go at it like bunnies.

I next dated an uptown preacher's daughter who I found irresistible because she wore stockings. No other girl I dated had worn stockings, and she was also the first girl I'd ever dated who lived with both her mother and father. Most everyone I knew lived in a single-parent household. She was very reserved, quiet, and proper. She was a virgin who was willing to have sex—on condition that she have a baby right then. Not knowing much, I had plenty of life examples teaching me that high school parenting wasn't for me. We broke up before we got too serious.

My next girlfriend, Belinda, and I were soul mates, and we became serious fast. She was beautiful, black as me, gorgeous, with delicious, luscious lips, statuesque like an African queen. But what most attracted me to her was how smart she was. She read and made me read more, and she would ask questions. Belinda broadened my worldview beyond the African American experience, steering me toward books about South Africa and apartheid, the history of events like the Sharpsville Massacre, setting up an awareness of my connection to people of color around the globe. Belinda wore an Afro hairdo, was stacked, and had a big beautiful smile. I loved her, especially her body, which was unbelievable. Her behind was spectacular, shaped like a basketball. Swear to God, every time I saw her from the backside I wanted to start dribbling. Not only that, she was sexually uninhibited, doing things like jumping into my lap in the living room of her daddy's house as he slept in the next room. For me at that point, that was doing the wild thing.

Belinda and I had a date planned to go to the movies on the afternoon of Christmas Day, a welcome chance for me to skip out

on the annual family holiday bash at the house of one of our relatives. Christmas, according to popular lore and actual accounts that
I had heard from normal people, was supposed to be an occasion
for family to gather to eat, drink, and be merry. Not in our family.
The routine was that everyone got together to eat, drink, and then
fight. Every holiday, religious, secular, patriotic, pagan, it didn't
matter, by the third round of drinks the battles began. So as Moms,
Sharon, and Kim followed Freddie out to his car, I just called after
them, "Merry Christmas! Y'all go ahead to the party, I'm going to
the movies with Belinda, so maybe I'll stop by later."

The house all to myself, a luxury, I go and put my clothes together for my date, then go into the bathroom and run a hot bath,
the anticipation of a great long Christmas Day soak putting me in
a serene, great mood. Moments after I lower myself into the water,
close my eyes, and begin to enjoy a series of meditative images that
take me out on the river on a hot day, relaxing without a care in
the world, I suddenly hear, "Motherfucker!" this and "Bitch" that,
coming from the front porch. Footsteps in the living room tell me
that Moms and my sisters are home, with Freddie too. It's like a
scene in that movie *Poltergeist* that came out some years afterward:
"They're baaa-aaack."

Lying in the tub, buck naked, I'm thinking, *Damn, I took too long.*
But before I can swing into action, the door flies off its hinges and
pointing dead in my direction is the barrel of Freddie's shotgun.
Never before has he looked so much like the meanest, drunkest,
craziest Sonny Liston as he does this day, raging at me with his
deadliest "Get the fuck outta my goddamn house! Get out of my
goddamn house!"

With no time to respond and ask what the hell I've done, and
as everyone in the house literally scatters to run upstairs or down
into the basement, I could kill myself for not bludgeoning him
instead of that goose now that he's finally going to make good on
his promise to blow me away. No choice now, I jump out of the

tub, heart pounding through my chest, and race out the front door and onto the porch. Buck naked for all the world to see in Milwaukee, Wisconsin, on Christmas Day.

Before I can figure out my next move, I look down and see a cute little boy passing by, bundled up in his winter coat for the fifteen-degree weather. He looks something like I did at his age, with ears somewhat big for his head that he'll no doubt grow into. As he spots me, his smile widens straight across his face. Sincere as you please, he says: "Merry Christmas, mister."

Not answering him, I watch him walk on down the street, soon disappearing into the wintry Wisconsin mist.

Belinda didn't attempt to cheer me up when we did get to the movies later. There wasn't an ounce of merry left in me.

That day marked the last time I bothered to celebrate a holiday in the Freddie Triplett household, and unfortunately, it pretty much ruined Christmas. For many years I didn't bother buying a tree, and if I did mark the season, it was in the effort to do something that honored the spirit of Christ, in some spiritual context. It has taken me the balance of my life to truly enjoy Christmas. By the same token, Freddie's gift to me that year was to start my clock ticking for how soon I could get out of Dodge.

A short while later, Belinda and I broke up, not for lack of love but more because of timing and my immaturity at helping her deal with the death of a mutual friend. By that summer of 1971, I was seventeen years old and going into my senior year of high school. When I happened to be walking down Wisconsin Avenue, my stomping grounds of this era, I glanced up into the window of the army/navy surplus store and saw a girl through the glass holding a T-shirt up to her chest, as if she was debating whether or not to try it on. One look and I just fell in love. Shot through the heart.

After I walked into the store and introduced myself, I learned that her name was Sherry Dyson and that she was from Virginia, a senior at Morgan State College, and in town with relatives. Light-skinned, with a full Afro and the most beautifully shaped breasts, just incomparable, she was not a movie magazine beauty, but in an understated, down-to-earth way a knockout. She was brilliant, kind, and had a sense of humor that put me at ease with her from our first conversation. After we met, we spent two days just talking.

At first, Sherry had no idea that I was four years younger than her, although after we went to see *Summer of '42*—a fittingly perfect romantic movie about an affair between an older woman and a teenage boy—I had to confess. For the rest of my life, every time I'd hear or even think of that theme song, I'd become seventeen years old again, crazy in love with Sherry Dyson, my dream woman from a well-to-do Richmond, Virginia, family. The daughter of a mortician father who owned the A. D. Price Funeral Home and a mother who was a high school teacher, Sherry had grown up all her life in one home, a gracious colonial house on Hanes Avenue, Richmond, Virginia—a street name I'd never forget, considering the deluge of letters and cards I addressed to her there.

At this stage of the game, having girlfriends had already provided me with some crash courses in basic economics. My last year of high school and the shocking discovery that I had amassed a nine-hundred-dollar phone bill calling Sherry long distance were all I needed to know that I had to do better than what I was earning as a dishwasher at Nino's Steakhouse, making at best a hundred a week.

After I hid the phone bill, Moms received a call from the phone company alerting her to the fact that our phone was going to be turned off for nonpayment. When she complained that she hadn't even seen a bill, Moms figured out fast what had happened. Staying extremely cool, she escorted me down to the offices of the phone company and made me confess why our phone bill was so high. A deal was struck to prevent the phone from being turned off that required me to turn over every cent I made for the rest of my teen years.

It was my own doing, but that didn't prevent me from throwing a fit at Nino's the next night when I reached a boiling point over being stiffed by the waiters, who were supposed to be sharing tips with me. This was from the same crew running back to the kitchen screaming for clean dishes. The manager shrugged and told me that I was lucky to have my job washing dishes as it was. Livid at everyone and delirious from the heat of "humping the hot Hobart," as we called running the dishwasher, I did the most disgusting thing that came into my head. I felt almost as bad afterward as the time I got into another financial rut from phone calls to Sherry and pawned Ophelia's television set. That night at Nino's I peed right onto the dishes coming out of the Hobart. Not once, but as many times as I could drink down enough liquid to make a statement of how I felt about my last hours on the job washing dishes at that steak house.

God must have had a laugh when the next job I obtained turned out to be handling bedpans and cleaning up pee and poop after old people. Even more important, I learned a new level of compassion that I had never known before, and I paid off the phone bill finally.

The person who helped get me the job as an orderly at the Heartside Nursing Home was Ophelia, now working there as a nurse's aide. For many reasons I wanted to do well, mainly because I was locking into a mind-set that whatever I was going to do in life, I wanted to give it my all, to go beyond what was expected of me. My first step, which would come in handy in the next pivotal chapters of my life, was to learn as quickly as I could from whoever was the best at doing the tasks I'd need to master. With that thinking, I really got into doing this kind of work: serving the food, changing people's diapers, making up the beds, emptying bedpans.

Pretty soon, I was thinking, *Yeah, I can do this.* Soon after that, I could do it better than the top orderly there. In fact, management saw how good I was and gave me my own wing. Of the thirty-

some-odd patients, all white, some were able to take care of themselves, while others needed a lot of help. The work was surprisingly
rewarding. It felt good to help people, and even better when people acknowledged how well I treated them. Unlike some of the
other orderlies and staff, I didn't ignore them when they rang my
call button but would go and help immediately. Nobody else there
was willing to give that kind of care. The truth was that I actually
liked helping them, liked doing my job.

Mr. John McCarville, an old Navy guy, had lost the ability to
speak. But he could salute. Every night when I put him in bed, or
anytime I attended to something he needed, he gave me a strong
salute. "Thank you," he was saying without words. "I appreciate
your kindness." Gratitude shone bright in his eyes. Two patients
whom we called the Flintstones—because one looked like Fred
Flintstone and the other like Barney Rubble—were mentally re-
tarded and middle-aged. The two had been on the wing so long
that after they became a twosome as homosexual lovers, no one
wanted to separate them. Fred was the aggressor and Barney was
the submissive one. I was rather freaked out when I saw one of
them eating his own feces.

"Is there any way to move them?" I asked my boss, thinking I
wasn't equipped for that kind of behavior.

"No, they need to stay on this ward, so you gotta try to deal
with it."

So I dealt with it.

Another patient was Ida, a tiny Italian lady with a gold tooth,
never seen out of her hospital gown and tiny hospital shoes. Sweet
as she could be, Ida was what we then called senile, probably suffering from Alzheimer's or some form of dementia.

The first time I saw her she padded up to me and asked, "Are
you my little boy?" I was really concerned about how confused
she was.

From then on, I answered, "Yes, Ida, I'm your little boy."

Serious as a heart attack, she then said, "Oh, that's funny. The last time I saw you, you weren't so tall. You weren't colored either."

Only once did I lose my temper and do something I instantly regretted. One of my patients, a wealthy woman from some blue-blood family, constantly complained, becoming louder and more obnoxious by the day. She berated everyone, me included, and refused to eat. Then when she did want something, she wanted it *now!* If you didn't jump to it, she was going to call her lawyer. The ghetto in me just flew out one day when she started saying really nasty things, and instead of leaving her piece of lemon meringue pie on her plate, I picked it up and put it *splat* right in her face.

Instantly mortified, I said, "Oh, I'm so sorry," as I grabbed a towel and carefully started wiping the lemon meringue off her cheeks and nose.

She just needed the attention as it turned out. She looked up at me gratefully and said, "Thanks, son, that's the first time I had my face washed all day."

———

When my sisters preempted my announcement to Moms that I had gone down and enlisted in the Navy, almost a year after high school graduation, she may have expressed her disappointment. Maybe if my last years of high school hadn't been so unfulfilling—especially with the administration treating me like a dangerous Black Panther outlaw—I would have pursued the college education that Momma never had. But by the time I came to give her the news, Bettye Jean Gardner Triplett flashed me her signature smile that could launch a thousand ships and asked if there was time to throw a party.

For the last few months I'd been working at Inland Steel, thanks to Uncle Archie helping me get a job there. As much as I had learned working at the nursing home, the union wages were a significant improvement in my pocket. And yet, I discovered a cold economic principle: the more you make, the more you spend. That was obviously something that I didn't have to leave Milwaukee to learn. But there was so much more out there I didn't know, and the reality was that I did have to leave my hometown, land of the familiar.

As to why I decided to join the Navy over the other branches of the service, it was possibly its superior marketing slogan, "Join the Navy, See the World," that did it. Or maybe it was all Jack Nicholson's fault, given the fact that I had just seen him in a role as a sailor in *The Last Detail* right before I went over to the recruiting center. Besides that, the Navy promised that I was really going to go see all the overseas places my uncles talked about. But the main motivation, even with Sherry not totally out of the picture, was getting to meet those women. I could hear Uncle Henry going on about the Italian women, and the Korean women who walked on your back to give you a massage that cured your spine of pain for the rest of your life. They had "feet like hands," I heard him say numerous times. I couldn't wait.

For the first eighteen years of my life, I'd guided myself without a father, believing that my fundamental responsibility was to protect my mother. Having failed to guarantee her protection by getting rid of Freddie, it was now time to put her lovingly and safely in God's hands and to go in pursuit of the happiness that was all my momma ever wanted for me.

PART TWO

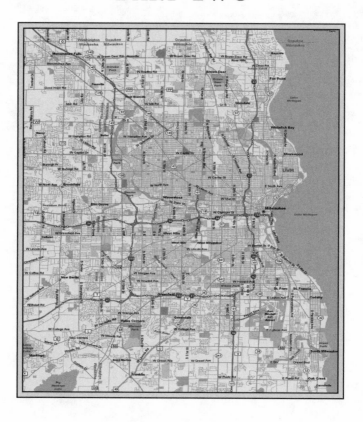

CHAPTER 6

The World Beyond

The USS *Chris Gardner* set sail—via airplane, the first time I'd ever flown—but instead of being sent to boot camp near a base like San Diego or in Hawaii, where all the recruiting photos were apparently shot, I was given a choice of going to nearby Great Lakes, Illinois, or Orlando, Florida. Opting for the farthest destination, imagining that would be a jumping-off place to all those foreign ports of call, I chose to go to Orlando. Land-locked Orlando. Hotter than hell with swamp-level humidity and steroid-fed insects.

Growing up on the roller-coaster ride engineered by Freddie Triplett, I was relieved by the institutional structure. Unlike an environment in which I could never do right, the Navy provided clear-cut guidelines for doing right or wrong and had a process for rewarding or punishing performance accordingly. There was definitely a part of me that resented authority and recoiled at the idea of having my individuality taken from me, but I understood the purpose and knew how to cope without losing a sense of who I was entirely. Of course, the transformation from being a nonconformist with my tie-dyes, beads, Afro, and light growth of facial hair to a clean-shaven, shorn, uniformed sailor was a shock and a half. The result was a terrible case of pseudo-folliculitis, for want of a better diagnosis, or big-ass bumps that a lot of cats, especially black guys, get from shaving for the first time. My hair was never the same after boot camp. As years passed I eventually gave up trying to grow it back right and was later grateful to Isaac Hayes for pioneering the shaved-head look.

The heat and humidity were rough from the start, but I didn't know what hot was until I had to stand at full attention in my dress uniform in the sun. My "training" in learning how to be still helped. I wasn't allowed to move or to react at all to the rivers of sweat running down my face and back, tickling my ass. Not a flinch.

In formation one afternoon I saw Senior Chief Petty Officer White, commander of Company 208, stride right up to me and braced myself for whatever he had to say.

"Son, you know what I know about you?" he asked, almost nose to nose with me as droplets of perspiration weren't just rolling down my face and body but touching me like long blazing fingers, like a parade of insects crawling and itching me. I didn't move. Officer White answered his own question: "What I know is that you've got a lot of self-discipline."

Not that I didn't make mistakes. Early on, in my enthusiasm, I saluted an officer indoors. Who knew you weren't ever supposed to do that? I didn't know. I was just saluting my ass off, chest puffed up, broadcasting—*Hey, I'm in the Navy, off to see the world!* As a consequence, I was sent to the deck—actually an expanse of lawn in front of the barracks—where I learned exactly how, where, and when to salute an officer. Surrounding this mock deck were statuesque palm trees inhabited by squirrels, a perfect setting for my superior officer to make me understand my station by ordering me to stand on deck and every time I saw a squirrel, run up to it, snap to attention, salute, and say, "Good afternoon, sir."

Please! Those squirrels must have had early vintage cell phones because the next thing I knew, squirrels seemed to just come out of nowhere, leaping from palm trees and scattering across the deck as I ran from one to the next, saluting and saying, "Good afternoon, sir." As intended, the humiliating part was the large audience of fellow recruits standing and watching from an upstairs barracks window while I dashed to and fro saluting a bunch of damned squirrels.

For the most part, however, I made it through boot camp with, as they say, flying colors. Graduates were given a choice of going either to a fleet or to an "A" school. Along with Jarvis Boykin, a fellow recruit I'd met at boot camp, I chose to go to an "A" school. This was a terrific opportunity, I thought, to build on the medical foundation that working at Heartside Nursing Home had given me. It was a stepping-stone to being a medic in the Navy's prestigious hospital corps, which I envisioned taking me to serve in the Philippines or Korea.

Boot camp had trained me well but had not gotten rid of my romantic streak. Not only was I ready to see the world beyond familiar shores, but I was beginning to think about the power of healing and helping the less fortunate, about changing and saving the world. Ironically, the school that I'd have to attend to set me on that path happened to be the U.S. Navy Hospital Corps School in Great Lakes, Illinois—not far from Milwaukee, Wisconsin.

There were more ironies to come. After doing that U-turn and ending up right back where I started up north, I faced the startling information that the U.S. Navy Hospital Corps provided medical backup and support for the U.S. Marine Corps. Actually, the Marine Corps was part of the Department of the U.S. Navy, something nobody had told me when I enlisted. My expectation was to be in an overseas medical naval facility, surrounded by slightly oversexed uniformed nurses like Hot Lips Houlihan from *M*A*S*H*. The last thing in the world I wanted to do was be in the Marine Corps. As I complained to Boykin and some of my other buddies I met in Great Lakes during the time we were being trained in the basics of first aid, "If I wanted to be in the Marine Corps, I could've joined the Marines. Man, please!" This was another reason I was increasingly concerned about where I was going to be stationed.

I started to get the sinking feeling that my vision of sailing off to sea was never going to happen. Hell, I began to worry, I might not even get out of the United States. That's why I was being careful to mind my p's and q's, just to be sure I was sent to one of the places I'd requested on my dream sheet and not shipped off with the Marines.

Fortunately, I had distinguished myself as a quick study when it came to the medical training we were being given. Everything looked promising on paper. As the twelve-week training period wound to a close, I had managed to stay out of the kind of trouble others had gotten into. I had already been discouraged from hardcore drinking by Freddie's example, in addition to the fact that I didn't really like the taste. But when the cats went out for beers off base, I went along and had a few. It practically went with the uniform. When my buddy Boykin and I headed off base to a bar called the Rathskeller one night, we had more than a few. We were drunk, sloppy drunk, which meant that we missed our ride and had to walk back to the base. Rather than walk the long way back through the main gate and be late, we decided to take a shortcut by jumping the fence.

It was pitch-black outside, moments before midnight, when we climbed the fence and looked down to see what appeared to be a solid landing spot, either the ground or a building top. Hitting down simultaneously on a heavy metal surface, we realized to our horror that we'd landed on a van. And not just any van. It was a van occupied by two brothers from the Shore Patrol. Judging from their groggy appearances, it was clear they'd both been taking a nap and we had awakened them. Now they were pissed.

"Goddamn!" said Boykin.

"Here we go," I said.

And so, the next morning, we had to go appear at Captain's

Mass—where the captain would decide our fate. Boykin emerged from his hearing with the bad news that he was being shipped off to Southeast Asia. Even though the War in Vietnam was winding down, there was a great need for medics in bringing troops home. Not that I wanted to go there, but it would be overseas.

As I walked in and waited for the captain, I stood tall, hoping that he'd look at my file and the destinations that I'd requested and see it in himself to look past the previous night's misdeeds.

The captain strode in, took a seat, and looked me up and down. He thought for a second and then asked, "You play football?"

"Yes, sir, I play football."

"Fine," he said, making a note. "You're going to Camp Lejeune. They've got a good football team down there, and they need a big guy like you." He put my file away and called out, "Next!"

———

Bad news and good news. The bad news, as I had started to suspect before leaving Great Lakes and arriving in Camp Lejeune, was that I really wasn't going to get out of the United States. Seeing the world was going to mean exploring the backwoods of Jacksonville, North Carolina—where Jim Crow seemed like he was alive and well anytime we stepped foot outside the base. Not only that, but Camp Lejeune was the biggest Marine Corps base in the world, populated by sixty thousand marines and six hundred sailors. So now, true to my fears, I was in the Marines. The only positive glimmer on this bad news was that I was sent to the Navy Regional Medical Center, as opposed to the Fleet Marine Force—only because the captain who had sent me happened to be a close friend of the Navy hospital's football team, one of the better teams in the Navy.

The good news was that for the next couple of years I served, worked, learned, and lived in an environment that was not too different from a college setting. While the Navy took care of my basic costs of living, I played some football, received an on-the-job education to rival what most premed students at top universities receive, and had a great time too. When I arrived, a coordinator explained that the barracks were full and there was nowhere for me to bunk as of yet. Together with a group of three other guys who hadn't been assigned to barracks either, I was taken on a tour of the hospital.

When we came to a wing that hadn't been officially opened for patients, the coordinator announced, "This is it. You guys will be staying here."

In no time we turned that place into party central. It wasn't the penthouse suite at the Palmer House, but we took advantage of the space, converting the patient sun deck and TV lounge into our bachelor pad, hooking up our stereos into an impressive, multiphonic sound system. All of a sudden, everything was cool. What had seemed like a bad break turned out to be a blessing no longer in disguise.

The hospital was state-of-the-art, and the staff, both military and civilian, were some of the best and brightest in the nation. Again, when receiving my job assignment, which could have been anything from orthopedics, podiatry, or proctology to psychiatric, among others, I pulled a lucky card and was assigned to work in the General Surgical Ward with Lieutenant Commander Charlotte Gannon, an absolute jewel.

Dressed efficiently in her white uniform with her Navy cap and its emblem of three-and-a-half braids, Lieutenant Commander Gannon had come out of Massachusetts General Hospital and ran her ward with authority, excellence, and compassion. It was an ideal environment in which to learn, and I thrived under her supervision. Throwing myself into every aspect of my work, I couldn't do enough to help the patients—mainly Marines and their family members, as well as some locals who needed specialized surgery not available at other area hospitals. By this point, I had learned the power of asking questions and knew that the best doctors didn't mind being asked them.

Gannon appreciated my focus and my desire to know more and embraced my litany of questions: "What is that called?" "How do you do that?" "Why do you do that?" "Would you show me?" "Okay if I try?" She taught me so much that influenced me in making all kinds of life-and-death decisions. Thanks to my experience at Heartside and some good instruction at the Great Lakes Hospital Corps School, I was clearly superior to anyone working in my position. Very quickly I became one of her favorite people and was respected by several other doctors too, all of which came in handy whenever I got into jams or needed an advocate.

None of the other doctors seemed to mind my questions, mainly because they usually only had to explain something to me once and I got it. Though I didn't know it yet, many aspects of my medical work would translate to other areas, perhaps none more important than knowing how to organize my time. Plus I loved what I was doing, everything from changing patients' dressings and hooking up IVs to providing postsurgical wound care, examining tissues, and debriding wounds—often doing several procedures simultaneously. Besides being really good with these specific duties, I was mindful of how what I did played into patients' overall healing and well-being. To that end, I placed great importance on maintaining detailed chart notes that helped the surgeons and nurses follow a patient's care—what time a dressing was changed, what an injury looked like, what it smelled like, whether a wound seemed to be clearing up, improving, or the patient complained of this, the patient complained of that.

After a short period of time, all the cats—from every background—were asking for "Doc," as they called me. My reputation was such that anytime anyone got shot, they were advised before they got to the ward to make sure they asked for me, that when it came to gunshot wounds, nobody could fix them up like I could. Even if I was busy or wasn't there, whenever someone else was assigned to them, they'd say, "No, I'll just wait for Doc." The same went for anybody who wanted their dressings changed. Seemed like I'd come a long way since I tried to dress my own wound with a Kotex.

One of my toughest early assignments took me to a crash site where a van carrying a dozen or more Puerto Rican brothers, all Marines, had gotten into a terrible accident on their way up to New York City for the weekend. Aside from the blood and guts, I had to help pull twelve unconscious and/or drunken Puerto Rican Marines out of the van, with glass everywhere. One of the guys, Dominguez, had so much glass in his face that I had to use forceps to remove all the embedded shards. Otherwise, he would have been horribly scarred for life, like a human Frankenstein. That was my call, even though others in my position would have most likely just sewn him up with the glass in there. He never forgot that I fixed him up, and the two of us stayed tight for quite a while to come.

In addition to the fact that I loved what I did and loved that feeling of appreciation that I'd helped, it was inspiring to see patients who were seriously hurt overcome the conditions that had brought on their hospitalization. To see some of these real cracker hillbillies suddenly setting aside their prejudices was incredible. Several of the Marines, you knew, would for sure call you a nigger in a heartbeat, but lying prostrate in excruciating pain, unable to move, they were having personal transformations simply by saying, "No, I'll just wait for Doc. What time's he comin'?"

They were waiting for a big black man like me to help them get through the crisis in which they found themselves. They seemed to be really changed, not because I changed them, but because they changed themselves by challenging their own beliefs. In turn, my own assumptions about folks who were different from me were challenged. For the first time since I had learned that the world wasn't all black, I really began to see people as people. Below the skin, I had learned, we're all pretty much the same.

Off the base, tolerance still had a long way to go. During an assignment answering the phone at the surgical clinic, I got a lot of calls similar to the one I received from a woman who barked, "My foot's broken. My foot's broken 'cause a two-hundred-fifty-pound nigger stepped on my foot."

"Okay, well, let me see if I got this right now? The foot is broken?"

"Yes!" she said.

"Now, did he break it because he was two hundred fifty pounds, or is it broken because he is a nigger?"

"Both!" she said.

Only every now and then did I meet people like that face-to-face. On a road trip out of town one weekend, my friend Pretty Willie and I—so much the opposite of pretty that he made my Uncle Doodabug look good—had to stop to fill up at a local gas station before we hit the road. Pretty Willie, who was from Aiken, South Carolina, warned that we might hit some unwelcoming spots farther away from base.

The local gas station didn't roll out the red carpet. In fact, no sooner had we pulled in than a skinny-ass old white woman came bearing down on us with a double-barreled shotgun, beady eyes blazing death as she announced, "I don't sell gas to no niggers! I sold gas to a nigger once, and he tried to burn my place down! So y'all just get out of here right now!" Nothing that overt had ever happened to me. Even Pretty Willie was as stunned as I was.

From my activism as a teenager, I knew that poverty and illiteracy made racism that much more pronounced. And there were a lot of poor folks, black and white, who lived in the vicinity of the base—even though I had little contact with them. Because I belonged to an institution now, I didn't have to suffer that poverty, something that made me want to help, even though I had no idea how.

In the meantime, a picture was beginning to appear in my head about my future in the medical profession, beyond the Navy. Sherry Dyson was not so much in the forefront at that point, probably because our communication wasn't as hot and heavy as it had been, although we did still talk. Even so, she fit the picture of a doctor's wife, and every time I thought of the image of her holding that T-shirt up to her chest in the display window of the army-navy store, I actually couldn't envision my long-term future without her. But for the time being, since I had missed out on the chance to romance women in foreign lands, I gave myself license to sow big-time oats.

One of the highlights was a trip that I made with three of my buddies to Howard University in D.C. We had a fantasy-filled introduction to coed life at Candell Hall. On one floor young men were housed, and the next floor housed young women. Young beautiful early 1970s liberated women. When we got to this dorm and saw what was happening, we said, almost in four-part harmony, "We ain't going back to North Carolina!"

We saw all those fine black girls and went AWOL. After spending all our money, we had no choice but to turn ourselves in to the Shore Patrol. We were issued orders, given fifty dollars to get back to Camp Lejeune, and promptly went AWOL again. Young and dumb, most of us nineteen years old, we couldn't stop ourselves. With all those sisters at Howard, we thought we'd died and gone to heaven! Finally, we partied ourselves out and had to turn ourselves in to the Shore Patrol a second time. Instead of giving us money, this time they took us straight to the bus station and escorted us onto the bus. Everyone got home intact except for crazy Haze, who managed to get into a fight and go AWOL a third time. When he returned, he was put on KP, had his pay docked, and pretty much had the book thrown at him. The other two guys didn't fare as badly as Haze but definitely suffered some consequences.

Just as I was waiting for my fate to be determined, Lieutenant Commander Charlotte Gannon appeared, brushed by me with a serious look, and went to huddle with the officers in charge of discipline. She went straight to the point, explaining, "Look, that's my right-hand man. That's Gardner. Leave him alone."

That was it. Charlotte Gannon had my back and she had juice. As soon as we returned to the ward, of course, she warned me, "Gardner, look, don't do that anymore. Just do your job and I will forget about it!"

From then on, I managed to keep on the straight and narrow. This was easier to do once I moved off base. After I met a sailor named Leon Webb—destined to be one of my best friends for life—we found an inexpensive trailer to rent and figured we could do our own thing and not get into trouble that way. Though I didn't have a car, I assumed that I could grab rides with Leon. It turned out to sometimes be more complicated than that, meaning I'd have to make sure I arranged rides from others when our schedules didn't coordinate. Although the Navy provided us with extra money for food and supplies, we lost the privilege of eating on base. We didn't quite understand that this was like real life—when the money ran out, we'd have nothing to eat. One memorably cold night—and it could get real cold out there in the sticks—our cupboard was completely bare except for a can of beans and an ostrich egg. Leon and I agreed that was the best ostrich egg we'd ever eaten in our lives.

Luckily, I was being fed and kept warm on some of those cold nights by a woman, ten years older than me, who lived off base not too far from where I was staying. Her cooking wasn't bad, she had a car, and she was fantastic in bed, a very kinky girl who introduced me to new things. It didn't bother me at all that there were other men in her life; to the contrary, that allowed me to play the role of a willing student without any relationship expectations.

One night in a moment of awkward timing, just as we start getting into it, I hear a knock on the door like a jackhammer—*boom,*

boom, boom, boom, boom!—and a voice saying, "*Open the door, open the door!*"

She ignores it, trying to get back to where we were.

Boom, boom, boom, boom, boom! This cat's not going anywhere.

Aw, man. I stop and ask, "Who is that? He's not going away."

"Oh, that's Leon," she says.

I know my roommate's voice and that's not him. "Leon?" Whoever it is, I'm here and he isn't, he's stopping me from getting my groove on, so I say, "Open the door. I'm gonna kick this motherfucker's ass."

"No, no, that's *Leon*, and you don't want to do that. Trust me, he's a boxer and you don't want to do that."

"*Leon* who?"

"Leon Spinks!" She sees that I still don't get it and then reminds me, "Heavyweight champion of the base?"

"Oh," I say. *That* Leon.

Leon Spinks!? Stationed at Camp Lejeune in the Marine Corps, he's already a boxing champ on the base, training for the next Olympics, and eventually will hold the title as heavyweight champion of the world.

Leon Spinks is outside drunk, cussing, wanting in because now it's his "turn." How'd I get into this predicament? How am I going to get out? No, I'm not getting into any duking match with Leon Spinks.

"*I'm going to knock this door down!*" he threatens, sounding like the Big Bad Wolf in the story of the Three Little Pigs. Next thing I know he's trying to huff and puff and blow down the trailer.

Because I'm a veritable walking encyclopedia of information, thanks to my long days spent in public libraries, I schematize the physics of this emergency and come up with a solution that maybe I've read somewhere or seen in a *Three Stooges* episode. So as he gets a running start to come batter the door down, my plan is that as soon as he hits the steps and puts his shoulder to the door, I'll open it and *bang*, he'll run into open space just as I fly out of there.

Just like clockwork, I time it right, opening the door as he runs in and collides with the table and then the wall, knocking himself out cold. Since he is so drunk already, it doesn't take much. Lying there on the floor, Leon Spinks has himself a good night's sleep, while my hostess shoos me out, not too pleased when I take her keys and her car but promise to leave it for her at the base.

The next time we're together, at my place this time, she convinces me to let her tie me up. Compared to all the missionary sex I've been having with other women, this is really forward. But since I've been tying her up, at her request, I agree. Using some intricate expert knots, she ties me to the bed, sprinkles baby powder all over me, and then tosses a big stuffed animal in the bed with me. "This is a little bit tight, okay?" she asks, but because we're just messing around and I'm thinking it's going to be quick, I don't complain.

There I am, spread-eagle, buck naked, covered head to toe in baby powder with a giant stuffed panda bear in the bed, and I close my eyes waiting for the seduction to continue. Nothing happens. I open my eyes and she has split. Gone. Just like that.

The only thing I can do is wait for my roommate to come home. Out in the country, who's going to hear me holler? Our landlady might, but I don't want her to see me this way. So I wait for literally hours, what feels like a day.

Finally, Leon's car pulls up. I have a fleeting panic that he's got Pretty Willie or Haze with him, or, God forbid, a woman. As still as I can be, I wait to see who comes in that door.

From the bedroom, unfortunately, I can't see who it is. Seems like he's taking forever messing around with something in the living room. Now I can't take it anymore and call out, "Hey, man, look here, can you come here and give me a hand for a minute."

"All right, hold on for a minute."

Several minutes pass. "Naw, naw, man, you got to come on right now. I need you to hurry up and give me a hand."

"All right, man, hold on, I gotta go to the bathroom," he says and heads in but then starts to walk right past me. At last, he gets the full inglorious picture and begins to laugh uproariously, asking what the hell I'm doing with the bear and all the white shit all over me.

Now I'm laughing too.

After Leon mercifully untied me, the two of us commenced to laugh for three days. The joke was absolutely on me.

———

One of the hardest yet most powerful jobs for any medic in a hospital caring for hard-boiled Marines is definitely proctology. Certainly this job requires a unique skill-set and involves principles that could probably translate to other fields of endeavor. Who wouldn't benefit from experience working around a bunch of assholes?

And so, from the General Surgical Ward to the surgical clinic, I eventually became the base's foremost proctology expert. This meant that every Monday morning every asshole with a problem was at my front door. Whether that problem was hemorrhoids, thrombosed hemorrhoids, peri-rectal abscesses, pilonidal cysts, anything to do with the rectum, anus, and vicinity, they came by me en route to see the actual proctologist. After a while, however, the doctors just left me in charge and headed out to the golf course.

No sweat. It got to the point that I could drain an abscess and eat lunch at the same time. It didn't bother me. My expertise included any kind of dressing application or change, plus a variety of procedures to treat patients with pilonidal cysts—basically a cyst that develops in the crack of the ass and hair gets in it and it becomes infected. Very common, the cysts can just blow up and look like a third butt cheek. I lanced, drained, and packed it, making sure that the infection was out and that the gauze was packed properly to continue to draw the infection out.

Full bird colonels with chests full of ribbons came to me with a range of these problems. Rarely did I get any respect from the officers who were there to see the doctor and didn't feel they had to be gracious to the medic—even though I was the one responsible for setting them up in the upside-down dental chair used for exams.

One colonel was in position, ass up in the air, when the doctor walked in and said, "Okay, I'm going to leave you here with Gardner, and he's going to set you up."

That was power. All of a sudden, the brass was completely vulnerable, his butt in the air, cheeks spread with tape, and I walked out, returning a moment later with the scope. The next thing I knew he was my best friend, saying, "Oh, Doc, oh, Doc, now, please, and, by the way, let me know if there's anything I can do for you?"

Sometimes, throwing in a little proctology humor, I'd claim to be out of lube.

Bad-ass Marines would turn into wimps: "Oh, Doc, oh . . ."

When the doctor wasn't in on one occasion, I prescribed suppositories for an officer, a full bird colonel. He was suspicious. "Don't worry," I told him, "I'm going to take care of you. Use these suppositories and we'll see you on Monday."

That Monday he and his wife marched into the ward, demanding to speak to my superior officer. Both looked at me with disdain, as if to say, *Who are you anyway? You're not a doctor and you're black!* Though I didn't know what I'd done wrong, I could see that he intended to write me up. Finally, he bellowed irately, "You don't know what the hell you're doing! You're dangerous! You shouldn't be here! And for all the good those pills did me, I may as well have been sticking them up my ass!"

It took all my self-control not to bust out laughing. He had taken the suppositories orally. This colonel was flying a $50 million jet, and he was taking rectal suppositories by mouth. Now his ass was still hurting and he was wondering why.

"Sir," I said calmly, "those pills that you took? You are *supposed* to be sticking those up your ass, that's the way they're going to relieve your pain and your swelling."

Sure enough, after I turned him upside down in my chair with his ass exposed, his whole attitude changed and he became a wimp just like all the rest of them. He also forgot about writing me up, and after his pain subsided, he was as grateful as the rest of my success stories.

In spite of an increasing level of self-confidence that my tour of duty at the Navy Regional Medical Center had given me, bouts of uncertainty arose from time to time, especially with the end of my term of enlistment just over six months away. Up until then, with an institutional structure providing me with four hundred dollars and change a month, free health care, and a sense of contribution, I had no worries. But suddenly, what to do beyond those six months had started to plague me with questions, conjuring up echoes of the no-daddy blues. Right or wrong, it seemed to me that if I'd had a father, he would have been able to give me concrete guidance. My uncles, my surrogate dads, had helped steer me into the service. Moms had told me that I could be successful at whatever I ultimately chose to do. What would my father, whoever this guy Thomas Turner was down in Louisiana—that name I had at some point gotten out of Momma—feel about the son he didn't know turning out to be a doctor? Wouldn't he want to claim me then?

Some of the enlisted guys I knew had decided to re-up, while others were heading home and getting set up in jobs, either engaged to be married and preparing to start families or returning to wives and kids already waiting for them. That was something I wanted one day, no question. But regardless of how worldly I thought I'd become, there was still a part of me that felt cheated about not getting to go off and see the world. Yet at this stage of my young adulthood, if I wanted to pursue a career in medicine, that would mean several years of schooling, which wouldn't exactly leave room for travel.

While stopping by the General Surgery Ward one afternoon, the answer to several of these questions arrived in the form of an offer from Dr. Robert Ellis. He was one of the doctors who had first heard good things about me from Charlotte Gannon and had then also taken me under his wing to train me. Truly brilliant, Dr. Ellis—or Buffalo Bob, as some of us sailors affectionately called him, on account of how intense he was and the fact that he was working in the Navy only under national duress—had received his training at Texas Children's Hospital in Houston with two of the world's most renowned heart and cardiovascular surgeons, Dr. Denton Cooley and Dr. Michael Debakey.

Now that Ellis was being discharged, he informed me, he was leaving for San Francisco to set up his own research lab at the University of California Medical Center and VA Hospital.

Knowing how well deserved and exciting this was, I shook his hand, congratulating him with all my heart—no pun intended.

"What about you?" he asked, aware that I had another six months to go.

I shrugged, letting him know that I was debating my options.

"Well," Dr. Ellis said, somewhat generally, "if you want to take a look at a career in medicine, I can help you with that."

My ears pricked up. I listened as he described the lab he was setting up and the research-assistant position he had to fill.

"You can come help me," he offered, letting me know the job was mine if I wanted it. "But it only pays seventy-five hundred dollars a year."

That was something of an improvement over my Navy pay. Not a dream salary. But a chance to be trained under one of the top doctors in the field, in San Francisco—about the farthest place I could go in the country and feel like I was visiting another part of the world.

"Think about it," he said. "Let me know."

I thought for two seconds and I let Bob Ellis know. "I'll take it," I told him. "I'll be there."

CHAPTER 7

Pictures of a Life

Y ou know, San Francisco must be the Paris of the Pacific," says the middle-aged, bespectacled, briefcase-carrying business-man standing next to me as I take in the sights at Union Square in the spring of 1976—a couple of years into my work with Dr. Rob-ert Ellis at both the University of California and the Veterans' Ad-ministration Hospital.

"You know," I say, thinking back over the time since I'd been out in the Bay Area, "you are right."

Of course, at this point, not long after my twenty-second birth-day, I've never been to Paris. But I am so impressed by this observa-tion that I start describing my new home turf to others as the "Paris of the Pacific," a phrase I'll eventually make my own.

This happens to be a beautiful day. And a beautiful day in San Francisco is like a beautiful day nowhere else in the world. The blue of the sky—with not a cloud to be seen—represents the dic-tionary definition of "sky blue." A warm breeze is rustling the trees in the parks, and everyone, locals and tourists alike, is out on the streets, like me, with nothing better to do than to marvel at this beautiful city.

It was also thrilling to be in San Francisco at that cultural, his-torical time. Even though it was no longer the heyday of flower children and free love, in the 1970s the city was still Mecca for a guy like me who was once the first black hippie in America. With many of the tumultuous changes of the sixties behind us, with the achievements of the civil rights movement evident everywhere, with Nixon exposed and Vietnam over, the protest era had seemingly given way to party time. Nowhere did that seem more true than in San Francisco's freewheeling, anything-goes, experimental, tolerant atmosphere.

After coming out of the military, where everything had been about discipline, process, order, and structure, I experienced the city that celebrated individuality and nonconformity above all else as if I was actually visiting a foreign country. My favorite stomping grounds became Haight-Ashbury, once the cradle of sex, drugs, and rock 'n' roll, still jumping with music clubs, restaurants, bookstores, head shops, and a crazy street scene that was colorful and alive.

Not only was the Bay Area in these years the perfect arena in which to explore and experiment, but I was at that perfect age when I wanted to try new things, explore new philosophies, taste different flavors, so that I could decide what kind of life I ultimately wanted to build for myself. As I figured out the externals of work, relationships, and money, this period was just as important for what it taught me about who I was internally, what I was really made of, what my authentic point of view was.

Not long after I arrived on the West Coast this was apparent when some friends invited me to join them at some sort of lecture. Three of us agreed to attend at the insistence of Bill, an extremely articulate guy as well as a hustler. The three of us represented the only straight guys who were then residents of the YMCA in the Tenderloin. We would shit, shave, and shower in rotation in order literally to watch each other's backs. We had to stick together, and if Bill was hip to go, we felt obliged to attend as well.

But I couldn't help asking, "What's the topic?"

"Chris," he promised me, "this seminar's gonna change your life.

My mother, Bettye Jean Triplett née Gardner.

Me as a baby.

Graduation day, me in the center with my navy class, Company 208.

My military ID, an eighteen year old eager to ship off to exotic lands.

My son and I enjoying free outdoor entertainment.

Chris Jr. sleeping.
The quiet before the storm.

Chris Jr. preparing to walk
in his father's shoes.

Chris Jr. finally in a new home after a year on the street.

Christmas in San Francisco—
Jimminy Cricket.

Shaking hands with President Clinton at the National
Teacher of the Year Award ceremony in the Rose Garden.

Uncle Henry, the first man I fell in love with.

Barbara Scott Preiskel:
My mentor, my hero, my patron saint.

Shoulder to shoulder with the great Nelson Mandela.

At the helm of my own firm. *(Photo by Leonard Simpson)*

My head is in my business, but
my heart is always with my children.

See, man, we're all conditioned to respond to things in a particular way—from our parents, school, government. It's the whole capitalistic programming of mind control that makes us chase after these material things. I'm talking about self-determination, about ending slavery to the almighty dollar, man."

"That's what the lecture's about?" I asked, reminding him that my work schedule was pretty tight.

"That's the problem," he went on. "Wanting material things, wanting to be middle-class, aspiring to be bourgeois. You think that your work is who you are, right? No, man, who you are is who you are, not what you do."

Sounded interesting enough to get me there. Even then, at what turned out to be a seminar called EST, run by a guy named Werner Erhard, nobody would explain what IT was all about. In fact, you had to get IT. And if you couldn't get IT, you had to be trained to get IT. And you had to pay a lot of money to be trained to get IT. Sitting on the floor, cross-legged, in a room full of nearly a hundred people, my three friends and I kept exchanging frustrated expressions as Werner Erhard and his lieutenants took turns yelling at us, just like in the military, and telling us how our lives weren't working and how we had all this baggage that we wouldn't take responsibility for. How could we do that? We had to get IT. But nobody could tell us what IT was! What was more, they didn't want us to basically leave until we got IT. No eating or going to the bathroom. With my three friends, Bill included, I soon began to roll my eyes in frustration. What I wanted to say was, *Look, just tell us what IT is, because maybe we could get IT if we knew what IT was. Maybe we got IT already.*

It occurred to me, that not even the seminar leaders seemed to knew what IT was. When that became apparent, after about an hour of all this berating, I stood up and finally said, "Yeah, I got IT." Just before the EST army could move in, I added, "Fuck IT. Fuck IT, and fuck you, and fuck that."

The four of us became very vocal. "Yeah, fuck IT!" repeated one of the guys. "IT ain't shit!" shouted another. Bill yelled, "I don't want IT!" I finished up by saying, "Keep IT."

As the only brothers in the room, we started to sense there was going to be a racial issue, but pretty soon most of the white people in the room began to give us looks like, *Ah, they do have IT.* All hell just about broke loose when one white guy stood up and joined us, saying, "Yeah, that's right! Fuck IT!" This was enough for us to be escorted quickly out because we had definitely messed up the game. That little experiment proved to me that I didn't need other doctrines to enlighten me. But Bill kept on searching.

A few years later I heard that he and his lady became followers of a charismatic leader who convinced his flock to turn over all their worldly possessions—to him—and leave the United States for Jonestown, Guyana. In November 1978, I would hear the news that Jim Jones had persuaded over nine hundred followers to drink cyanide-laced Kool-Aid in a mass suicide. Bill was among those who died that day. It really made me wonder how someone who was so street-smart and who could challenge the belief system of the status quo could then adopt such a radical belief system like the Jonestown thing without questioning it.

Part of my defense mechanism was the need I had for control that had been with me since childhood. This was also why I continued to resist the excesses of drugs and alcohol in these experimental years. Of course I tried stuff now and then, like the one time I smoked some angel dust and had to talk myself out of believing that I could fly. The moment the PCP reached my brain, I proceeded to do one hundred pull-ups on the heating pipe in my building—a supernatural feat when I stopped to think that in the Navy I could only do twenty-five pull-ups on a good day.

When I started looking out my window and trying to decide what landmark I should fly toward, something sober and wise inside me recommended: *Forget flying, how about a walk?*

From the Tenderloin, I walked and walked and walked, effortlessly, feeling that I was rising up with the angle of the hills, then coasting down them, being pulled toward one bridge and then toward another. Magically, I arrived in Chinatown, like I'd been sailing and had come ashore, coincidentally in the middle of a holiday marked by a lavish parade. Without being invited, I joined right in, dancing in the street with everyone in costumes and masks, many holding Chinese lanterns and papier-mâché creatures, many looking at me strangely, no doubt wondering, *Who is that happy man? He's not Chinese.*

By the time I started to come down, I was in a bar in North Beach, grooving to an eclectic band that comprised a snare drum and a harmonica. Man, I thought I had to be in Carnegie Hall. It was a good thing that I recognized how dangerous that high was. Music in itself can be a mind-altering experience, so to be on an even more altered level, the music was just mind-blowing. Out of control! When it came time to finally return to the Tenderloin, I trudged home not so effortlessly, sobering up fast and realizing that this wasn't a drug I needed to try again.

The reality was that for all my exploration during off hours, my major focus of experimentation was in the laboratory doing the work that Dr. Ellis had brought me out to do for him. My friend Bill who took me to the EST meeting had accused me of having bourgeois aspirations, and it was true—I was seduced by the idea of a potential career in medicine. If that was what I wanted, if I was passionate and dedicated, Bob Ellis was willing to place an incredible amount of trust in me, to teach me, and to open up an entirely new world in medical research, one that was different from the Navy world I'd worked in.

The project was being conducted in conjunction with the Veterans' Administration Hospital—located at the farthest beachhead of San Francisco at Fort Mylie, out by the Golden Gate Bridge—and the University of California San Francisco Hospital, near

Golden Gate Park and Keysar Stadium. At the VA, where I spent most of my hours, the research aim was to create a laboratory—basically from an old operating room—that duplicated the environment in which the heart functions during open-heart surgery. Specifically, we were trying to determine what concentration of potassium best preserved the high-energy phosphates in the heart muscles. We would do a set of experiments with a high-potassium solution, a set with a low-potassium solution, and a set with a minimal-potassium solution, taking samples of heart tissue over time and using those results for our findings. Ultimately, it was the high-potassium solution that we found to be most conducive to preserving the high-energy phosphates—information that would transform how heart transplantation and surgery were done, as well as influence cardiovascular science. For an information sponge like me, this work put me right in my element.

"Gardner," said Dr. Ellis on one of my first days of work, "I want you to meet Rip Jackson."

I turned to take in the startling appearance of Rayburn "Rip" Jackson, imported to San Francisco by Ellis from back in Jacksonville, North Carolina. Just as Dr. Ellis looked the part of a young brilliant surgeon—average height and build, glasses, balding, with a nose like an eagle's beak, meticulously sniffing out details, passionate, and sometimes high-strung—Rip Jackson had the megawattage intensity of the medical scientist-technician genius that he was. Slim, short, and clean-shaven, with shocking white hair and small, piercing blue eyes, Rip extended his hand to shake mine and greeted me in an accent that was purebred country boy, straight out of the North Carolina backwoods. "Nice to meet ya'," he said, with barely a smile. "Heard a lot about ya', Gardner."

My instincts told me that Rip could have been a Ku Klux Klansman in his younger days. Something about him reminded me of that old woman at the gas station who threatened us with a shotgun. He wasn't so extreme, but as time went on certain comments he let slip confirmed that he was a bigot all right. Having worked for many Jewish doctors, he apparently was careful not to make anti-Semitic remarks. But perhaps because he'd had little exposure to black doctors, Rip didn't censor himself, for example, when it came to expressing how he felt about seeing an interracial couple at the hospital. He shook his head in disgust, commenting to me, "I think I'd rather see two men together than a black man and a white woman."

Interestingly enough, it may have been a function of how well we got along that he made comments like that in my presence. In any event, from the beginning he saw not only that I wanted to learn from him but that I was quick to get IT, and he treated me with the utmost respect. The way we progressed was that he came out initially for a month, trained me to oversee everything that Dr. Ellis needed done for the next six months, and then came back at various intervals as needed.

His personal racist hang-ups aside, Rip Jackson was so great at the mechanics of building a laboratory and teaching me how to run it that he earned the utmost respect from me. Even though he wasn't a licensed medical doctor, his technical expertise equaled that of a top surgeon, and he trained me in this highly specialized area to do everything to support Dr. Ellis. Our responsibilities ranged from excision of hearts to catheterizing blood vessels and suturing, from ordering equipment and supplies to administering anesthesia, performing biopsies on heart tissues of patients, and analyzing the results.

Adding to the extraordinary education I was getting from Bob Ellis and Rip Jackson was a third exceptional rocket scientist in the medical laboratory—a guy by the name of Gary Campagna. Gary didn't have a medical degree either, but did for a vascular surgeon named Dr. Jerry Goldstein what Rip did for Dr. Ellis. A San Francisco native, Gary was witty and hip, an Italian American gentleman, and he took me under his wing, teaching me about technique and the importance of finesse. I now saw that it wasn't enough to know what you were doing; you had to have the hands, you had to have the right touch.

Gary had memorable sayings to emphasize certain techniques. In grafting veins, for example, precision was mandatory in first being able to control the blood flow—to shut it off, basically, like a spigot—in order to excise the portion where the graft needed to go, then to suture it all the way around without any blockages. In the clinical setting, I learned how to do that, to determine the kind of slice required for excising a portion of the artery, what type of sutures to use, what type of ties to make, what kind of graft ultimately would be needed depending on the condition of the vein. Gary warned me off making the common mistake of trying to handle the vein too abruptly, cautioning, "Stroke it, don't poke it."

These three—Gary, Rip, and Bob Ellis—were providing me with the equivalent of a medical school education, at least in this specialty. As the game plan now unfolded in my mind, I imagined that once our work was completed and I took the time to knock off a college education, I would be a prime candidate for any top Ivy League medical school in the nation. The prospect was thrilling. Could I really do that? Could I reach that far? My mother's words echoed—*If you want to, you can.*

The excitement didn't come just from the potential status and money that a career as a surgeon promised. To me, it was the challenge, the quest for information, the opportunity to apply my focus in a venue that required me to learn what amounted to a foreign language. It was starting to dawn on me that there was a language specific to all things and that the ability to learn another language in one arena—whether it was music, medicine, or finance—could be utilized to accelerate learning in other arenas too. Scientific language was fun to master—not only the medical words and meanings but also the prose, with its rhythm of urgency and its precise way of describing phenomena and processes. That understanding of process—how to get from here to there—was the real bait for me, what hooked me and made me want to learn more. Because I was so motivated and naturally curious, the learning felt easy.

Once I had learned the language, doors at the VA and the UCSF Hospital literally opened as Dr. Ellis brought me in to sit and talk with the top tier of his medical colleagues. In those settings few had any notion that I hadn't been to medical school and wasn't a doctor, let alone that I had never been to college and had barely finished high school. Sure, there were moments when I felt my lack of education, but I discovered that rather than pretending to know something I didn't, there was a way to ask, "Now, I'm not following you here, can you explain?" that most doctors were more than happy to answer.

In time, Bob Ellis developed so much faith in my mastery of our research that I went on to co-author several papers with him on the preservation of myocardial high-energy phosphates—papers that were published in various medical journals and textbooks. Even some Harvard Medical School grads can't claim to being as widely published.

"Where did you go to med school?" was a question that inevitably came up, especially from the interns working under Dr. Ellis and Dr. Goldstein. It confounded Ellis that so many of the interns who were starting their residencies in surgery had so little practical awareness. They didn't have the hands, didn't have the eyes, didn't know the controls or the procedures. Some didn't know how to handle instruments. Instead of wasting his time on these basics, he started sending them upstairs for me to train. Suddenly, all those questions that I had been asking—"What are you doing?" "How do you do that?" "Why are you doing that?" "Can I try that?"— became questions that I was answering.

The interns were all bright and knew anatomy and physiology, biology and chemistry. But only a few had the hands. I frequently caught myself sounding just as intense as Dr. Ellis, Rip, and Gary combined. During tests that involved open-heart surgery on dogs, it was maddening to witness rough handling, as often was the case, of the canine patient's arteries and fragile organs. In my lab, as Dr. Ellis called it, I was free to say, "No, don't pull. You apply pressure gradually."

When an intern gave me that look that said, *Who are you to tell me what to do?* I was even more adamant, raising my voice and saying again, "No, you don't do it that way. You're not up under the hood of your car."

There may have been some bigotry involved, given the fact that the interns at the time were all white males from Ivy League medical schools and I was some black dude without a medical degree saying, "No! I don't want that. Give me the scissors!" But what really seemed to get on their last nerve was that they had to do what I said. Dr. Ellis made it clear to every intern he brought upstairs to me: "This is Gardner's world. Whatever he says goes. He's in charge."

My feeling was that if someone wanted to learn or was willing to try, I'd bend over backward to help. But some of the interns were so arrogant, they dismissed my input out of hand, as indicated less by what they said and more by their body language, which showed they didn't want to listen to me. In those situations, all I had to do was to tell Dr. Ellis, "You know what? This guy Steve—I can't help him." That was it. After that I'd never see the intern again. On occasion I was even more specific: "That guy Richard—he doesn't want to listen. You know what, don't waste my time, don't send him back to my lab." Dr. Ellis only nodded in agreement, respecting my opinion and appreciating that I was as passionate as he was.

Dr. Goldstein's interns in vascular surgery were some of my tougher challenges, giving me big-time attitude when I called their lack of finesse into question, reminding them of Gary Campagna's "stroke it, don't poke it."

"What exactly are your qualifications?" some of these interns were indignant enough to ask out loud.

My matter-of-fact response was: "I don't have a degree, but this is my room. You've been invited here. You're a visitor, and I'm doing my work. If I can help you, I will, but you have to listen."

In certain instances, I could see by the expressions of resentment on some of their faces that they had never had any black person in authority telling them what to do—they had never encountered a black person in control. Some were able to get past that hurdle; some weren't. For my part, I had to learn not to take some of their superior attitudes personally, in the same way that I couldn't take it personally when my mentors put me in that position of control. The powerful truth that emerged for me was something Moms had tried to tell me when I was younger—no one else can take away your legitimacy or give you your legitimacy if you don't claim it for yourself.

Before leaving for the Navy, I had apologized to her that I hadn't gone on to college, thinking how proud that would have made her. Momma surprised me by saying, "Boy, it's better to have a degree from God than from anywhere in this university system. If you got your degree from God, you don't need all this other stuff."

In my mother's language that didn't mean that an intricate knowledge of the Bible or religion was required. Rather, she was talking about self-knowledge, about an authentic belief system, an inner sense of oneself that can never be rocked. Others may question your credentials, your papers, your degrees. Others may look for all kinds of ways to diminish your worth. But what is inside you no one can take from you or tarnish. This is your worth, who you really are, your degree that can go with you wherever you go, that you bring with you the moment you come into a room, that can't be manipulated or shaken. Without that sense of self, no amount of paper, no pedigree, and no credentials can make you legit. No matter what, you have to feel legit inside first.

Momma's point of view certainly resonated during this period, not only when I was being questioned but when I questioned myself. There were times during meetings of more than one hundred doctors—some of the brightest minds in medicine—when I'd look around and notice that I was the only black man in the room. But if it wasn't an issue for me, it didn't have to be an issue for others. My blackness was a fact of who I was, yet the more comfortable and secure I became in my expertise, the less my color defined or distinguished me, and the more comfortable I became holding my own with white people further up the ladder than me or lower down. What distinguished me was my knowledge, my command of the information that was the focus of the research Robert Ellis was pursuing. This awareness gave me incredible confidence that I could succeed in this field of endeavor, and succeeding meant the world to me. That was why I was prepared to hang in for the long haul, even if it took me another fifteen years to attain the degrees necessary for me to practice medicine. Whatever it took, I was worth it, as was the effort to study and learn, day in and day out, repeating tests sometimes over and over again, like a blacksmith hitting an anvil every day.

There were only two clouds on the horizon—money and sex. Even though Dr. Ellis kept increasing my salary, up to around $13,000 a year by early '76, there was very little more he could squeeze out of his overall budget for the project. Even for someone who was willing to slum it, San Francisco was a costly place to live. Believe me, living in the Tenderloin—in the same neighborhood as the Y but in an apartment of my own at 381 Turk Street—I was definitely slumming it. My salary was stretched even without car payments or insurance. Since I couldn't afford a car, I hadn't even gone out to get my license yet, although I did know how to drive and sometimes ran errands for work in the hospital van. The necessity of getting a second job loomed. Then again, that would use up whatever free time I had for enjoying something of a social life.

The constant money crunch I could handle. But the sudden halt to my heretofore successful pursuit of the opposite sex was a shock to my system. What was going on? In a city like San Francisco, full of beautiful single women, I couldn't for the life of me figure out why nothing was clicking. Not that I wanted to fall in love, but what I really wanted, to get laid, wasn't looking good. There was a doctor I'd started seeing, one of the few African American women I'd met at the hospital. She was attractive in a smart, ambitious way, but she was uptight about sex. The chemistry never happened.

Then there was a pretty sister that everybody at the hospital was into. Sweet and curvaceous, with long wooly hair and a rich caramel complexion, she finally accepted my invitation to go to the movies, and we started hanging out. Seemed like it took forever to get an invitation back to her place, but when it happened at last, in a cruel twist of fate I was so tired from work that day I actually lay down on the bed to get comfortable with her and promptly fell asleep.

The next thing I knew this lovely woman scorned was shaking me by the shoulder and pointing to the door. Glumly, I scuffed on out of there, apologizing all the way. As I stepped outside a gust of wet wind smacked me in disdain. "Sure is cold out here," I said, hoping she'd change her mind.

"That's too bad," she replied, "because it's hot in here." Then she slammed the door in my face.

That was the sad state of my extracurricular life on that memorably beautiful spring day when I was out on my own at Union Square and the middle-aged guy with the briefcase struck up a conversation with me about San Francisco being the Paris of the Pacific.

As it's getting toward late afternoon, there is nothing out of the ordinary when he says, "Hey, I'm going around the corner to have a drink. Care to join me?"

Even though I don't drink much, I figure—*Why not?* I'm still getting to know the city and not sure where the women are hanging, so I tag along enthusiastically. The bar, a joint called Sutter's Mill, turns out not to be where the women are hanging. In fact, as we step inside the pitch-black interior of the place and I try to focus my eyes in the darkness, I don't see any women. What I do see are nothing but men, and two of them are in a corner kissing. Of course, I realize that this is a gay bar.

"You know what," I say to the guy, as if I just looked at my watch for the first time, "I got an early shift tomorrow, and, uh, great to meet you, but I gotta go."

Before he can say a word, I'm gone.

This isn't the first time I've been hit on by gay men in San Francisco. Usually, I have no problem explaining that I don't work that side of the street. Actually, compared to the attitudes in the Navy, I think of myself as extremely tolerant. Yet with my bad case of the no-woman blues, I'm not even in the mood to be polite.

Unable to establish a relationship here in San Francisco, I find myself picking up the phone more than usual to call my long-distance girlfriend, Sherry Dyson, who I have never quite gotten over since that first time I saw her with the T-shirt in the window of the army-navy surplus store. In this time period, she has returned to Virginia with her master's degree and is working as an educational expert in mathematics. Besides our regular phone contact, she has been out to visit a couple of times, although neither of us has made any moves to indicate that we should be getting more serious.

So we're talking one night and it hits me that there's no one who gets me like Sherry, no one who can just say, "Chris, you're full of shit," when I'm being too full of myself, and no one else that I've ever pictured with me in the life that I'm working toward. In a romantic rush, out of the blue, almost just to hear myself say the words, I change whatever subject we're on and ask, "All right, so when we gonna get married?"

Without skipping a beat, Sherry says, "Well, how about June 18?"

So much for sexual exploration and experimentation. Not sure what I had just gone and done, I said good-bye to the no-woman blues and prepared myself to enter into the institution of marriage.

———

For the next three years I lived what could have been called in some respects a storybook life. The wedding, held as planned on June 18, 1977, was picture-postcard perfect: beautiful, tasteful, and simply done in a park near Sherry's parents' home—a place that had become synonymous in my mind with stability and security.

Moms was there, glowing with pride. She and Sherry bonded immediately. My Navy buddy Leon Webb, soon to head out to San Francisco, flew in to be my best man, and he couldn't have been happier for me. We were all impressed with the Dysons' home. Nothing over the top, the house looked like something out of a magazine—exquisitely decorated with southern charm, rare artwork on the walls, chandeliers throughout the two-story space, gourmet food in abundance, and a bar stocked with wine and liquor imported from around the world.

The Dysons' way of life represented the ideal of home that had been in my dreams from the time I'd seen *The Wizard of Oz* as a kid. For a while, I'd even dreamed of moving to Kansas when I grew up because of that portrayal of safety and serenity. In Oz there were witches and maniacal flying monkeys and the same sense of imminent insanity that was in our household. Back in Kansas, folks were normal and kind, and there was no threat of not knowing what could happen next, how far it was to the pay phone, would the police come in time, would your mother and siblings be killed when you got back.

Part of the attraction, unquestionably, was my longing to belong to the world that Sherry came from—a world in which she had grown up adored as an only child, with the same mother and father together, the same house, with a sense of being anchored and with none of the chaos and violence that had afflicted my childhood. Her parents didn't seem to mind that I came from a different world and were as gracious as they could be in welcoming me to their family. Certainly, like Sherry, they saw that I had potential and was on a solid path to becoming a physician, even though I had a ways to go.

Still, I had begun to have misgivings about this marriage from the moment I spontaneously popped the question, much of which I passed off as typical prewedding jitters.

The first person I had told in San Francisco was Dr. Ellis. If I was looking for someone to beg me to reconsider, Robert Ellis wasn't that person. Genuinely pleased for me, he went on to loan me the hundred bucks I needed for a suit to get married in, and then he shocked me even more by suggesting, "Take an extra day off." For a guy who was as obsessed with work as Buffalo Bob, that was unheard of.

My next stop was the jewelry district on Market Street, where I miraculously found a diamond ring for nine hundred dollars that I bought on credit. It looked old-fashioned, with clusters of little diamonds in a flower shape and a band that turned out to be white gold. En route to Virginia on the airplane, I was so nervous carrying a diamond ring in my pocket that I had to check on it every five minutes to make sure it hadn't been mysteriously stolen during that time. It was the nicest thing I'd ever bought for anyone, and I was sure Sherry was going to like it.

My misgivings vanished the moment the two of us embraced upon my arrival. We had a deep connection, a comfort and fondness for each other that was really all that mattered. Watching Sherry take charge of the wedding made me admire her even more. She had planned everything, her Pops had written the check, and all I had to do was show up. I loved how she carried herself, her confidence, intelligence, and humor, her vivacious manner that attracted people to her in general. She was gorgeous in a wholesome, distinctive way, and her legs were great. I loved her strong personality and the fact that she had definite opinions about what she liked and didn't like. Therefore, it didn't bother me that she wasn't so crazy about the ring.

"Oh, it's beautiful," she reassured me. "Just not the cut I had in mind."

I had no idea what that even meant, but I wanted her to have what she wanted, so we agreed to exchange it when we went back to San Francisco. For all I knew, they might have been cubic zirconium, not even diamonds. That was something else I appreciated about Sherry, that she could educate me about the finer things in life. Caught up in the festivities, we both were in one major whirlwind, and it was only the next morning, after a farewell brunch, that the two of us had a chance to be alone as newlyweds. Neither of us said as much, but the reality had finally settled in. We were both probably wondering if we really had done the right thing.

Nonetheless, with our lives together ahead of us, we packed all of Sherry's earthly belongings into her blue Datsun B210 and hit the long road to San Francisco. Even though my mother-in-law had insisted that I get my driver's license while I was in Richmond, Sherry did most of the driving. In spite of the summer heat that hovered from start to finish across Interstate 80, the lack of air conditioning in the Datsun, and my frequent naps, we had enough to talk about and plan to make the trip at least a little less arduous.

Sherry had visited me before in the Tenderloin and was somewhat prepared for the seedy atmosphere that greeted us, although she was adamant that we move from 381 Turk as soon as possible. In no time, she got a job as an insurance claims adjuster, and shortly after that she greeted me with the breathless news, "I found a place on Hayes. I fell in love with it. It's a third-floor walk-up with hard-wood floors, bay windows, and French doors!"

This was all foreign to me, but if it made Sherry happy, I was happy. Still in the 'hood, the area was known as Hayes Valley and had a lively black community feeling to it, not to mention that we were out of the 'Loin. Thus, we entered into a nesting phase as Sherry turned our new apartment into a warm, welcoming environment. She decorated amazingly on our budget—with potted plants like ficus Benjamins and wandering Jews adorning shelves and hanging from the ceiling, a nice brass bed, a wicker rocking chair, a stylish couch, new cookware and serving pieces. I was as into transforming our living space into a home together as she was.

In the kitchen, Sherry was a fantasy come true. Man, could she cook: soul food including the best fried chicken ever, pasta in every shape and form, and gourmet dishes to rival any of the great chefs of San Francisco. She was always coming out with new creations too. "Remember the way they made that dish at the Vietnamese restaurant?" she'd say. "I'm going to try doing something like that." And it would be even better.

We moved up in the world again after Sherry met me at the door one night and announced, "Wait until you see the place I found on Baker. It's in one of those Victorian buildings I've had my eye on. Chris, you'll love it! It's got five rooms, great sunlight."

I only laughed and went along with the plan, thinking not only how much she enjoyed re-creating for us in San Francisco what she'd grown up with in Virginia, but also how lucky I was that she was educating me, elevating my sense of culture and style. She wasn't just giving me an awareness of what a Victorian-style building was, something I never knew, she was opening me up to a lifestyle that included theater, comedy, and social gatherings with fascinating, intellectual conversation. We filled my few nights off with trips to comedy clubs to see the likes of Richard Pryor or to dinner parties with a serious, creative crowd at the home of Sherry's cousin, Robert Alexander, a writer. Whenever we were there, I gravitated to the same group of three guys, very smart, hip, and active in the arts. One was a brother named Barry "Shabaka" Henley, and the other two were cats named Danny Glover and Samuel L. Jackson. Little did I know the three would later be in the top tier of actors on stage and screen.

But even while our portrait of a happily married life seemed to be what we both wanted, within a couple of years I began to confront a feeling deep down that something was missing. If I had been better at communicating my feelings or if I had taken the time to try to resolve what wasn't working, it would have been so much better than what I did by trying to ignore and run away from the problems.

Some of those problems had to do with basic differences in where we came from and in our likes and dislikes. Sherry liked the better restaurants on Fisherman's Wharf; I liked the countercultural vibe of the Haight. To me, the better restaurants were predictable; to Sherry, the anything-goes, hippie atmosphere of the Haight was too wild. Fairly conservative, she was a good churchgoing Episcopalian. That mentality was nothing like where I'd come from: straight-up Baptist, and that's all I knew. Episcopalians reminded me of Catholics in church, always doing calisthenics on cue—standing up, kneeling down, standing up again, kneeling back down again, reciting lines appropriately, in unison. Quiet, dignified, subdued. Being demonstrative with feelings seemed to be discouraged. Tears were dabbed away by handkerchiefs or simply held in. Not like in the Baptist church, where there was competitive shouting. No comparison. In the Baptist church where I grew up, when my big sister and I were taken there by Aunt TT, folks sang, danced, sobbed out loud, spoke in tongues, had dialogues with the preacher and God at the same time, and caught the Spirit in the most dramatic ways. Women threw up their arms, screamed, and fainted!

Men jumped and shouted! Every Sunday somebody got carried out. As a kid, I didn't know intellectually what was going on, but it was exciting and real. Oh, man, it was hot too. Episcopalian churches were cool, hardly a drop of sweat to be seen. In the church where I grew up, you got high on the heat. Those fans everyone had didn't do a damn thing to cool us off.

Of course, I enjoyed going to church with Sherry, knowing it would open me up to new things. But there was a loudness, a wildness that was lacking. In my heart of hearts, I was slowly coming to face the truth that I didn't want to live a picture of a life—whether it was by having to live up to the role of doctor that I was striving for, or whether it was in my marriage. Sherry had to have been having similar concerns, especially when a parade of houseguests started descending on us.

When my best friend Leon Webb came out to get work in radiology, the path he'd begun in the Navy, that wasn't a problem, even though he stayed for three or four months. Sherry and Leon got along just fine. But when my childhood buddy Garvin came to stay for a while, she and he didn't mesh at all. This was her home, after all, so I was in the position of encouraging Garvin to find somewhere else to stay, soon, which unfortunately hurt our friendship. Of course, if things had been just peachy with Sherry in other respects, it wouldn't have been an issue at all.

The real problem that took me forever to admit had to do with what was or wasn't happening in the bedroom. We loved each other deeply, profoundly. We were presidents of each other's fan clubs, cheering each other on more than anyone else. But our sex life was nice, predictable, quiet. Not hot. I wanted to compensate for not getting to go around the world and meet all those foreign, exotic women. I'd had a taste or two of the X-rated versions, and I wanted more, what else could I say? But rather than say something or initiate what I wanted, I became aloof.

We might have been hamstrung from the start. After all, we had built our romantic relationship over telephone wires and on letter paper, always with that theme music of *Summer of '42* playing in the background. Early on, it had been a major turn-on to be the younger man with the more worldly, college-educated woman. Now I was looking to her to introduce more spice. But she didn't know that, and I didn't know how to shake up the routine.

Ironically, the safe, stable home that I'd wanted since childhood turned out to be too structured, too orderly, too rigid. Later I was able to take the long view and realize that I had gone from one institution, the Navy, to another, marriage, with barely a break in between. At the time, I didn't stop to think about it in those terms, except to realize perhaps that I'd learned the classic lesson: *Be careful what you wish for because you might just get it!*

Obviously, I had some serious inner conflicts about what really was the good life for me. Those qualms were put to the side when Sherry became pregnant, something that was as exciting and different as it was terrifying. Instead of questioning my marriage, I put those doubts on the back burner and suddenly began to question, for the first time, how married I was to the idea of becoming a doctor. Even though I was up at sixteen thousand dollars per year now, that wasn't going to support a family and pay for me to go to college and then med school. I went out and got a second job.

Not out of her first trimester, Sherry miscarried, a disappointment to both of us, but one we took in stride. Now that I'd faced the need for more money, I kept up my second job working as a security guard at nights and on weekends, not doing too badly. That was, until I was sent to fill in on a graveyard shift at the pier as the guard of a creaky old unused ship. With nothing but a flashlight, I took up my post at a chair, freaked out by the horror movie sounds but too exhausted to stay awake, only to be nudged back into consciousness by something rubbing up against my leg. My first thought was of those cats in my nightmares about the witch woman's house back in Milwaukee. Instead, when I felt that same thing scratch me, I looked down and saw a rat the size of a large cat, its jaw unhinged and preparing to munch on me. As God was my witness, my time in the Navy notwithstanding, I had never been on a boat before and had no idea that there were rats on boats and had never dreamt that rats could be so goddamned huge. Screaming like a girl, I jumped straight up out of my chair. The rat screamed too and ran, and so did I, the two of us in separate directions. So much for my stint in security.

From then on, I managed to grab odd jobs here and there in my off hours, doing things like painting houses on the weekends and working for moving companies.

Though she said nothing, Sherry may have noticed that I was spending less time at home, not just because of these extra jobs, but because I was looking to break up the routine. Some nights I went by myself to hear music on Haight Street; other times I hung out with some characters I'd met in the neighborhood, watching football games, smoking some weed, passing time. Sherry wasn't overly fond of some of these cats, especially a couple of the guys who had moneymaking enterprises that weren't all on the up-and-up. In one of my covert acts of rebellion against too much structure, I actually went so far as to try to make extra dough dealing on the side. Besides the fact that I was a complete failure at it, I practically got myself killed when some big-time gangsters came waving guns to collect cash that I didn't have. Somehow I got hold of that cash real fast. It wasn't more than three hundred dollars, but to a ghetto boy like me, that hurt. When a couple of my friends next proposed that I go in with them on an insurance scam, I politely declined.

My short-lived life of crime had the fleeting effect of making me grateful for what I had at home and at work. It also taught me the major principle that there ain't no such thing as easy money. Banging on that anvil, that was the way. Even so, it was frustrating after five years that I hadn't been able to buy a car. Sherry's Datsun

B210 still was our only means of shared transportation, though fortunately we could both take advantage of San Francisco's excellent public transit system. There were also morning rides to work that I hitched with my coworker and friend, Latrell Hammond.

"Chris, listen to me," she'd begin every morning when I jumped into her much-abused, lime green 1961 Ford Falcon after she arrived to pick me up. Every morning she had some new advice she was selling, and it was usually good. A force of nature, Latrell had the gift of gab as one of the fastest-talking, most scandalous women I'd ever seen in my life, with the ability to sell you anything—including your own shoes that you had on your feet at the time.

Latrell and I were strictly platonic friends. She and Sherry were tight, so she had the best interests of my marriage in mind at all times. There were occasions, however, when I'd wonder if she had the best interests of me surviving her driving in mind. Latrell was outrageous. But because of her gift for gab, no matter how late we arrived at work—and she was chronically late—she could always pull it off. From the minute I hopped in the car, as I tried to follow her latest line of conversation, and as the two of us slid around on the Falcon's seatbelt-less bench seats, Latrell gabbed away, putting on her makeup, drinking coffee, smoking and gunning for the green lights, all at the same time.

She acted completely unaware that I was praying aloud, "Oh, my God, don't let me die in this lime green Ford Falcon."

If we caught all the green lights, we could make it to work in fifteen, sixteen minutes. That's still not good if you're already late. But if one red light caught us, we were shit out of luck. Remarkably, while I didn't even bother trying to make excuses when a whole room full of interns were waiting for me to arrive, in her department Latrell had a new and exciting excuse every day—which her superiors never questioned.

Sherry was such a contrast. There was only one morning, to my knowledge, that she left the house without being organized and in control. That was revealed later that evening when she returned from work and confessed that something was wrong.

Was this the conversation that I had been hoping for and dreading at the same time? "What's wrong?" I asked.

"I think something's wrong with my ankles."

"Your ankles?"

"I've been walking funny all day," she explained. "I can't figure it out."

Being the investigative medical guy that I was, I suggested, "Let me take a look." When I did, at first I saw nothing. Then I realized, cracking up as I did, that she had become a fashion victim of what I called her shoe garden. Because she had amassed such a collection, she kept the shoes neatly arranged in a basket in our bedroom. But somehow in her haste to get to work on time, she'd grabbed two different shoes.

She joined in laughing with me when she saw it for herself. That was so unlike her. But it was indicative of how together and consistent her routine normally was.

A short time after that incident, I had a reaction to a Richard Pryor line that was indicative of how much I was dying for a change in our sexual routine. Pryor was talking about some of the crazy things that doing blow could do to people. At the time, I had only tried it once and didn't get what all the hype was. Now Pryor was talking about how it affected your sex drive, and he was telling a story about how he'd be high and make up wild stuff to do, telling his lady, "Now, baby, I want you to go up on the roof. I'm going to run around the house three times, and on the third time I want you to jump off on my face."

Sherry didn't laugh. I didn't laugh either. Instead, I thought to myself, *Aw, yeah, that would be cool.*

That's where my mind was lurking. So when I meet this kind of cute, kind of plump, but fairly hip woman with a short tight natural who happens to have a nice little place and who happens to tell me, "I really want to give you a blow job," I do not say no. And when I say yes, and this kind of cute chick turns out to be a fellatio expert, I start to mess up bad. Really bad. It's stupid enough to be stepping out to get my dick sucked, but worse, I invite this woman to where I live when Sherry's at work one day and I have the afternoon off.

The whole time I'm doing it, I feel so good, but the minute I come sanity returns, and I know that this is one of the worst mistakes I've ever made in my life. Not just because it's wrong every which way, but because in the last few times we've gotten together, I've come to understand this woman is stone cold crazy. The next time I see her at her place, I let her know that while it's been swell, we shouldn't get together anymore.

"What are you trying to tell me?" she asks, fury in her eyes.

"Well, I don't want to see you anymore."

"Are you breaking up with me?"

Realizing that she's not getting it, I try to remind her that we weren't together that way to be a couple in the first place. "Look," I say, "you're the best, and I'll remember our time together, but nothing else is gonna happen between us. Let's just be friends."

Now, either she is not satisfied with how I've broken it off or she is really nuts, because a few mornings later I wake up in the morning to find that Sherry's car, the Datsun B210, has been brutally vandalized. A can of white paint has been dumped on top of the roof, spilling white stripes of paint right down the windows and the windshield wipers, everything. The tires are slashed, sugar's in the gas tank, and prominently etched by finger in the paint is a message that reads: *FUCK YOU!*

I know who's done it but I can't prove it. I can't let Sherry know. Standing there pissed off at myself more than anything, I decide that I've got to now lie big-time and say that I've got no idea who would have done something so violent. A random act, no doubt.

A brother from the neighborhood approaches as if to make conversation. "Hey, man," he says, "let me holler at you for a second."

Not wanting any chitchat, I turn away, letting him know, "Yeah, okay, talk to me later."

With a shrug, he insists, "I was just trying to tell you who did that to your car."

"Oh?" What else am I going to say?

"It was that little fat bitch with short hair," he says with a snicker. "Okay?"

Well, I know who did it, the street knows who did it, but thank God Sherry doesn't know, and the insurance agrees to cover it, only after they ask, "Mr. Gardner, what happened?"

"I don't know," I say in my most indignant voice. "I came out and found it like this. I must have made somebody angry, but I don't know who it was. Maybe whoever did this just made a mistake. I just don't know." The insurance claims person points out that a message like that is usually personal, not a random act or a mistake, but leaves it at that.

In the days that followed it was obvious from the whispers and looks that word had traveled through the grapevine. The incident soon passed but remained an ugly memory for me. Sherry never indicated that she knew anything about it, but she did seem to be picking up on my discontent, asking me more often than not where I was going or where I'd been out late the night before.

When we finally did have a talk, toward the end of 1979, with my twenty-sixth birthday not too far down the road, it was to confront a change of professional plans. I had decided that I wasn't going to be a doctor.

Baffled, Sherry groped for words. "Why? I mean . . ." She just looked at me. "Isn't that what you've been working toward?"

She knew that the challenge was gone. We had talked about that before. I was already the medical whiz kid. It was going to be ten years more of education before I could officially do what I already was doing. But it wasn't just that, as I explained to Sherry. My mentor, Dr. Ellis, had raised his concerns with me, opening my eyes to some of the trends that were about to radically alter the health-care field. In plainer language, he had said, "Chris, you really need to reconsider being a doctor because it's going to become a vastly changed profession."

What was coming down the pike at the time were versions of socialized or nationalized medicine, precursors to what became HMOs. As Dr. Ellis rightfully predicted, this meant that a top surgeon who might make several thousand dollars per surgery then could be looking at as little as a few hundred dollars for the same services in coming decades. Not only were the new insurance plans going to cover less, but they were also going to emphasize non-invasive procedures and create bureaucracies that set fee structures. Bob Ellis made it clear that he believed in me, that I had the talent and energy to succeed and, even more important, to make a contribution to others.

Except for the time that Moms had told me I couldn't be Miles Davis, no one else had ever put a hand on my shoulder to steer me in one direction or another. I had to listen. As I went on to explain to Sherry, there were plenty of options for me in the medical field, perhaps in administration, sales, pharmaceuticals, or the insurance business. I would start checking out some of those options as soon as I could.

There was even a sense of relief that flooded me. No longer did I have to play the part of a future doctor. But Sherry was anything but relieved. That future had been part of the package she married: Chris Gardner, college graduate, medical student, doctor. She had every reason to be disappointed, even though she expressed her support for whatever I decided to do.

After cheating on her already, I had made up my mind 100 percent never to repeat that mistake. Yet we were starting to drift further apart, our differences showing up in stark ways.

This comes crashing in on me on a Saturday after we head down to Fisherman's Wharf, just to do some sightseeing and some shopping, when I can't help but notice this fine woman out for a stroll. I don't want to ogle, but my penis stands up at attention to salute, rock hard. Everybody in the vicinity on Fisherman's Wharf gets a full view of me walking around with a major piece of wood bulging in my pants.

One brother walks by and comments, "Still strong, huh?"

What can I do? Kind of embarrassed, but not really, I glance over at Sherry and am shocked to see how livid she is. "That's disgusting," she says, mad as hell.

There's a part of me that wants to get mad too and tell her it's not disgusting, it's normal. There's another part that's regretting not having taken the time to be single and sow my wild oats a little more.

It's funny how life can turn on such an unplanned minor event as a spontaneous boner or a thoughtless comment. In that moment the stage was set for my marriage to be over. I would always love Sherry Dyson to death. What she had given me was so much more than the picture of a life I was looking at, maybe more than any woman, other than Moms. Sherry gave me the gift of believing in me, of pushing me to set the bar high for myself, of sending me the message that I was worth it—sometimes when I had forgotten. Whether she was ready to admit it or not, back before we were married, she too had definitely felt some ambivalence about our long-term prospects, but her love was always unconditional. In years to come, she would become my best friend in the world, even though in the short term she would suffer terrible hurt for which I was sorely to blame.

The real turning point that changes everything in our marriage and our lives comes shortly after that day on the pier when we go out to a party together and my future—in the form of an exotic black goddess named Jackie—sees me checking her out and gives me a look. She is five-ten, statuesque, stacked, wearing a shimmering dress like she's poured into it, just oozing sexual energy. And without hesitation or premeditation whatsoever, I reach over, grin, and grab her ass. My favorite kind of ass, it feels just like a basketball. My hand lingers. She doesn't slap me, doesn't flinch. Just raises her eyebrow and smiles. As if to say, *What took you so long to find me?*

I hurried headlong as a door opened into a world that promised absolute sexual joys I couldn't even begin to imagine, a world that was also destined to turn into a horrendous nightmare, and that's putting it lightly.

CHAPTER 8

Turned Out
(an intro)

For the second time in my adulthood, I was preparing to re-learn that lesson about being careful what you wish for. Over the next thirty days, everything that I was and everything that I hoped to become flew out the window. I barely knew my name. After spending twenty-six years fighting powerlessness with a need for control, a need for clarity of vision, I eagerly tossed whatever control of my senses remained and took a flying leap off the plank into whatever unexplored depths lay below. Somewhere in the back of my mind I recalled tackling *The Iliad* and *The Odyssey*, thanks to a fondness for mythology that got me started reading early on. And even as I remembered the story of Ulysses—who tried to resist the call of the Sirens, those sea nymph creatures whose irresistible song destroyed the minds of sailors and sent them and their ships crashing on the rocky shores of the Aegean—the warning signals went right over my head.

Within days of meeting Jackie—who lived within walking distance of me and Sherry, five blocks away around the corner—the ship that I'd been sailing turned into wreckage as I boarded a new vessel to destinations unknown. This was the beginning of the end of everything that had come before and the beginning of the beginning of everything that would happen from then on.

Over at Jackie's apartment, on her Murphy bed with a brass

headboard, on the floor, in the kitchen, against the wall, under the shower, sometimes all in the same night, we made love like there was no tomorrow. For thirty days in a row, after or before work, for hours at night or in the early morning, for whole days at a time when I skipped work, even as I tried to maintain the appearance of normalcy when Sherry and I crossed paths at our place or when I tried to recover my focus in the lab, my life became a blur. A sex-induced hypnotic haze. In my feverishly aroused state, I kept thinking that I'd get my fill, that I'd come down off this high, but Jackie kept on upping the stakes, taking me further to the outer limits. When her relatives came to visit and were in her apartment, she invited me up to the building's rooftop—where she opened her coat to reveal that she was wearing nothing but stiletto high heels, fishnets, and a garter belt. Dazed, mesmerized, in a trance, I could hardly wait to find out what was next. Everything that seemed missing before burst into being, like in *The Wizard of Oz* when the movie goes from black-and-white to Technicolor. The sex was so out of this world, so unbelievable, I had to tell myself, *Chris, man, you are not in Kansas anymore!*

The 1980s were upon us, and the drug de jour that was suddenly as all-American as Coca-Cola was its illegal cousin, cocaine. The first time I did it, I hadn't been impressed. But I tried it once a little while before getting it on with Jackie and as she started to go down on me, using her tongue, mouth, lips, hands, fingers in ways that ought to have earned her a Pulitzer Prize for poetry, I now understood what all the obsession about blow was. Talk about hot, loud, and wild. Talk about being turned on and turned out. With Jackie, I was a goner. She took me and turned me all the way out.

Reason and rationality, my old friends, had split at some point in those thirty days. My moral compass, as they say, went on the blink too. Once we started to come back down to earth after that crazed month, Jackie began to press me about what my long-term intentions were. Probably I was hoping our adventure would run its course because I honestly didn't want to get divorced. But it was plain to me that I was nowhere near ready to break things off with Jackie.

At one point, she talked me into going back east to see relatives of hers. We had an enjoyable time meeting everyone and seeing a little bit of New York City—which towered in my senses like the Emerald City of Oz, magical and dangerous, as if you needed a special password to be allowed to enter—but staying with family members put a major damper on our sexual odyssey. After making love anytime and anyplace for thirty days and thirty nights, we had no privacy to do anything and I was in pain. When we finally headed to JFK to fly back to California, I was starting to count the minutes until we returned to her apartment.

Not Jackie. She was not going to wait. At Kennedy Airport, just as we happened to be walking along in a corridor near a baggage carousel where no one was around, she gave me that arched eyebrow and a look I now knew well, pulled me toward her, as she leaned back against a column, lifted up her dress, slid her hand down, and started to play with herself, commanding me in a low but urgent smoky voice, "Do me, right here, right now!"

This was partly what turned me on so much and also what freaked me out—that she was the aggressive one sexually. I would rise up to match her, but she would almost always initiate, determining when and where to have sex. I had heard of the mile-high club before and had wondered about getting it on in flight in an airplane lavatory. But an empty baggage claim corridor at JFK wouldn't have occurred to me. Making sure no one was around, since we did have time before our flight, I had at it.

Amid the "oh yeah baby"s and the "c'mon now"s and the escalating sounds of pleasure, of course I was embarrassed and freaked out, but the more she undulated, the more abandoned my thrusting became, and the thrill of how good it was getting—her with her back against that pole, me standing there, working it—I forgot where I was. She then took it up another notch, wrapping her legs around my waist, until we were both lost. Humpin', gruntin', sweatin', moanin'. This was way-over-the-top good. Beyond my wildest imagination.

Heaving and breathing as all systems were go, out of the corner of my eye I saw, to my horror, a lone baggage handler who had come out of his office to watch the show in disbelief. But instead of remaining an audience of one, he pivoted around in such a way that told me he was going to invite a crowd in, maybe charge admission.

Jackie had her eyes closed, and I couldn't stop now that I was so close to an orgasm, even though the next thing I knew there was a posse of four more baggage handlers gawking and grinning at us. It couldn't have gotten any worse, but it did when one of them hit the button so that the carousel started to move and the baggage belt revved up as one of them decided to cheer me, yelling, "Get that shit, brother! Get it!"

That wasn't all. Now here came the bags. And here came the people! Talk about coitus interruptus! Flashing me nothing but a sly smile, Jackie covered up real fast, having gotten some satisfaction. I regrouped as fast as I could too, much madder than I was embarrassed—but still doing all I could to avoid the shocked faces of the passengers who certainly got an eyeful. To this day, I don't like baggage handlers.

A showdown was coming. In a perfect world, my wanderlust for the wild side would have run its course. But the reality was that the world wasn't so perfect, something I was beginning to realize big-time. Having my cake and eating it too wasn't going to happen. My hand was eventually forced, unfortunately, which added another layer of regret to the awful guilt I felt in the late spring of 1980 when I told Sherry I was leaving. What I did and said, how I did and said it, just destroyed her, and it will hurt me for the rest of my life how I bungled what would remain one of the most important relationships in my life. Sherry soon moved to Oakland, and though we had little contact, it took nine years to be legally divorced, partly because of how painful it was and partly because of the other drama that was going on.

Even if Jackie hadn't become pregnant within nineteen days of our meeting—a determining factor in my moving in with her because that's where I thought my responsibilities rested—I probably would have made the same decision. It was about sex. I had been turned out, and there was no going back in.

———

OJT—On-the-Job Training—was destined to be my watchword as I journeyed into fatherhood. The arrival of Christopher Jarrett Medina Gardner Jr. on January 28, 1981, at San Francisco General Hospital changed every focus, every priority of my existence. He had to be the most beautiful, the most brilliant, the most agile, the most intuitive, the most musical, the most soulful, the most athletic infant in the hospital ward. He had a wisdom and greatness about him from day one, no question. When I cradled him in my arms the first time, I had a strange feeling of familiarity, as if he and I knew each other from a previous lifetime. Without words, I swore on everything and everyone that I cherished in this world, reaffirming my lifelong promise that I would always care for him and that I would never be absent from his life.

Chris Jr. stared right up at me, knowingly, as if to say, *All right, Poppa, I'm counting on you.* Then he studied me, in a way that I never knew babies could do, as though he was seeing me when I was a little boy not knowing who my father was or where my mother was. It was my imagination of course, but he seemed to be saying, *And you can count on me too.* My son made me a better person, bringing purpose and meaning to my life, to an extent I'd never known before and would only fully appreciate later.

In the months leading up to Chris's birth, I got some OJT with Jackie, who revealed hitherto unknown aspects of her personality. When we met, she had been finishing up dental school at the University of California. Once she graduated, she expected to be able to take time off, chill for a minute, and then delay having to work so that she could study for her boards. Now that the smoke had cleared somewhat after our initial fireworks, it was apparent that she had a definite game plan, with quite an ambitious view of moving on up in life. At first she didn't pressure me so much as point out that it was time for me to cut the cord at the VA, something that I'd been delaying during the period that my personal life had been so turbulent. Since we were already rolling with an upwardly mobile circle of young black professionals—each of them some form of doctor, lawyer, or Indian chief—the fact that I was already in the medical field was cool with Jackie. Still, even though she acknowledged that I was doing significant work in research under Dr. Ellis, she didn't refrain from mentioning that the pay wasn't comparable to what her friends and their spouses were making.

Those comments didn't bother me because I already knew I wasn't earning enough to support a family. Publication in several prestigious medical journals may have been a thrill, but it didn't pay a bill, to borrow a line from the great Berry Gordy—one of my heroes and one of a very few black business entrepreneurs I knew about, who happened to have written the song "Money: That's What I Want." It wasn't the money conversation that bothered me. What did bother me was the question Jackie started asking with increased regularity about halfway through her pregnancy, a remark that seemed to come out of nowhere when she said it the first time one evening over dinner.

"You know, Chris," Jackie began, and I could tell from her tone of voice that I wasn't going to like what I was about to hear. She continued, "I have to ask you, how are you going to be a father when you never had one? How do you know what it means to be a father?"

Not saying a word, I sat and stared at her, my heart pounding. How could she ask me that? From the very beginning she knew one thing about me: that I had a real intense issue about not having a father. She knew I would do anything I could to be the father I never had. I was floored.

"Well?" she asked. I knew she was trying to push my buttons, but why I wasn't sure. Was it a test to make sure that I wouldn't leave her? If so, it was cruel because she knew from my history that I would never leave a child. Never.

We changed the subject and the tension passed. When she brought up the same question again, using exactly the same wording, "How are you going to be a father when you've never had one? How do you know what it means to be a father?" I caught on that this was another way to push me. Obviously, when it came to her pushing me sexually, I was a willing participant. But this line of questioning left me resentful, even though, in her defense, she was expressing practical concerns for the future.

The third or fourth time she brought up the issue, I barked back, "Don't you think it's a little late to ask me to fill out a father application?"

"What's that supposed to mean?"

"Maybe you should have asked about my résumé before you got pregnant. Because you knew I didn't have a father of my own!"

In a flash, Jackie turned silent and cold.

In spite of this unsettling dynamic, she did succeed in getting me to think about what it really meant to be a father—a theoretical part of the equation that was moot the moment Christopher was born. Now that we had a baby, the reality was that we were a family and I had to learn what it meant to be a good father OJT— on a practical, immediate basis. This was do or die. If I couldn't do or provide for him, it would be a betrayal of everything I had promised myself from as young as I could remember.

A major logistical problem was space, as our one-room studio was soon taken over by an oversized bassinet, changing table, and all the other infant-care items I never knew about until now. The next problem to solve was finding a day care situation for the baby while Jackie was at school and I was at work. The process opened my eyes big-time to the complex disparity of the child care pecking order—starting at the very top with the full-time live-in nannies, the part-time au pairs, and the live-out nannies to the on-call babysitters (with a wide range of hourly wages and various levels of qualifications), then the private, high-cost day care schools with waiting lists, to the less expensive but still credentialed city-funded child care programs, to probably the least costly: unlicensed care at the homes of women who took kids in for a daily fee. Fortunately, we were able to afford the next-to-the-last option by enrolling Christopher in day care at the Parent-Infant Neighborhood Center not too far from where we lived.

The quality of care was really great, even though I confessed to Jackie that I wanted something more upscale for our child.

"You know, Chris . . ." she began. I knew that tone. Her patience was wearing thin about when was I going to leave the VA. Before the baby arrived, she'd been subtle about it; now she was in full-court press. "What are you holding on to? You know you're not making any more money. Ellis told you he doesn't have any more to pay you." This was true. The National Institutes of Health, which funded our research, had turned down recent grant requests to raise my salary.

"I know," I said, trying to head her off at the pass.

"Stop saying you know and do something! You've got to accept it. You're not planning on a career in medicine, right? You've made up your mind you're not going to pursue this, right? You've got a baby to support and you need more money. So quit and get a better-paying job!"

She was right, though that didn't make it any easier to find a new position. It didn't make it any easier to give up my top-dog status in the laboratory and go to the back of the line at something new where I would have to work my way up again. But finally I began to look in earnest for whatever that next job was going to be. Jackie had every reason to be frustrated, after all. Now that she was studying for her boards to become a practicing dentist she obviously had her own issues with being thrust into motherhood. All her female friends from dental school had gotten board certification and were setting up their practices or marrying into situations with husbands in professional practices. I wasn't there yet, even if I had potential. Trying to understand her feelings, I also had to hold on to my confidence, to know that even if I was still on the come, my time would arrive sooner or later.

Two opposing drumbeats begin to sound. One of them is the steady, firm bongo beat of family and work, the familiar routine, putting the word out that I'm job hunting, hitting the pavements. The secondary beat is erratic, sometimes barely there, other times booming like a bass drum with the crash of cymbals, the ominous sound of domestic stress. Little arguments arise. Money, not enough of it, not fast enough. Sometimes it's me getting frustrated; sometimes it's her. Jackie runs hot and cold, giving and withholding. She works me; I call her on it. I shut down; she gets defensive. I yell; she punishes. Then it passes, we make love, we move on. Everything's okay again.

Then the arguing picks up, and the dynamic shifts radically one day when I arrive home and am greeted by her announcement: "Chris, this isn't working out, and I don't believe it's ever going to work and maybe you should just move."

Shocked into silence, I glare at her. *What the fuck?*

"You should just move. You shouldn't live here anymore."

That's not going to happen, I promise her. I need to be with my son. She knows that. Looking around, I don't see Christopher. "Where's the baby?" I panic.

"You can't see the baby now."

CAN'T SEE THE BABY? Those words strung together totally infuriate me. What has been a basic family movie with some conflict but mostly humor and love now turns into a horror flick. Dark, powerful feelings of fear and helplessness flood me. I'm standing there not knowing what to do, with anger I can't even quantify or verbalize, when the storm clouds break just as suddenly as they came over. No resolution. No apologies. Almost as if it was some kind of test.

The storm passes. Whatever provoked her ire subsides. We go back to normalcy. But I'm jumpy, not knowing if the next time she's going to threaten to take him and actually do it. All the old fears haunt me. Freddie's on the other side of the country, getting too old and sick to hurt Momma anymore, but I'm still caught up in the cycle of waiting for an ax to fall, not knowing what shock is around the corner. We're heading out to see some friends one day, arguing about whether we should go, and I'm outside on the sidewalk waiting for Jackie to bring six-month-old Christopher out in his baby carrier, and all of a sudden it looks like they're not coming. Oh no, we're not playing that, I roar to that effect, calling up at the apartment.

The minute she emerges from the house, I shock myself by marching over and grabbing the baby carrier with Christopher in it, instigating a tug-of-war between us, while I tell her, "You not gonna take my child from me!"

This may be the ugliest thing that I have ever done in my life, an act I will never forgive myself for. There aren't even words to explain to her, to my son, or to myself how wrong I am. But this is primal shit. That big banging drum of discord is all I hear as I finally wrest the baby carrier from her and carry him down the block and the next and the next until I spot a church and take a seat on the steps. I complain to my six-month-old son, "Man, this is fucked up! Is it gonna be like this forever?"

Christopher furrows his brow, as if trying to understand, gurgling unintelligibly.

I explain, "I can't let nobody take you from me."

He understands, I think, by the way he squints his eyes in rec-ognition. Or maybe he's exhausted and needs to sleep.

In any case, there's only one truth that matters: he's my son and I love him, and I'm never going to leave him, no matter the cost.

Eventually I walk him back to the house, facing the fear thing, the weight of the unknown, that has come back with a vengeance, as I mentally square off with the problem, just as I did as a child, by giving myself something pragmatic to do. Money, that's the remedy, I realize.

In the months that followed, I supplemented what I was mak-ing at the VA with odd jobs, anything extra that came up, as I had in the past. To save on the cost of rent and give ourselves more floor space, we moved to Berkeley, where we were able to find a small house off an alley that had an unlikely patch of rosebushes in front. With the money situation eased, we were able to get an economy-sized sedan, nothing fancy, so we could commute to San Francisco for work and school.

Still looking for a position that would be a step up from re-search and keep me in medicine, I tried to cheer myself on, figur-ing that if I could just apply myself to the right thing, the money would be there and the pressure would ease up. Things weren't great with Jackie, but at this point the need for more money was coming from me, not her. As the sole breadwinner, not only was I responsible for the three of us, but I was paying much more atten-tion to what was coming in and what was going out. In the past, when I basically only had me to think about—even when Sherry and I pooled our resources—it was a very different ball game. This was about putting food on the table for my growing child, Jackie, and me. More important, it was about creating a plan to provide for them in the future so we didn't have to live paycheck to pay-check.

I was hopeful, determined, focused. But something was holding me back, an old ball and chain that I had refused to recognize all this time—even with Jackie's doubts about how I couldn't know what it meant to be a father if I never had one. Had it not been for Christopher and a book I was reading to him out on the stoop one afternoon a short while after his first birthday, I might never have acknowledged how much the no-daddy blues was still plaguing me.

Earlier we'd been sitting outside in the shade, playing with a ball, spending some time together, letting the California breeze cool us off, and I had an overwhelming feeling of joy as I paused just to look at Christopher. We hadn't cut his hair yet, and it was a long floppy 'fro that waved like a flag in the wind as he played without care or fear. The thought that flashed in my senses was, *God, this must be what heaven is like.* Nothing mattered except that I was here in this time and place, being with this beautiful little boy who was everything in the world to me. The idea occurred to me that this was something that was supposed to be passed down from generation to generation, fathers playing ball with their sons, sitting side by side to look at books together. It just hadn't happened when I was a son.

But now I had a son who loved to read and wanted to look at one of his favorite picture books.

In his slightly coherent babble, Christopher asked, "Who 'dat, Poppa?" or something along those lines as he pointed to an illustration of a colt standing with his family of horses.

To explain the concept of family to him, I pointed too, showing him the colt, the stallion, and the mare: "That's the little horse, and this is the horse's father, and the horse has a mother."

Christopher nodded, eyes bright, pointing with me as I repeated the identities of the horse family.

"Right! And, Christopher, you have a father and a mother. The little horse has a mother, and the little horse has a father. Just like you."

As if he understood exactly, he pointed and said, "Momma," and, "Poppa."

Well, this was amazing. So I went further, telling him that everyone in the world had a mother and father like that little horse. "Momma has a mother, and Momma has a father," I began, wondering how best to explain the concept of grandparents to a one-year-old.

Just then Christopher turned his face up to mine, and with a questioning look in his eyes, he pointed to me, as if waiting for me to say that I had a mother and a father too.

The way he looked just rocked me off my seat. The irony was that I had always imagined I would meet my father one day, even if it was just to confront him about where he'd been. But here I was, almost twenty-eight years old, and I had never met him. How could I meet him? I didn't know. Was he alive? Didn't know that either. Didn't know where he was or what he looked like. But the moment my son made his precocious comment, I knew it was time.

At work in my office at the lab the following day, I called directory information for Thomas Turner in Monroe, Louisiana. That was all I had finagled out of Moms all these years.

The operator had five listings. I asked for all five, deciding to just go down the list and take my chances.

When I made the first call, I asked the elderly person who answered, "Is Thomas Turner there?"

"Thomas Turner is dead," said the elderly person, to whom I apologized.

Hoping that I hadn't missed the boat, I made the next call, explaining to the woman who answered that I was looking for a Thomas Turner who may have known Bettye Gardner.

The woman felt comfortable telling me, "You know what? I can think of two Thomas Turners. One drinks, and the other one used to drink, but he quit."

Going with my gut, I asked her how I'd get in touch with the sober Thomas Turner and found out where he lived. I gave the address to an information operator to make sure I had the right phone numbers.

Looking at it, I took a deep breath, not sure how to start if the real Thomas Turner answered the phone. Not knowing, I dialed the number and heard the sound of a phone being picked up and a deep male voice answering, "Hello?"

All I could think to say was: "Do you know Bettye Gardner? I'm her son Chris and I'm trying to find my father. Do . . ." Before I could finish, I was interrupted.

"Yeah," my father said. "I've been waiting for you to call a long time."

———

Just by virtue of having gotten to the bottom of a nearly twenty-eight-year-old mystery, a dramatic shift in energy took place in my life almost overnight. The man I'd met on the telephone wasn't much more than a voice, but he had encouraged me to come down to Louisiana to meet him in person, along with several siblings I never knew about.

While I promised to do that as soon as I could make the arrangements, what had been an insurmountable process of finding my new niche in the working world was all of a sudden a cakewalk. With my sights fixed on the possibilities of making my way in the business world, I quickly landed a job as a sales rep for a medical equipment and supply company called CMS. Based in San Bruno, in the heart of the then-developing Silicon Valley, CMS sold primarily to laboratories and hospitals. I was going to be starting out at just under $30,000 a year, nearly twice what I'd made in research, with the potential of making twice that—what the top earners were making.

Of course, those earners had been in the trenches for twenty years—building up their territories, books, and relationships—and I never thought of myself as a natural salesman. Then again, I'd been to college with every person I'd ever met, as Will Rogers said about myself, and had known some unbelievable characters who could sell you the raindrops falling on your head. I could learn to sell. Plus, I knew the power of information and knew how to spot the leaders and how to learn what they did and how they did it to be successful. Adding even more to my confidence was the fact that although I didn't know the business lingo, I was extremely proficient in medical language and understood the mind-set of the buyers as well as the sales veterans at CMS.

So, good-bye to the future Dr. Chris Gardner, good-bye to wearing scrubs. My only lasting regret was the fact that I did have the hands. But looking at myself in the mirror in my business attire—a nice jacket, not a bad-looking tie—I was encouraged. This was a whole new venue, a challenge. The feeling of potential lit my fire again.

As a sales rookie, I had the triple whammy of being handed a brand-new territory in which to build relationships, representing a company not established in this territory, and being the only black person employed by CMS. By this point, I was a seasoned veteran at being the only African American in a cadre of white professionals, so that was a non-issue. The main issue was that I was starting from absolute scratch, which I discovered overnight by picking up some fundamentals about sales: (a) buyers like to buy from people they know, and (b) they like to buy established products.

Instead of being discouraged, I found the competition exciting. As far as I was concerned, I was really happy to have a shot, so rather than honing in on the challenges, my focus was fine-tuned to the questions: How do I get more business? What information do I need to expand my opportunities and build relationships? In the past I'd been able to find an expert and ask those questions, but at CMS that wasn't the case. As it turned out, the sales managers—

who made a percentage of what the reps made—spent most of their time reinforcing their top producers. With rookies like me, the manager handed me my book, patted me on the shoulder, and said, "Go get 'em."

OJT once again, I dove in, clocking hundreds of miles a week on my sporty new maroon Nissan hatchback packed to the gills with brochures, supply samples, and equipment to show in demos, traveling daily from Berkeley to every far corner of Silicon Valley and back, unloading and loading sales materials countless times a day. Building on the philosophy of hitting that anvil, I agreed with the belief that sales success came down to a numbers game. What I also learned in making repeat calls was that the more down-to-earth and personable yet respectful I was, and the more I remembered names of secretaries and little details about buyers, the better my chances. My sales figures started to take off.

On the downside, the competitive atmosphere extended to after hours, when managers and reps headed out to see who could drink the most. The schmoozing and drinking thing was part of the game, I understood, but it wasn't for me. Now that I was in business, I was serious about increasing my numbers, about making money. That didn't earn me any awards at CMS, but the guys in hiring at Van Waters and Rogers, a better-established competitor in the medical equipment and supply field, were impressed with my ambition and hired me on.

Not too long after starting the new job, I was able to purchase a plane ticket for me and Christopher to travel to Monroe, Louisiana. During a long, nerve-wracking flight from San Francisco to Memphis and then another puddle-jump to Monroe—with Christopher unusually calm, sitting on my lap the whole way—I reviewed the indignities of a childhood filled with being told by Freddie Triplett that I didn't have no "goddamn daddy." What was I going to say to my biological father? On the phone, I hadn't gotten around to asking why he never called or tried to meet me, even when he said that my brothers and sisters had heard so much about me. And what was I going to do if the scene got too heavy and I wanted to split? If Christopher got antsy?

Really clueless about what to expect, the moment of truth arrives as I lead my son down the rolling stairway of the prop plane and look over to see *him* standing there. Six-six, 280 pounds. Black as night. A country man who has been in Louisiana forever, he towers in front of me—nothing like I imagined.

The first thing that crosses my mind: well, I guess I won't punch him—which as a kid was always the first thing I envisioned doing to him.

His presence is huge, stunning. Beside him are two of his daughters, my half-sisters. Between me and Christopher and those three, we all look just like each other. Thomas Turner looks like he had just spit me out, there is no doubt.

As awkward as this encounter is, he seems fairly comfortable with it. That's because, I later learn, this scene has been repeated more than a few times before. The joke my sisters tell me later is that it's pretty much like the Olympic games: every four years somebody shows up. No need to ask questions, you just look at them, see the family resemblance, open the door, and let them on in.

Even with my scientific background now, I am still amazed by the miracle of genetics. My sisters Deborah and Janice and I really do look like identical triplets. When we get to Thomas Turner's house and sit down to talk, Deb says, "You know what? You look more like Pop than any of us. You even got hair on the back of your hands just like Pop."

Laughing, I can't believe they're checking me out to that degree, and I look at my hands and over at his. They're right!

Over the next four days of our visit I get to know the cast of characters who inhabit this very different version of an all-black *Happy Days* show, Louisiana style. With it hot and humid like nothing I've ever experienced, not even in the Navy in Orlando, our clothes could have just come out of the washing machine. Even our hair and fingernails are sweating.

As the days flew by, I couldn't help calling Moms to let her know that I'd made it over to Rayville, her old hometown, and was spending time with my father. Before coming, I had told her that I was going to Louisiana—not only to meet him for myself but so Christopher could meet his grandfather. Now that I was actually here, it was important to let her know that I'd put the pieces together. She was happy for me. But when I asked, "Momma, you want to say hello to him?" she didn't hesitate before answering, "No." Her unqualified response told me little more about their relationship, whether or not it was a relationship, and that was the full, final stop to the discussion. I would never know. The legacy of the family's "don't ask, don't tell" policy continued.

Getting to know the soil from which I had first sprung included a trip out to Delhi, where the absence of lights, neon, street signs, and cars turned the nighttime blacker than anything I'd ever seen; the stars looked like lightbulbs clearly outlining all the famous constellations. Blown away, I couldn't stop staring up, wondering what my life would have been like if I had been raised here. We met the family matriarch, my grandmother, a tiny, exquisite black woman named Ora Turner. Though she had never set eyes on me before, her greeting was to spread her arms wide and hug me to her. I was her grandchild.

"I use to ask yo' daddy where you was," my grandmomma said, stepping back to take me in, nodding in approval. "He didn't know nothin'. I use to always ask him where you at."

The next thing she needed to know was where I had been baptized. For a moment, I couldn't remember.

Alarmed, my grandmother, a fervent Christian woman, proposed, "Boy, I ought to take you out there right now, take you outside, back out to that creek, and baptize you myself. Lord, have mercy!"

That scared the shit out of me. A pitch-black night, nothing but the stars and the moon for light, and me getting dunked in a creek? That was all I needed to hear in order to remember being baptized at TT's church when I was six years old. Lord had mercy and my grandmother was satisfied.

Besides getting to know Deb and Jan, I met my other half-siblings—my brothers Junior and Dale and my sister Mary, who lived over in Shreveport. There were aunts and uncles and cousins too—one cousin so fine I regretted that we were related. Wherever we went, everyone was generous and hospitable, treating me like a celebrity. The social habits and pace of life seemed different from Milwaukee, but the more we hung out and talked, as the family stories and the jokes started to roll, the fewer differences I saw. As much as I considered myself a Gardner through and through, there were aspects of myself that I could now see had come from the Turner side of my family.

The most remarkable moment in the trip came one night close to the end when I decided to take Christopher with me on the train to Shreveport to meet my sister Mary, and my father went to the station with us. Not too late yet, it was already one of those tar-black country nights with only twinkling slivers of stars and moonglow to light our surroundings as we waited out by the tracks behind the station. Off to the side was a set of tracks heading off in another direction that Christopher found interesting. We were early, so I saw nothing wrong with my son going to check out the rails with his grandfather, especially since the two had gotten comfortable with each other right away.

The sight of the two of them walking along the railroad tracks made me catch my breath. There was my father, then in his midfifties, massive like a black oak tree, patriarch to more offspring than any of us may have known, walking with my son, a fourteen-month-old toddler, energetic and talkative. My father held Christopher's little fingers protectively, proudly.

As one of those memories that you capture and that remains

unchanged through the years, the image of the two of them walking along in that night produced a surprising reaction in me that would come back every time I recalled it. What first flashed in my brain and my heart was—*How come that couldn't have been me? How come I never got a chance to do that?*

As time went on, I recognized that it wasn't anger of course. But I was jealous of my little boy, ridiculous as that was. Below that layer, in the core of my being, was simple hurt. The reservoir that stored all those years of abandonment had been stirred up by that sight and now hurt like hell.

At the airport, as the Louisiana contingency of my family came to see me off, with my sisters making me promise that we wouldn't lose contact, I looked down at Christopher and marveled at how our exchange about fathers and mothers had gotten me here. In that regard, I could take away with me a sense of completion. Even though I couldn't see it yet, a nearly twenty-eight-year-old load of resentment had been lifted. At long last, I let go of the no-daddy blues. I had a daddy, albeit one I didn't know well and never would, but I was no longer a fatherless child. That wasn't my song to sing anymore.

Christopher and I flew back to California—a trip that seemed to take half the time it had taken to get to Louisiana. There was no denying that a circle had been closed. It was somewhat fractured, not a perfect circle, but gaps had been filled in my understanding of who I was and where I came from. Though many questions lingered about what might have been if things had happened differently in my upbringing, my preoccupation wasn't with that part of my past anymore. Yes, on that plane I was still hurting bad, thinking of my father and my son walking along those railroad tracks, hand in hand, as I turned and twisted that question in my mind like a Rubik's cube: *How come that couldn't have been me?*

But by the time the plane touched down, the hurt had begun to fade, and I felt renewed and revived—ready to take on the world, with a level of confidence and clarity of vision that I had never had before. Great things were right around the corner, I just knew it.

CHAPTER 9

Turned Out
(advanced)

Bob Russell—the guy at the top of the heap at Van Waters and Rogers—walked around like he was the God almighty NBC peacock.

I didn't get what it was about him that made him such a fantastic producer, but when I found out that he was not only getting all the business but making $80,000 a year—compared to my $30,000 starting salary—I had to figure out what his secret was.

While I had thought that my trip to meet my father would give me and Jackie the break we needed to appreciate each other more and help put everything in perspective, the stress picked up exactly where it had been before—the same patterns, the same arguments. Her frustration with herself, with me, and with how her dreams weren't panning out always translated in my mind to the need for more money. So when I found out what Bob Russell was grossing, $80,000 became the magic number for me. *If I can ever get there, that's all I'll ever want,* I thought. At that time, I couldn't even dream any bigger. But if Bob Russell could do it, I could too.

My confidence was apparently not shared by my sales manager Patrick, who had also apparently not been involved in the decision to hire me. It probably didn't help that I was a tall, black man and he was just a little bit taller than a midget.

A fussy Irish American, Patrick was what I called a "pen guy."

He punctuated every sentence he uttered with a *click-CLICK* of his pen, emphasizing each and every point he made—and they were numerous since he knew everything and the new guys like me didn't know anything—with additional clicks.

What I learned wasn't so much how to be a better salesman as how not to be intimidated. So when Mr. Pen Guy started sending the message that he wasn't digging me, I found a way to let him know, *Hey, I'm not digging you either.* If he made a mildly snide remark, instead of really barking back, my reaction was to bend down, subtly reminding him that I was tall and he was short, and to say, in mock politeness, "I'm sorry. What was that?"

Patrick's face inevitably turned red. Of course, when he really pissed me off, I was less subtle as I cupped my hand to my ear, bent over, and said, "What? I can't hear you down there, all the way down there."

His only response in those instances was to *click-CLICK* away. Somehow my antagonizing him convinced him to teach me a thing or two about selling the Van Waters and Rogers line. During the middle of a sales call with a buyer, after I'd already started to take the order, he'd interrupt, reminding me, for example, that it was important to stress that even though competitors had the same products, Van Waters and Rogers had the superior products at a lower price. Then there was the time he stopped me and asked, "Gardner, where are the samples? You should have brought out the samples before writing the order."

In situations like that, I couldn't go off and ask why he didn't wait to tell me later but had to humiliate me in front of a buyer. Infuriating though it was, I learned by default that it was vital to distinguish the product I was selling from the competition as superior and less expensive. What was more, I learned that there were stages to selling. There were also numerous intangibles. Some of the skills could be learned and developed, but I soon saw the truth of the matter—that the best salespeople are born that way. Not everybody can do it, and not everybody should do it. Did I have what it took? I didn't know yet. But damn, $80,000? What did Bob Russell have that I needed to have?

Whatever it was, I refused to be deterred, even with having to drive outrageous numbers of miles from Berkeley to every whistle stop in Silicon Valley, from San Mateo to San Jose, mostly down the road from the San Francisco airport. But the most important call I ever made was in the city proper at San Francisco General Hospital, where I went to deliver samples and a catalog to Lars Nielson, who ran a lab we should have been doing some business with. Even though the call went well and I expected to come back for the order, when I exited the building, the math I was doing in my head was telling me that I still had a long way to go to compete with Bob Russell. Yet what options did I have?

Just then, after being momentarily blinded by the sun's glare, I see the red Ferrari 308 circling the parking lot. The owner of the car, dressed in that perfectly tailored suit, who is the beneficiary of my parking spot after he answers my questions—"What do you do?" and "How do you do that?"—is a gentleman by the name of Bob Bridges, a stockbroker with Donaldson, Lufkin & Jenrette, who commands a salary of $80,000 a *month*!

Stop the presses. I don't have to be a math whiz to compare and contrast that with Bob Russell's $80,000 a year. Fuck Bob Russell!

At this stage of my life, I know as much about Wall Street, stocks and bonds, capital markets, and high finance as most people know about the preservation of myocardial high-energy phosphates. But even before I sit down to lunch with Bob Bridges in order to learn more about what exactly a stockbroker does and how to do it well, I'm already seeing myself in that arena. How can it be any different from everything I've ever done before? From working at Heartside Nursing Home and the Navy Hospital at Camp Lejeune in general surgery and the proctology clinic, to heading up a laboratory at the

VA Hospital and the University of California Medical Center, to being the up-and-comer doing sales in the Silicon Valley, I've walked into jobs with no knowledge of the fields but have succeeded and done well in all of these areas. Not just done well. Done absolutely fucking fabulously well. No, my monetary success hasn't been overwhelming. But in growth and skill, I've excelled beyond my own expectations.

All that is enough for me to think I can do the same as a stockbroker. Despite the fact that this is the first time the notion has even come up on my radar screen, from here on out there is not one doubt that I have found my calling and that I'm going to be in hot, relentless pursuit of a career in that arena. For reasons I can't begin to explain, I know with every fiber of my being that this is IT.

To the average man or woman on the street, this certainty probably sounds crazy. Besides not having gone to college, I don't know anybody and have no connections or special privileges to help me even get a foot in the door. That is, except for Bob Bridges, who I don't know from Adam, other than the fact that I gave him my parking space.

Nonetheless, when we go to lunch and I ask, "What does a stockbroker do?" he patiently and generously describes his average day.

Basically, Bob says, every day he goes to his nice little office and he sits there, takes a couple of phone calls, and writes something down.

"Let me get this straight," I repeat. "You take a call and write something down. That's it?"

Bob goes on. "Well, yes. And I call people too, and we talk. I tell them stories about companies, and they send me money."

Another light flashes on in my head. This dude—wearing another custom-made, beautiful suit, at a cost of a couple thousand dollars easy—is selling, just like I'm doing. But instead of having to drive all around, up and down highways, to find obscure facilities and labs, carrying a small warehouse in the trunk of his car, he gets to go to one office, sits there, and talks on the phone. I want to say, *Damn, that's slick!* but only listen attentively as he conveys the secret to his success.

Bob is self-motivated, he says, setting his own goals. "Every day when I'm sitting there talking on the phone, I say to myself: *I'm not leaving until I make four or five thousand dollars today.*"

Again, the math is overwhelming. He sits there and talks to people until he makes four or five thousand dollars *that day.* I'm killing myself to gross four or five thousand *a month*! To be sure that I haven't misunderstood, I ask, "Bob, let me see if I got this right. You talk to people, some of whom you know, some of whom you don't know, some of whom you have to get to know, and you tell them stories about these companies and these investment ideas and opportunities, and they send you money?"

"That's what I do," he says, with total sincerity.

With total sincerity, I announce, "I can do that." Just for emphasis, I add, "Yep, I can do that. And you know what? I *want* to do that!"

Laughing, whether he believes I can or not, Bob offers to introduce me to some branch managers at the different brokerage firms in town. The fact that I haven't been to college is a liability, he admits. But he also tells me that there are training programs at these various companies for which I could qualify, even without a degree, and receive training in every aspect of the job—from the fundamentals of investment to financial planning and the full spectrum of economics and high finance—while I'm studying for the licensing exam. But in order to be hired on full-time—to do what he's doing—I have to be licensed.

Done, I thought. Chris Gardner, stockbroker. This was where I was supposed to be. Period. Despite the logistical nightmare that ensued, I knew from that lunch forward that it would be worth it.

Geography became my first major obstacle. When Bob started setting meetings up for me, most of them were scattered across the financial district in downtown San Francisco, all of the meetings during the nine-to-five prime time of the working day. No early breakfasts and no meet-and-greets for drinks. Since my sales calls for Van Waters and Rogers were mostly all down in the Valley, also during the nine-to-five working day, that meant either being late or missing meetings that my pen-wielding boss Patrick was scheduling for me.

Most of my interviews were at the larger firms with training programs, like Merrill Lynch, Paine Webber, E. F. Hutton, Dean Witter, and Smith Barney, companies where Bob knew the branch managers. If there was any possibility that the hoops I had to jump through were going to discourage me, that was eliminated the moment I stepped foot in the first brokerage firm I visited. Talk about being turned out! One hit and I was hooked. It was something in the air that was instantly invigorating.

Sitting there waiting for my interview, I could feel my adrenaline pumping, like a contact high, just from watching all the activity that was happening simultaneously: phones ringing, ticker tape running, stockbrokers hollering out orders and transactions and stamping time clocks. It was all at once like visiting a foreign country and like coming home.

The impact was exactly what I felt the first time I heard Miles Davis and saw how his music could totally change the mood of everyone hearing it. The trading room had a similar kind of power. It was a nerve center, hooked into the doings and happenings of millions of other people all over the world. What a rush! Some rushes came and went; this didn't dissipate. This was sustained intensity.

Waiting for the appointment that day didn't bother me because the more I absorbed what was going on, the more certain I became that I could do this. There weren't any other black guys in the office, or at least not any that I could see. But that didn't alter my confidence. Not when there was a chance to make $80,000 a month!

Of course, I may have been naive about that being the going rate for most stockbrokers. Still, it was part of what had fired me up. Momma had told me that if I wanted to make a million dollars, I could. Eighty grand a month times twelve, with some overtime and bonuses thrown in—I figured it was only a matter of time and I'd be making that million in a year! Again, if Bob Bridges could do it, so could I.

Now that I had found the vehicle and venue to do what I believed I could do, it was only a matter of getting one person at one of the firms with a training program to agree with me. That wasn't so easy. Interview after interview, the answers varied, but they all translated to no. N.O. And with every no, as a parting gift, I invariably spotted the ubiquitous pee yellow parking ticket under the windshield wiper when I dashed out to my car. Another fifteen to twenty-five bucks that I didn't have, another reminder that I'd have to take time off from work one day and go to court to plead my case to have the tickets reduced or cleared. Still, I wasn't going to give up.

Racism wasn't the main issue, although it was a part of it. My understanding eventually about why I kept getting turned down was that it was "place-ism." The questions boiled down to connection, placement. What was my connection to the market? What was my connection to my peers, since I never went to college? My résumé showed lots of experience, but the objections piled up about what wasn't there. You're not from a politically connected family. You've got no money of your own. Who's going to do business with you? What's your connection to the money?

Place-ism. It made sense. But I just kept telling myself, *I know I can do this.*

At the San Francisco office of Dean Witter, a friendly broker named Marty made himself available to me. He was someone to whom I could turn for advice now and then, even if I didn't have an appointment. When he referred me to the Oakland office of Dean Witter, I assumed it was because I was black, even though when I got to that office, set in a mainly black section of town, there were no other employees of color to be seen. By that point, nothing mattered but getting in their training program. It had been a few months, and no one had given me any indication of interest, while I was starting to really jeopardize the job that I did have, with the Pen Guy on my back. The reality was that I was getting tight, and with that in mind I marched into the Oakland branch manager's office prepared to close the deal, not to pitch myself but to ask: "When can I start?"

Under the heading of the worst job interview ever, I sat there in this cat's office overlooking Lake Merritt, and as I was talking, he stared right over my shoulder, interrupting me to say, "Oh, that's so interesting, a horse has jumped into Lake Merritt."

I wanted to say, *Fuck that horse.* After all, Lake Merritt wasn't deep, so the horse wasn't in danger of drowning. But it was all too clear that he could have cared less about me. As professionally as I could, I stood and said, "Obviously, I've gotten you at a bad time, so why don't we try and do this again at a later date?"

He agreed, and I excused myself, only to gallop horselike out to my car, pluck the parking violation ticket off the windshield, and haul ass down to the Valley, where I was supposed to be picking up Patrick to go call on an account. In my haste, I forgot to hide the pile of annual reports I'd been amassing from these stockbrokerages—Dean Witter, Paine Webber, EF Hutton—that was sitting on my front passenger seat.

It was in that split second when Patrick started to get in the car that I realized they were there. With veiled panic, I went to grab the papers just as he sternly asked, "Gardner?"

"Yes . . ." I began, sure that I was about to be busted.

Patrick peered at me with suspicion, asking, "Are you going to open a brokerage account?"

"Oh, yeah . . ." I answered, trying to look really cool, feeling relieved. "Yeah, I'm thinking about opening up an account."

But then, just to show he didn't quite buy it, he gave me a funny look and a click of his pen. In the days that followed, Patrick started to check up on me more closely. Though he didn't actually know that I was interviewing with other companies, he was obviously beginning to suspect something, especially when he found out that I'd been canceling appointments and showing up late for others.

To make matters more stressful, Jackie had been hinting that I was fooling myself into thinking I could make it on Wall Street. Her point of view, valid enough, was: "Well, most of the guys there in that business, don't they have MBAs?"

No matter how many times I explained about the training programs and that you didn't always have to have a master's degree, she had no evidence that was true. Her friend at this firm had his MBA, and her friend's husband at that firm had his MBA. "Chris, you don't even have a bachelor's. Don't you have to have some kind of degree to work in that industry?"

It was the credentials argument all over again: "You ain't got the papers." This from the woman with whom I was living, and the mother of my son.

You watch, I kept promising. I'm going to do this. I saw it, tasted it, smelled it. Even so, with money tighter than it had been in a long time, the Irish midget waiting to nail me, and Jackie worried, I knew something had to give.

Just when I thought I had exhausted all my options, I had a follow-up interview at E. F. Hutton: the culmination of several conversations was that the branch manager did not say no. He said, "We'll give you a shot." Walking me to the door, he shook my hand and told me that he'd see me two weeks later, at seven o'clock in the morning, to start the training program.

I could have tap-danced out of his office, Gene Kelly style, into the San Francisco midsummer rain. Practically on wings, I kissed the parking ticket left on the car and called it lucky, promising myself to finally take a day off to go to court and take care of all the tickets. At long last, the validation that I wasn't crazy was here! My mental bank account started ringing up my stockbroker commissions.

Though I intended to close up some Van Waters and Rogers pending sales over the next two weeks, there was a slight wrinkle that turned up a few days later when Patrick announced, "Gardner, we don't think this is working out. You don't seem to be making any progress. We're trying to grow this territory, and you're just not cutting it."

Relieved, I admitted that the feeling was mutual and that I had other opportunities lining up that I wanted to pursue. *Big mistake.* The minute I said that, even before I could wrap up diplomatically, Patrick cut me off with a click and prepared to hurry me out. Just to clarify, I asked if this was a two weeks' notice, and Patrick explained that we were terminating our arrangement then and there. They would mail me the check.

Beautiful. A perfect plan: go home, wait the two weeks, start collecting unemployment, spend some time with the family, then head off to Wall Street, where I'm going to make more money than even Bob Russell, not to mention Patrick.

When what I thought was my severance check arrived but turned out to be a reduced amount for time I'd already worked, I learned that because I had "quit," there was no money for the two weeks that I would have worked and also no unemployment. That was a drag, but since I planned on conquering the stock market soon, I didn't sweat it.

In an experience to be filed under the heading of "best-laid plans of mice and men," after enjoying those two weeks—during which I don't get around to taking care of the parking tickets—to make a good impression I show up thirty minutes early on the appointed Monday morning and no one seems to know who I am.

Surprised at the lack of organization, I ask for my new boss, who is also the branch manager, the guy who hired me, the person who told me, "We'll give you a shot."

Oh, says one of the brokers, he was fired on Friday.

Standing there at the reception desk, for the first time as an adult I become conscious of the strength of my own sphincter muscle. To some, this could be a cause for irony, even humor. Not for me. There is not one iota of humor in me as I freak out, exiting the building to see that it's pouring rain but not bothering to use my umbrella. How could this have happened? The job that I left my other job for doesn't exist. I got no income. I'm having beefs with my woman. What the hell am I going to do? I don't know.

What I do know in the hours and days that follow is that nothing puts more stress on a relationship between a man and a woman than if the man has no job. At least, in the world I come from and inhabit, that's so. A man without a job, as far as my upbringing taught me, is no man at all. Any man that was a man had to take care of and provide for his family. Even old drunk-ass Freddie basically went to work every day. So it was unacceptable for me to wake up in the morning and not have anywhere to go to work—after being so sure that I was on the way to Wall Street and knowing that it was my responsibility because I made the decision to do what I did. I could only imagine how Jackie was going to take it.

Later I would refer to what happened next as a series of incidents and circumstances that taken all together might be seen as the perfect example of Murphy's Law. Complicating those principles was the crumbling foundation of my relationship with Jackie. When I first came home to tell her what had happened, she said absolutely nothing. What could she say? "Sorry, old chap, hang in there," but she didn't. We had no savings, no income, only bills. Not anything extravagant, just your normal run-of-the-mill living bills: food, rent, car note, day care, Pampers.

My first order of business was bringing in some bucks, imme-diately. Returning to some of the odd jobs I'd done when I was supplementing my salary at the VA, that same day I made fifty bucks painting houses all day for a friend in the contracting busi-ness. Fine. That meant we were going to eat that day and pay the gas bill. The next day my buddy hired me to work on a roofing job, and the next day I cleaned out a basement, and the day after that I did yard work. Whatever work I could scrounge up, I did it, not joyfully, not with expertise, but willingly.

This was, in my mind, a lousy setback, an unfortunate rut in the road. But it wasn't the end of the ride by any means. In fact, while I worked those jobs, all I could think about was getting back on track, finding that open door, that one break that would pan out.

In the midst of money arguments and increasing daily tension at home, all the while that I was painting houses, junking, and mowing lawns a semblance of a strategy emerged. The one remain-ing possibility that I had going was over at Dean Witter, where they hadn't said yes but hadn't said a final no. My challenge was over-coming the placement argument: what was my connection to the business, my experience? A bigger challenge was having to explain that I was currently unemployed, after having been dropped by my last sales job. My thought was that if I could get someone to vouch for me, someone like maybe Joe Dutton, an African American en-trepreneur in the high-tech field I'd met at a business seminar, that could make a huge difference.

When I called Joe to ask him for the favor, he was happy to help a brother. With that, I was able to set up the interview at Dean Wit-ter. If they told me no this time, I wasn't sure what I'd do after that, so the interview loomed as though my life depended on it.

Later I would wonder how different things would have turned out if the first training program had gone forward or the guy who hired me hadn't been fired. Would that have changed the turbulent dynamic in my household? The lack of money made everything worse, but there were other problems. In Jackie's view, my smoking weed to take the edge off was intolerable, as were my sometimes loud and critical comments. In my view, she had no confidence in me, which was infuriating. And my gut instinct warned me that she was capable of using Christopher to retaliate against me.

The showdown came on a Thursday night after we heard the news that my friend Latrell's little boy Sebastian had been killed on the street when he was playing on his tricycle and a car hit him. It wasn't what we were arguing about, but the tragic news compounded our emotional state when we began to bare all our complaints in an epic verbal argument that was so exhausting, we finally both fell sleep without any resolution. On Friday midmorning, the minute our feet hit the floor, everything picks up where it left off.

When she starts getting dressed to leave, an indication to me that because I'm not going anywhere I need to get Christopher dressed and over to day care, where we have no money to pay for his care but need to keep him so we don't lose our place when we get the work, I panic. Moving quickly, Jackie heads out the front door, and I follow her out, demanding to know, "Where are you going? We gotta work this out, and you ain't going nowhere until we do!"

Refusing to acknowledge me, she starts down the steps and I run after her and attempt to take her by the hands and turn her toward me. As she pulls away, I grab her by both wrists and she pulls back again, trying to get away. Upset that I've stooped so low, I release my grip and let go, only to watch her fall back into the rosebushes.

I watch her stand up, brush herself off, looking slightly scratched, and as I start to swallow my damn pride to apologize, Jackie seethes, "You're getting the fuck out of here."

Now I'm back in the fight. "No, I ain't. I'm not going nowhere." Seething myself, I slam the door and go back into the house to get Christopher into his bath.

What follows is a series of events that spiral meteorically out of control, resulting in legal complications that to this day remain ambiguous—due to Jackie's ultimate decision not to press charges over the rosebush incident. Initially, however, it was apparent that was what she intended to do, when some ten minutes after she split, there was a knock at the front door and, with Christopher wrapped in a towel and in my arms, I open it to find two young Berkeley police officers, in uniform, on my doorstep. Behind them, on the sidewalk, is Jackie.

One of the officers asks, "Are you Chris Gardner?"

"Yes," I answer, with a shrug. Not following.

The second cop explains, "We have a complaint from the woman who lives here. She said you beat her."

What? "No, I didn't beat her," I say, adamantly.

The first cop asks how she happened to have scratches on her body, so I point to the rosebushes, explaining how she fell. But the second cop says, "No, sir, she said you beat her, and the State of California treats domestic violence as a serious offense."

Just as I'm about to explode over the fact that I know domestic violence is a serious offense and that I know what a woman who's been beaten looks like and how I would turn myself in to the police before I committed that crime, I watch the first cop walk over to my car and write down my plate number.

After he verifies that it is my car, the two announce that they're taking me in to the police station.

When I object, saying, "No, I gotta get my baby ready and take him to day care," they announce that they will hand the baby over to his mother and she can take care of that. In shock, I helplessly watch as they hand my swaddled son to Jackie and watch her carry him inside the house, closing the door without a glance in my direction. In the meantime, I am handcuffed and put in the backseat of the police car.

In a state of total disbelief, I cuss under my breath at Jackie the whole way to the station. Whatever I'd done to deserve her resentment, I could accept responsibility, but the further we drive away from Christopher the more I start to lose it. Making matters worse, I learn next that besides the possibility of battery charges, I am definitely being charged with owing $1,200 of unpaid parking tickets. Now I go out of my mind, my anger giving way to fear and an overwhelming sense of powerlessness. Those two demons have lurked in the wings whenever circumstances have spun out of control and have suddenly emerged centerstage.

After they book and fingerprint me, I'm led to a holding cell where I'm informed that Jackie's complaint isn't the cause—since if it was just that I could sign myself out. But unless I can pay the parking tickets, I have to plead my case to a judge. This is where the screw gets turned, as I wait to be taken into court. But it's Friday. Soon it's Friday afternoon. After waiting and pacing in my holding cell, I see one of the desk guys heading back my way and listen as he explains, "Oh, about the parking tickets. The judge says it's too late today to do anything about this. He'll see you on Monday." He pauses, then adds, "You have to stay here. You can't leave until you see the judge."

"ARE YOU FUCKING TELLING ME I HAVE TO WAIT IN JAIL UNTIL MONDAY TO SEE THE JUDGE?"

Like I've offended him personally, the desk guy says, "You owe the State of California money, and while we've got you here we're going to get this resolved."

The dictates of Murphy's Law demand that things get worse. And they do immediately as I'm escorted now to another cell and I see that they've put me in with three of the meanest, ugliest, freakiest motherfuckers I've ever seen in my life: a murderer, a rapist, and an arsonist. And now I'm in here on parking tickets? With heavy-duty flashbacks to the only other time I was put in jail, for stealing pants at the Discount Center, and was ridiculed for reading my books, I'm not saying a word as I listen to everybody taking turns telling their little jailhouse story and why they're in here. Of course, the first thing I learn, a lesson soon to be reinforced by other convicts, is that nobody did the crime for which they're serving time. It's all a case of mistaken identity or somebody who didn't tell the truth. Each of these badasses says the same four words: "I didn't do it."

In unison they then turn their thick necks slowly toward me, leering my way, asking at the same time why I'm in here. Not about to admit that I'm in jail on parking tickets, I reach down to my lowest vocal register and squint up my eyes menacingly as I say, "I'm in here for attempted murder, and I will try it again, all right?" To establish my turf, I point to where I'm going to sleep and let them know, "And that's my bunk over there."

I'm jet black, mad as hell, and bigger than anybody there. My ruse works so well that I am able to obtain the most important coin of the realm for anyone incarcerated: cigarettes.

Ironically, I had started smoking back in the Navy while working on long night shifts in the hospital. By this point, I've quit because I can't afford it, but apparently a weekend in the slammer is going to get me back on the habit again. Smoking is far preferable to the stale bologna sandwiches and cold coffee we're served over the course of the longest, most excruciating weekend of my life.

Monday morning can't come fast enough. When it does and I'm standing before the judge, he barely looks up from his paperwork as he says, "Mr. Gardner, you owe the state of California $1,200. How do you want to settle this?"

He asks if I'm working, and I shake my head no. He asks if I can pay, and I again shake my head no.

For the first time in this ordeal, more than fear and anger, I feel unbelievably sad as I grapple with the reality of these circumstances. "I don't have the money," I mutter, at my wit's end.

"Well, Mr. Gardner, you give me no choice but to sentence you to ten days at Santa Rita." With a bang of his gavel, he calls out, "Next case!"

A guard appears instantly and chains me up, ushers me out of court, marches me to a bus that drives out to the boonies of the heat-trapped northern California Central Valley to the over-crowded, decrepit county prison, Santa Rita, where the current most famous convict is the crazy Mexican ax murderer Juan Co-rona. In shock, I look around at the pit bulls sitting next to me on the bus. My crime? Not the alleged battery, which was Jackie's initial complaint, and about which it was still unclear that she would go forward, requiring still more legal wrangling. But the parking tickets? There's no trial. They are a fact, proven documents of my disregard for the law because I was trying to get ahead in the world. If you can't pay, you've got to stay. Period. The end. *For ten days.*

Where is my attorney? Everybody else has a public defender, somebody. *That's it,* I think. My recourse, my way out. They didn't give me an attorney. So as they're letting me off the bus, I try to explain to the sympathetic-looking African American driver of the bus that he needs to take me back to court. Or maybe, I actually hope, he'll let me go. Well, the second I step out of line, prison guards start jerking the chain, dragging me right back in line.

If there was anything that helped me survive the dehumanizing effect of incarceration, it was my time in the military. It wasn't just the prison uniform of orange PJs and clear jelly sandals, it was the total control and regimentation, the diet consisting of more unpal-atable bologna and nasty coffee, and the acclimation to ovenlike conditions. There were no Pacific Ocean breezes, no Santa Anas. Hot. Hot. Hot. It was a perfect recipe for me to get into an argu-ment with one of the guards when I realized that my new contact lenses were hardening in my eyes like fish scales since there was no saline solution to be found. Convinced I was going to go blind, I demanded to see a doctor, and when the guard wouldn't respond, I muttered something brilliant like, "Fuck you."

That was rewarded with a fast trip to isolation, what turned out to be a brick hut without a roof, the size of a bathroom, not even large enough to lie down in, what they called "the hot box," where I was alone, suddenly missing the same prison conversations that had been driving me crazy earlier. Good thing I'd been talking to myself most of my life, as I began a two-way conversation by saying out loud, "Oh, man, this done gone from bad to worse, bro."

"No shit, man," I commiserated as best I could.

"So why they say they got to cool you off in the hot box? That's some kind of an oxymoron." With the sun baking down, it was demonically hot. Then again, it could rain, and there would be nothing to do but get wet.

When I ran out of small talk to make with myself, I started singing, then eventually just made noise, all in an effort to block out the fear: How did this happen? What was going to happen now?

The hot box cooled me off only to the extent that I tried to reasonably request a hearing to get to the funeral for Sebastian, knowing what it would mean to Latrell. But after quietly and calmly making my requests, I was turned down.

After serving my ten days, in lieu of paying the parking tickets, they were no longer an issue. Now, as I wearily awaited transfer back to the Berkeley jailhouse where I could have my hearing to find out if there was a charge from Jackie's complaint, I faced what I considered the biggest problem of this whole ordeal. The interview at Dean Witter was scheduled for the next morning. All those months and months of effort had come down to my last shot with the fellow who could say yay or nay to my future as a stockbroker. But upon arriving at the Berkeley jailhouse, I learned that I couldn't see the judge until the next morning. What to do? How could I show up at Dean Witter when I was still in jail?

The answer came in the form of a guard, a Latino brother, who must have gotten up on the right side of the bed that morning and who agreed to let me make a phone call to try to reschedule my meeting. Perhaps it was my begging. Perhaps it was my explaining that I had a real chance at this job, and I really needed it.

Whatever the reason was, he dialed the number and handed me the receiver through the bars into the cell. There I was, behind bars, calling Mr. Albanese at Dean Witter. When he answered, I greeted him warmly, with a "Hello, Mr. Albanese? This is Chris Gardner, how're you doing?"

"Fine," he said.

I went for it: "I've got a meeting with you tomorrow, but something's come up. I need to know if I can reschedule for the following day?"

Heaven smiled on me as he replied, "Fine, no problem. Be here at six-thirty in the morning."

Thank you, Lord, I prayed right in front of the guard. Mr. Albanese had said he was looking forward to meeting me. I told him that I'd see him the day after next.

My legal ordeal with Jackie continued the next morning when we had to meet in court. It was my intention to take the high road, apologize, and find a fair way of sharing equal responsibility for taking care of Christopher. Obviously, our relationship was over. My plan was to head home, get my stuff, and find a place to stay. But Jackie came armed with a desire to punish me, apparently, which resulted in a subsequent court date that was set for several weeks later. When I watched her leave that day, despite what I perceived as an icy cold demeanor on her part, I still had the hope such a court meeting wouldn't be necessary.

My other comfort was the prospect that lay ahead, the possibility that the interview would be the open door to my future. By the time I hit the train heading back to our house, where I planned on packing up fast, spending some time playing with Christopher and figuring out how I could have him come stay with me, wherever I landed next, I was cheered up enough that I was willing to dismiss a gut instinct about how Jackie behaved toward me that day—as if there was another shoe that was going to drop. But after what she'd already put me through, that didn't seem plausible, so I let it go.

Nothing was out of the ordinary as I walked down the path to the house and up the steps to the front door. It was only when I glanced at the window that it struck me as odd that there were no curtains there. Hmmm. What was wrong with this picture? The bombshell exploded when I peered inside the window and saw that the house was empty. Bare. No Jackie. No Christopher. No furniture, stereo, pots and pans, clothes. No car on the street. The locks had been changed.

In a frantic, anguished daze, I stumbled down the sidewalk, approaching anyone who'd talk to me. "Where's my son?" I asked neighbors and strangers alike. "Where's Jackie?"

One woman, her close friend and a semi-landlord, wouldn't tell me anything. "You shouldn't have beat her," she scolded. "Don't ask me, 'cause I don't know nothing."

Obviously she knew everything. In fact, I was doubly mortified that everyone seemed to know what had happened except for me. It was too late to defend myself against whatever Jackie had said about me. All that mattered was that Jackie and Christopher had seemingly fallen off the face of the earth and I had to find them.

And first I had to find somewhere to sleep that night, and I had to go to the job interview the next morning in bellbottom blue jeans, T-shirt, maroon Members Only jacket (which matched the sporty maroon car I used to have), and the paint-speckled Adidas sneakers that had become my work shoes for odd jobs—the same outfit I'd gone to jail in and spent most of the time wearing, other than the prison orange PJs and jellies.

Days after she had buried her son, a subdued Latrell Hammonds took my phone call and said it was no problem for me to come over, wash my clothes there, and stay on her couch that night. Falling to sleep was difficult, especially as it came over me that these days and nights ever since the police drove me to the station had marked the first time in his life that I had been physically separated from Christopher. When I did finally give in to sleep, I didn't dream at all as the conscious question rammed insistently all night long in my brain: *Where is my son?*

CHAPTER 10

California Dreamin'

D elivery's in the rear," says Mr. Albanese of Dean Witter, glancing up at me from his cup of coffee and his *Wall Street Journal* as I approach his desk at 6:15 A.M. that next morning.

Fortunately, no one else in the firm is in yet in this part of the office, so I don't have to endure any more embarrassing reactions to my jailhouse attire. True, my jeans are washed, and my Members Only jacket isn't too wrinkled. But the paint-speckled sneakers make me look like exactly what Mr. Albanese apparently thinks I am—a delivery guy or some dude who's wandered in from the street.

"Mr. Albanese," I say as I step forward and introduce myself, "Chris Gardner. We've got an appointment this morning at six-thirty, and I'm sorry I'm early."

"That's all right," he says. "I'm an early riser."

"I am too." I nod, go-getter that I am. Now I see that he's taking a closer look at me, my cue to come up with a genius explanation for my lack of professional attire. After a beat, I begin: "Today might be the most important day of my career, and I must admit, I'm underdressed for the occasion."

Apparently not amused by my attempt at irony, he agrees: "So I see," then adds, "What happened?"

None of the lies that I can conjure in this instant are either bizarre or plausible enough to answer him. So I tell the truth, minus the part about going to jail, but including pretty much everything that's happened recently: Jackie emptying the house, taking everything, including my car, and especially how she has my son and I don't know where either of them are.

Listening intently, Mr. Albanese interrupts me before I can get out my last sentence: "You think what you're going through is rough? Try having to put up with three different broads pulling the same stuff!" Turns out, he's been married and divorced three times, taken to the cleaners each time, and he launches into a series of stories about his ex-wives. For twenty minutes he rants and raves. Just when I think we can segue back to the main question of my future, he remembers something else: "And then this gal I was seeing, let me tell you what she did."

The truth is that I'm here to tell him why I'm going to be an asset to Dean Witter in the firm's training program, and I am not so much interested in commiserating. But obviously this is a very cool guy, so I listen and nod and say at appropriate times: "Oh my God!"

Finally, he spends his wad. Instead of hearing me out or asking me questions, he stands up from his desk, takes a slug of coffee, and says, "Be here on Monday morning, and I'll walk you into the training session personally."

Just like that. The heretofore-locked gates to Wall Street had opened. I was in! It wasn't a million dollars in my pocket or the keys to my own red Ferrari, but it was validation. The funny part was that after worrying about my clothes—and only later learning that Jackie had taught herself to drive a stick shift in order to get our car, which I never saw again, and take Christopher to the East Coast, along with the key to the storage locker where she put all my stuff—the story about why I was underdressed was how I bonded with Albanese. It just went to show that God does work in mysterious ways.

Of course, there were no guarantees. As a trainee, I would make a stipend of $1,000 a month, and between putting in the actual training hours, assisting the brokers around the office later in the day, and studying every other waking hour for the exam, there wouldn't be a moment left over to earn any additional income. That was going to mean some very lean living. It also meant that until that first stipend check came in at the end of the first month, I had some major issues to tackle.

By that next Monday I'd been able to secure some nights on various friends' couches, line up some meals, borrow enough money to ride BART to work, and find a buddy willing to loan me a suit and a pair of shoes that would get me to that first check. The suit was two sizes too small, and the shoes were two sizes too big. Even so, I walked tall and proud into work that first day, surprised to see a face I'd first seen there several months earlier. A brother named Bob—or "Bow Tie Bob," as I had dubbed him on account of his ever-present bow tie and horn-rimmed glasses and milquetoast, country club demeanor—who was a Stanford graduate and the first African American ever put in the training program. After I'd met him back when I first started stopping by, I was just eager to talk to anybody and happy to see another brother in there. Introducing myself, I'd said, "Wow, you're in here? Wow! How did you get in? What do I need to do to get over? What did you do?"

At the time of those first conversations, Bow Tie Bob had only recently started the training program and seemed more interested in talking about how he had graduated from Stanford, where he played on the golf team, than about how he had broken the color barrier in the financial world. Since it was obvious that I had no credentials, hadn't even gone to college, belonged to no clubs, and didn't play golf. He didn't have much reason to talk to me at all, although the looks he threw at me were quite articulate, saying in essence: *Where did you come from?*

For all I knew, Bow Tie Bob could have grown up in Watts. But he had gone to Stanford—which I wasn't knocking in the least—where it appeared his whole life history had begun and ended, and he had molded himself into the whitest black boy I'd ever met. At least that was my take earlier on.

In an interesting twist, I discovered that Bob was still in the basement, in the same training program, because he had yet to pass his test—after three tries. In the process, he had been transformed from preppy Bow Tie Bob into a radical Bobby Seale. Instead of welcoming me into the program, he greeted me by conveying just what the challenges were and letting me know that the test was culturally biased.

"Really?" I said, wondering if that was true.

"That test will beat you down, oh man," he warned me. "It'll beat you down."

From day one, it was clear to me that I had to do well my first time out of the gate on the test. Business was business, and no matter how much a company wanted to promote equal opportunity, I was sure there was no way they were going to have two black people on the payroll who flunked the test. Circumstances being what they were, I would have one shot. That was why I avoided even associating with Bob, as if his problem, whatever it was, might be catching. After he launched into his culturally biased complaint one too many times, I eventually called him on it, quipping, "Bob, didn't you go to Stanford? Culturally biased? What the hell! You of all people should know that stuff because that's where they teach it." That pretty much was the most contact we had from then on.

In my habit of seeking out individuals from whom I could learn, I hooked up with Andy Cooper, a corner-office guy, one of the top producers at the firm who was selling tax shelters—before the tax laws changed in this era. These deals—usually in real estate, oil, or natural gas—could yield huge write-offs, anywhere from two-to-one up to four-to-one. The basic way these tax shelters were sold was to call and invite prospective investors to a seminar.

From the advice given to me by Bob Bridges, I established standards of discipline as to how many phone calls I made every day, with two hundred being my daily requirement, no matter how discouraging the responses. Since Cooper had seen that I was pretty disciplined on the phone, he gave me the job of calling the tax shelter leads and getting them there in person, where he made the pitch, closed the deals, and took all the commissions. As a trainee, I was doing the grunt work for free, something that I didn't quite grasp until later. But it actually didn't matter to me. All I cared about was succeeding in this business, learning everything I could, and getting as much experience as possible.

When I wasn't training, working, or studying, all I cared about was finding out where Christopher was and reuniting with him. But that worry raised the ongoing problem that I had nowhere to live other than at Latrell's, at her mother's back house, where I had a room to myself; at Leon Webb's crib, where I crashed on the floor; at the apartment of my childhood friend Garvin's briefly; or occasionally with a couple of different women who didn't mind sharing their beds and their cooking, though I didn't have much to offer in return other than my lasting appreciation.

Unbeknownst to me, I was fine-tuning the ability to move frequently, even constantly, unaware of how critical these skills were going to become. After that first stipend came in, I went out immediately to buy a better suit. With the suit I wore on my back, the other one on a hanger in a garment bag slung over my shoulder, a few toiletries, and my books, I was self-contained. Rather than leave my stuff at anyone's house, I got in the habit of keeping everything with me. One evening at work when I hadn't lined up a place to stay that night, it occurred to me that since I was usually one of the last to leave the office, no one would be the wiser if I slept under my desk. After all, I was usually the first one there in the morning too.

That first night was strange, like I was going to get found out—

not for sleeping at work, but for not having anywhere else to stay. But the fact was that I wasn't like Bow Tie Bob, who kept getting more chances, and I wasn't like Donald Turner, who was in the training program with me and whose big brother was a top pro- ducer at the firm: True or not, the other guys had infrastructures in their lives that I did not. Donald was high-strung and intent on passing, but if he didn't, his brother had his back, no question. Not that I felt sorry for myself, because that wasn't going to help me. But I had to face facts: there was no backup plan, no safety net, nobody needing me to succeed to make themselves look good. This was all on me. If I needed to sleep under the desk, then that was what I would do.

After a couple nights, I discovered that sleeping at work was not only convenient but cut down on train fare and there was no bed to make. I would just lie down, sleep, get up before anyone got there, wash my face, freshen up as best I could, brush my teeth and hair, splash water from the sink on my body, paper-towel off, and get some deodorant action going. Sometimes I had the same clothes on, and sometimes I changed my suit and shirt—which I had in my hanging bag. By the time others walked in, I was already on the phone, making sure I got a head start on those two hundred calls a day. I would finish up relatively early in the evening, making sure I didn't call too late. Then it was back to studying.

During the weeks that followed, whenever worries about what I couldn't control overcame me, my focus saved me. If I could just put my head mentally in the call—being positive and friendly but sticking to business, in a time-efficient, productive manner—and create that discipline to keep going, keep dialing, keep putting the phone down and picking it up, then I could survive until night, when I could hit the books, which were really mind-numbingly technical but which I convinced myself were as captivating as the greatest stories ever told. Years of hearing Momma tell me that the public library was the most dangerous place in the world because you could go in there and figure out how to do anything *if* you could read, I also convinced myself that all this information I was learning in preparation for my exam was going to give me that competitive edge so I could pass it that first time.

When my brain wanted to give up, my attitude was that I had to study like I was in prison—because knowledge was power and freedom. An image rode along with me of Malcolm X in prison, teaching himself by studying the dictionary, starting with "aardvark."

With all this moving around, though, I hadn't had any luck locating Jackie and my baby. In fact, she was the one who actually managed to track me down and begin a series of torturous phone calls. At Latrell's, when she first called and asked for me, I got on the phone and was met with sheer silence from Jackie and the sound of Christopher screaming in the background. So I replied with sheer silence, my stomach tied up in knots. It was the first time but not the last, and whether by coincidence or not, every time she called, wherever she found me, Christopher would be crying in the background. Every time, I was in full-blown anguish, but my training from the Navy, and from the stillness I saw in my mother when she was under assault, kept me from saying a word. Finally, unable to provoke me, she would hang up. The *click* echoed for a long time after I put the receiver down.

Each time I went through the process of mentally changing the channel, dialing into the frequency that tuned me into what I was studying. Sometimes the thought of Bow Tie Bob helped me kick into overdrive, reminding me of the test's requirements. With a 60 percent or higher failure rate, it covered the Wall Street gamut—financial instruments, products, stocks, bonds, municipal bonds, corporate bonds, convertible stock, preferred stock and regulations—to a depth rarely covered in college business courses or even in some MBA programs. Containing 250 multiple-choice questions, the test had several sections, and I would have to pass 70 percent across the board—options, equities, debt, municipal finance, corporate finance, regulations, rules. Failing even one section was automatic failure of the whole test.

With enough money from the stipends, I found a low-cost rooming house in Oakland, not too far from downtown and Lake Merritt. For all intents and purposes, it was a flophouse, though decently kept up, that included three meals a day or whatever I could eat while I was there. This was a different world than any I'd lived in before, with people just barely scraping by, some with mental problems or addictions, one stumble away from falling through the cracks. Not that I was judging, but I couldn't relate. The rooming house was just a temporary, low-cost option where I could sleep, study, and eat on the occasions that I made it back in time for the evening meal.

For a while I was able to eat during the day whenever tasked with gofer work to set up the conference room for Andy Cooper. As trainees, Donald Turner and I were responsible not only for making the initial calls to leads and following with mailings and more phone calls but for putting out the sandwiches and other light refreshments before the seminars began. If people didn't show, the sandwiches definitely didn't go to waste. Constantly hungry, I didn't mind being asked to do that job at all.

At the same time, I had started to look beyond my exam, at climbing the Dean Witter ladder, and wasn't sure it was such a good idea to cast myself too much in Andy Cooper's crew. For Donald Turner—whose brother was already established and aligned with Cooper, there wasn't much choice. Part of the reason he was so high-strung was the very real pressure on him to live up to expectations based on his brother's star performance.

He had to produce, especially when he was already being spoon-fed business—not all the time, but often enough—from his brother's contacts. This seemed to only make Donald, already pale, go whiter. About my age, clean-shaven, with his red hair combed like a schoolboy's across the front, he had a small, thin voice and a way of finishing up his pitches and his phone calls by saying, "All right, bye-bye."

I wanted to lean over and say, *Who the hell are you saying* bye-bye *to?*

And he had the good leads. Me, I made the cold calls. I didn't know them, they didn't know me, but they knew the name of the company and took my call. OJT allowed me to develop three important skills. First, I had to make my call quota. Next, I had to learn how to quickly assess whether this was someone who was just chatty or really worth pursuing. Finally, I had to know when it was time to wrap up. This became a game for me—to know if the prospect was getting ready to say no or hang up on me. My internal mantra was: *I'm going to hang up on you before you hang up on me.* But to my prospect, I said "ThankyouverymuchHaveaniceday" as if it were one long word.

This way, no matter the outcome, I could win. In order to not seem rude, I'd always say the same thing: "Thank you very much, have a nice day," as clearly and quickly as I could. Polite and businesslike, I didn't have to hear no or the angry sound of the phone being hung up, the call didn't reflect badly on me or the company, and I could be on to the next call—dialing the old-fashioned rotary phone, like cranking away at a lottery wheel.

Whenever I stopped, with nothing else to concentrate on, there was nowhere else to go in my head except for my powerlessness at finding and seeing Christopher.

The other trainees knew I was intense, obviously. But I saw no reason to confide in anyone where I was staying or what drama was playing out in my personal life. It helped me to reflect on something Momma had said to me way back when I had illusions of becoming an actor—the time I asked her for five dollars and instead of giving it to me, she made a point by suggesting that I act like I had five dollars. That had cooled me off being an actor real fast. But there was something else in her message that became relevant now. No matter what I had in my pocket, no matter what my suit cost, nobody could prevent me from acting *as if* I was a winner. Nobody could prevent me from acting *as if* my problems were all in the process of being solved. Pretty soon, my acting *as if* was so convincing that I started to believe it myself. I began to think futuristically, *as if* I had already passed the test as I weighed what would happen next.

This was what I puzzled over while riding BART over from Oakland and back every day, every night. The patronage system of favors done in return for favors owed had started to make me wary. I realized that, by sticking with Andy Cooper, I'd end up more or less working for him and catching his overflow. That was one route to go, the stepping-stone path, maybe safer, but ultimately less lucrative. The riskier approach was to carve out a niche of my own, to build my own base from scratch. For a new guy who hadn't even passed his test yet, deciding to take that approach would be a couple notches past cocky and just shy of foolhardy. Still, from what I was learning around the office, the major players were the few brokers who did their own thing—putting time into research and combining traditional and nontraditional ways of getting the biggest bang for their clients' bucks and themselves.

Dave Terrace was one of the cats I kept an eye on. With one of the biggest offices at the firm, he traded back where all the heavy hitters sat, behind the floor where us newcomers were, and whenever I could, I turned around to watch him do his thing. Pure business—no flash, solid, consistent. He might not have been making more than Andy Cooper, but he was in solo flight. That appealed to me. My choice was made. As it later turned out, to have gone and hitched a ride on the tax shelter bonanza that Andy and his guys were enjoying would have sent me into the same crash they all faced when the tax laws changed.

The day of the exam arrived. Donald Turner, wound up tighter than ever, looked so stressed I thought he'd kill himself if he didn't pass. Bow Tie Bob wasn't taking the test again at this exam, possibly because he was busy filing complaints about its cultural bias. Maybe to Donald and some of the other trainees I appeared to be annoyingly relaxed. Not so. Inside I had the raised adrenaline and tension of a warrior going into battle, a gladiator ready to take on his most lethal opponent—if need be. But I was prepared. Nothing stumped me; there were no tricks. No cultural bias either. I knew the answers. The test was easy. In fact, I whipped through the first half with time to spare, took the break, and did the same when we came back for the second half of the test.

We had to wait three days to find out the results. That was just enough time for the delayed-reaction freak-out to take place. What if I only thought it was easy? What if I didn't spot the trick questions or the cultural bias? What if the test was about to beat me down after all? Scolding myself, I repeated my mantra that there was nothing on there I'd never seen before and just to leave it alone.

The phone call couldn't have come fast enough. One of the associate branch managers was on the other end when I picked up the phone in my room.

"The suspense is over," he began, waiting for my reaction.

I waited too, saying nothing.

"You passed, Gardner," he chuckled, probably aware of the monstrous sigh of relief and release that came from my lungs. "Overall you scored eighty-eight percent," he went on. "You did great."

Neither surprised nor elated, I was grateful. Sitting on the edge of my bed in the rooming house, I let my mind go blank and just let myself breathe. There was no one to go celebrate with, nobody who understood what this meant. Whether or not Donald Turner passed, I never knew. But I did know that my colleague Bow Tie Bob wasn't going to be thrilled.

What did it mean? That I passed the test, but only one test. Like

I'd won a qualifying race for the Olympics. My training was over and I was ready to compete. Now I was going back to scratch, back to cold-calling out of the white pages. I was going in to build my own book, whatever it took, cranking out calls that I'd pitch and close, finding my niche. In some ways, the stakes had just gotten higher than before when the company had an investment in training me. That was done. Now I had to produce. But something had changed. No longer did I have to prove a damn thing. My confidence was as big as the Pacific Ocean. I had passed. Finally, I was legitimate. I had my papers.

———

Jackie sits across from me at the Berkeley coffee shop, a month or so later on a Friday afternoon, as I try hard not to be rattled, no matter what she throws at me.

It has been four months since she left with my son, and our car that I'll never see again, putting me out into the cold. That alone is bizarre, but we have also just come from court, where things have taken an additionally strange turn.

In the days leading up to the court date, she had placed a few calls to me and had actually spoken, refusing to let me talk to Christopher or to give me any information as to his whereabouts, but baiting me with some details—like the fact that she taught herself to drive a stick shift in order to drive across the country and that she had lots of lawyer power. The lawyer was a "brother," someone I'd come to refer to as a "poindexter"—a dry, bland, non-threatening eunuch. Though I suspected that she meant her brother the lawyer, when I walked into the hearing with my lawyer—whose fee cost me most of my salary that first month as a broker—I saw that her representation power consisted of someone from the local DA's office, representing the state, and the arresting police officer.

The next surprise was that Jackie decided not to bring charges. Just like that. In my analysis, right or wrong, it seemed that all of this had been Jackie's way of having contact with me. That was supported by her suggestion that we go somewhere and talk.

Fine. Here we are. She seems to know where I live, like she's been keeping tabs on me, which indicates that she knows I passed the test. But she's got nothing to say about that. Sure, maybe she has some sour grapes. After all, she never believed I could do it without the college degree, or possibly she was projecting her own insecurities, or maybe she has other people telling her that she's missing her dream while I'm chasing mine. Whatever is the case, of course she doesn't congratulate me that I have the license and the job. But then again, she has something that I don't have—our son. Oh yeah, and she has my stuff. Not that there's much I could use at the moment, given my temporary lodging, which in the foreseeable future isn't about to change.

My decision not to be part of the Cooper Clan wasn't the most practical initially. In terms of commissions, I was at about $1,200 a month now, though I could have made more had I been willing to help set up bigger deals for Andy to commission for himself while taking over some of his smaller deals as they became available. Instead, I wanted to nab bigger and smaller deals for myself, even though there was no promise that I'd get either. That was my choice—I had a higher ceiling but less of a floor. I approached the numbers game with eyes open, knowing full well that X number of calls equals X number of prospects equals X number of sales equals X number of clients equals X number of gross commissions, or dollars in my pocket. Out of two hundred calls, a great batting average was ten first-time clients, with half that many turning into repeat customers—where money was made. Doing my own thing, I was the assembly line, cranking, dialing, and smiling. I was good, so good that several more senior brokers made overtures to me to collaborate with them, to help boost their numbers. Whenever they did, without being ungrateful, I typically responded, "No, I don't think I'll take you up on that. I just want to build my own book. But thanks for thinking of me."

This entitled me to be named, nearly continuously, the "Broker of the Day." At first, this sounded like an honor, a step up. Broker of the Day was the point man for any office walk-ins who didn't already have a broker or an account at the firm. Usually walk-ins wanted specific information or had an idea of something they might want to buy. In San Francisco, where peace and free love had ruled not many years earlier, there were nonetheless racial biases in 1982, and it was soon clear that these walk-ins weren't expecting to see a black man as a stockbroker. That added another layer of challenge, but I acted as if it wasn't an issue and offered my full assistance. "How do you do? I understand you want to buy a Ginnie Mae?" We'd go over the particulars. Or: "You want to put money away for your grandkids? Yes, I have some suggestions."

A few times, after I had laid all the groundwork and basically written up the ticket, I subsequently learned that I hadn't gotten the commission. Why? "Well," the branch manager said on those occasions, "they wanted someone with more experience."

The first time this happened I steamed. The second time I confronted my boss. "Let me see if I got this right? They're basically buying stock in Commonwealth Edison, correct? To get the dividend yield, the income, it's not going to change based on who gets the commission. Same stock, same company. But they wanted someone with a little more experience? He gets the commission that I set up?"

It wasn't rocket science. The reality was that people had never dealt with a black person before and didn't want to, even though I'd done a great job and made them some money. But I was learning that I could turn down being Broker of the Day. Back I went to smiling and dialing. The lesson here wouldn't necessarily apply to other guys, but for me it was apparent that I did better on the phone. If I could get someone excited about the opportunity to make some money, if we could make the connection, that was the way to go. Besides, though I could resort to the vernacular any time, any day, I was not audibly black on the phone. Maybe that stemmed from the knack of learning other languages—musical, medical, financial, Anglo-Saxon, whatever. And a name like Chris Gardner? No telltale ethnicity there. I could have been anybody from any background.

The phone became my color shield. I actually discouraged new clients from coming into the office in person, which was one of the ways other brokers liked to close their deals. "Okay, here's what we're going to do," I'd say once we established that we were going to do some business. "Let's open the account, send me in the check, and we'll get the company to send your confirmations out, and we'll just get going. Will you be mailing the check today or would you like to do a wire transfer?"

When folks wanted to come in, I had an easy way of saying, "No, that's not necessary, because it's so hectic and crazy in here. Let's do it over the telephone."

After the four months since Jackie had split with Christopher, the ball was definitely starting to roll, but it hadn't translated into much of a change in my income yet. I had no outward symbol of my success so far to wave like a flag in front of Jackie.

Instead, I give her as little insight into where I'm at as she's giving me about my kid. Finally, she slides a key in my direction and tells me where the storage locker is that contains my stuff. But what I want most, she refuses to offer—my child. With the least amount of reaction I can give, I pocket the key and leave, reeling inside.

Well, I think, before I truck back to Oakland, I don't have anywhere to put my stuff yet, but at least I can go dig out a couple items of clothing and my trusty briefcase that I purchased almost a year earlier when I first made my foray into the business world.

Later that night at the rooming house, as I'm airing out the suit and shining the shoes that I pulled from storage, I pause to admire my stylish, brown-leather Hartman briefcase—something I'd spent what seems like an exorbitant $100 on. Just then, I'm startled by the sound of firm knocking at the door. The rhythm of the three knocks—short, short, *long*—reminds me of Jackie's way of knocking. But then again, that's highly unlikely.

Sure enough, as I open the door, there she is. Not alone. In Jackie's arms is Christopher. My son, my baby! He's nineteen or twenty months now—looking more like three years old, more beautiful than I had remembered him in my every waking and sleeping recollection. Between my shock and my euphoria, I don't know what to say.

There is more shock and more euphoria to come as Jackie hands him to me and as she does says, "Here." From behind her she produces a huge, overstuffed duffel bag and his little blue stroller. Again she says, "Here."

I'm holding Christopher, hugging him tight to me, still not following what's happening.

Slowly it dawns on me that this isn't a visit but that she's actually leaving him in my care. Though she says little, I know her well enough to realize that this is it and that she just can't do this anymore.

From our brief exchange, it's apparent that she is feeling the pressure of raising a child as a single mother at the same time that she is establishing herself professionally. I also sense that she regrets taking him out of state and not working out a joint arrangement earlier on. But none of that is spelled out exactly in words. She does tell me what's inside the duffel bag, including the monster package of Pampers, what he needs to eat and how often, what he shouldn't eat—"no candy"—and then she tells Christopher goodbye and leaves.

"Christopher," I tell him over and over, "I missed you! I missed you!"

"I missed you too, Poppa," he says, talking in a full sentence now and with one of his wise expressions, like he's already a veteran of change and knows we may be in for a rough ride.

Or maybe that's what I'm thinking. Whatever is going to happen, two things I know are true. First of all, I have my son back with me and nobody on this earth is going to take him away from me again. That's a principle of the universe now. Second—and I already know this to be a fact—we have just become instantly fucking homeless.

———

Time changes when you're homeless. Seasons turn out of order, all in the course of a day. Especially in San Francisco, which has all four seasons all year round. During the daylight hours of the working week, time feels sped up, passing way too quickly. Nights and weekends are another story. Everything slows to an ominous crawl.

Your memory changes when you're homeless. Always moving around, changing geography, having no address, no anchors to tie to when events take place. It becomes hard to recall whether something happened a week before or a month before, yesterday or three days ago.

How did I become instantly homeless, especially now that I was a stockbroker working for Dean Witter? Because children were not allowed at the rooming house. No exceptions. The days of crashing on the couch at my friends' homes were over too. I'd imposed enough when I was in the training program, but to ask to stay for a few nights and add, "Oh, by the way, and my baby too?"—that wasn't going to fly. The ladies I was seeing may have been fond of me in the sack but weren't going to be pleased about me showing up with an inquisitive, active toddler.

The one lucky break I caught in trying to figure out how to navigate a whole new terrain was the fact that it was a Friday when

Jackie showed up with Christopher, giving me at least that night at the rooming house before being thrown out the next day. That also gave me the weekend to find us a place to stay and a day care situation starting on Monday.

We hit the streets Saturday with all of our gear, him in the stroller, as I practice the new balancing act that's going to get all too familiar, heading down toward the "HOstro" to check out the price of some of the HO-tels—emphasis on first syllables no accident. I'm having a major internal debate over the questions: *What* am I gonna do? *How* am I gonna do this? One line of thinking says, *I've got my baby, I'm not giving him up, that's not an option.* Another voice reminds me, *Ain't no backup here, no cavalry coming in for reinforcement.*

The day care center in San Francisco at $400 a month is out of the question. With rent at least $600, that would take up what I'm earning after taxes, leaving nothing for food, transportation, and diapers. At a pay phone I call a few friends to see if they've got any inside scoop on day care facilities in the East Bay. One of the places looks wonderful. It too turns out to be over my budget; besides, they don't accept kids who aren't potty-trained.

"Okay, Christopher," I tell him as we start to leave, "we'll work on that, okay, baby?"

As I'm looking around, hoping that it won't be too long until I can afford having him here, I notice that the day care management has a sign on the wall declaring the center to be a place of "HAP-PYNESS."

For a minute, I start to question in my mind how good a child care facility can be that can't even spell "happiness" correctly. Of all the things I have to worry about, that's not one of them. Even so, back out on the street, I feel the need to make sure my son knows that the word is spelled with an *I* and not a *Y*. H-A-P-P-I-N-E-S-S.

"Okay, Poppa," says Christopher, repeating the word. "Happiness."

"That's a big word," I say with approval, wishing that I could ensure Chris's and my own happiness in the immediate future.

The ability to spell is not my main concern when I call the numbers I've been given for Miss Luellen at one house and Miss Bessie at another and a third place on Thirty-fifth Street—babysitters who keep kids on a regular basis but not any kind of day care centers with licenses and registrations. The woman on Thirty-fifth says to bring Christopher early on Monday and says that I can pay her by the week. One hundred bucks. There's no real money savings except that I can pay as I go. Though this doesn't do a lot to reassure me that he's getting the best care possible, it's better than nothing.

For a place to stay that night, I get us a room over in West Oakland on West Street at The Palms, so named for the one palm tree in the courtyard and a second one on the corner two hundred feet away. From what I can tell, the only residents besides us are the hookers. Later, this doesn't bother me, but for the time being all I can do is get us into the room as fast as I can, double-lock the door, and turn the volume up on the TV to make sure we don't have to hear the sound effects of any tricks being turned.

It costs me $25 a day for the room, which comes with a color TV, one bed, a desk and a chair, and a bathroom. But okay, we're here. That's my new philosophy: wherever we are, we're here, this is where we're at, and we're going to make the best of it. For now.

When I managed to step out of the blur of space and time to look at the big picture, the reality was that I had the job and the opportunity that was going to change our circumstances and lives forever. Nothing was going to shake my conviction, not even the mental and actual calculations of what I'd have left over after the cost of The Palms and babysitting, and not even the screaming and sobbing that Christopher began the minute we walked into the babysitter's place.

That killed me. He could probably feel my reluctance to leave him with strangers, but I had no choice. All I could do was reassure him, "I'll be back. I'll be back." Backing out, practically in tears myself, I kept repeating, "I'll be back."

When I came to pick him up that evening, he ran up and almost jumped into my arms. "See, I told you," I reminded him.

But the next morning it was worse. Getting him out of the hotel and into his stroller was a struggle, and he started wailing the second we rolled around the corner onto Thirty-fifth, me chanting all the way in the door and out: "I'll be back. I'll be back. I'll be back."

The days and images begin to streak by as the nights get longer and the air becomes colder and wetter. After picking him up, I usually take him for something to eat, somewhere warm and cheap where I air my concerns with my little sidekick, telling him, "Naw, this ain't gonna work. The Palms is too expensive, man. Remember the house? Yeah, in Berkeley, our little house. It was ours. This transient thing's no good."

Christopher gives me one of his furrowed-brow expressions.

How can I explain to him or myself? It's not just the whores, the dopeheads and winos, and the street lowlifes, it's the feeling of not being settled, of having no home base or support group. It's about the noise and the lights constantly going from the outside because The Palms is right on the drag, the "ho" stroll, with car horns honking, music playing, and people hollering. The TV helps drown some of it out, enough for me to chew on any and all options, to focus on what to do and how.

Every now and then, kindness sprang up out of nowhere, and in the least likely places, as it did one evening when we came back to The Palms and one of the sisters working the street approached us. She and her colleagues had seen me with Christopher in the stroller every morning and night and probably figured out our deal. A black man with a little boy in a stroller, a single dad—it wasn't anything they'd seen before.

"Hey, little player, little pimp," she said as she came close, a candy bar in her hand to give to Christopher. "Here you go."

"No, no," I insisted, maintaining Jackie's rule against sugar, "he don't need any candy."

Christopher, unfortunately, was disappointed and started to cry. "Don't cry," she said and reached down into her magical cleavage and produced a $5 bill, handing that to him.

Did I object? No. Christopher was so happy, he looked like he preferred the money to candy. Smart boy.

"Well, thank you," I muttered, not knowing if she knew that her $5 bill was going to buy us dinner around the corner at Mosell's, a soul-food kitchen both my son and I loved.

The same sister and a couple of the other ladies of the night started giving Christopher $5 bills on a regular basis. In fact, there were some days when we wouldn't have eaten without their help. At my hungriest moments, when we were running on empty, I would roll the stroller by their stretch of the sidewalk, on purpose, moving real slow just in case none of the familiar faces were working the street yet. There was a purity in the help these women gave us, with nothing asked in return. Kindness, pure and simple. On uncertain days, I thought of us as wandering in the desert, knowing that we were being led to a promised land and that God was sending his manna to feed us in a most unique way.

From this point on, nobody could demean a whore in my presence. Of course I don't advocate prostitution, but that's their business and none of mine.

My business was Wall Street, nothing else.

Dialing and smiling, at work I am soon the Master of the Phone, the ultimate cold-call salesperson. It's my life force. My way out. With every single one of those two hundred calls, I'm digging us out of the hole, maybe with a teaspoon, but bit by bit. The urgency increases, driving me that much more when I look at my son and have to leave him every day, knowing I don't have the luxury to just be positive and persevere. No, I've got to get there *today*. It's not like I can cruise for a bit, then crank it up tomorrow. Hell, no. It's *now*. There's nobody handing me business, I'm not Donald Turner with a brother upstairs, and I'm not one of the veterans with existing books just servicing clients. This is all on me. Every phone call is a shot, an opportunity to get a little bit closer to our own place, to the better life I want to live, a life of happiness for me and my son.

Without offering an explanation, on various occasions I brought Christopher to work with me, another sign to my coworkers of my diligence. After everyone left, usually by 5:00 P.M. on the dot, 5:30 at the latest, I would stay on, continuing to call, and then we'd both stretch out and sleep under the desk. The rest of the office was used to my staying late and never seemed to suspect anything. Some were amused, and most of them cheered me on with their usual parting words of, "Go get 'em, go get 'em."

In the morning they reacted the same way when most of them arrived around 7:30 or 8:00 and I was already at my desk, making phone calls, Christopher occupied with a picture book or scribbling on paper. For not even being two, he had an uncanny knack for playing on his own and not distracting me from work.

The only person who seemed puzzled at all was the branch manager, who was typically the first person in the office every day. He never said a word, but I was sure he wondered how I managed to beat him there on those days, with my baby in tow no less.

To my knowledge, no one there knew that I slept under the desk with Christopher on those nights when I didn't have anywhere to go—whether I took him to the babysitter early in the morning, picked him up in the evening, and came back to the office that same night, or whether he stayed with me in the office that day. What they did know was that I was hungry for success. How literally hungry they didn't imagine.

Part of what was driving me were my circumstances. Because

I'd made the decision to build my own book, it was going to take longer to see the dollars in my pocket. I was starting small, building trust, developing relationships; it was like planting seeds, watering them, letting them grow until it was harvest time. It was a process that had its own cycle, often a four- to six-month cycle, sometimes longer. That farming metaphor took me straight into winter, when I knew it was going to be extremely tight until spring. So I cut back on everything, making sure that I carried all our stuff with me every day, juggling the duffel bag, the briefcase, my hanging bag, the Pampers box, and an umbrella as I moved us downstream from The Palms, where a room and a color television cost $25 to a trucker motel that got us a room and black-and-white TV for $10 a day. The neighbors were now mainly truckers and the prostitutes catering to that clientele, right off the freeway. Heavy-duty turnover. After eating, we came home each night and locked up tight, refusing to go out even in nicer weather.

On weekends, when there's no rain, we take advantage of San Francisco's many public parks and opportunities for free entertainment. One of our favorite stops is the children's playground in Golden Gate Park, where Christopher can play in the sandbox or climb on the jungle gym while I sit in a swing, mulling over how to get from today to tomorrow. One day I only have enough money to either get us back to Oakland on BART and stay in the trucker motel or get us a drink and a snack from the refreshment stand.

"No drink, Christopher." I try to calm him down as he starts to cry. "We'll have a drink and popcorn next time." This kills me.

The next time we have the same dilemma, I buy him what he wants, unable to say no this time. That's one of the nights that's balmy enough that we sleep, or try to sleep, on a grassy corner of Union Square, not far from the same spot where the guy who tried to pick me up once called San Francisco "the Paris of the Pacific."

We sleep close to the side of the park that's underneath the

Hyatt Hotel on Union Square, not as luxurious as some of the other hotels in the neighborhood, but clean and modern, a beacon of security and comfort that somehow makes me feel better, even sleeping in its shadows. Diagonally across from our corner is the city's truly dangerous real estate, particularly at night, bordered by the Tenderloin, the part of town where I first lived, back when it was easy to rough it.

But roughing it takes on a whole new meaning in this period. After thinking that I really knew San Francisco, I now come to know the city on a far more intimate basis—not just where there are and aren't hills, but the degree of their angle and grade, the number of steps it takes to push the stroller up them, or how many blocks to walk the long way around to avoid a hill, and even where the cracks in the concrete sidewalks are. Cracks in the concrete. Becoming familiar with cracks in the concrete is not some obsessive-compulsive pursuit, it is a matter of survival for maneuvering a child in a fragile stroller with everything I own on my person—under time and weather constraints.

The rains come hard this winter of 1982 and early 1983, eliminating the options of outdoor free activities or sleeping in the park. Though I've avoided food lines, I can't anymore, not with a hungry little boy, and we soon start making our way over to Glide Memorial Church in the Tenderloin, where the Reverend Cecil Williams and activists in the community have been feeding the homeless and hungry down in the church basement, at Moe's Kitchen, three times a day, seven days a week, three hundred sixty-five days of the year.

The best part for me is that on Sundays after church services, instead of standing outside in the lines that go down the street and around the corner, we can take a different route through the building and down the steps to Moe's. But no matter how we get there, as I take a tray and start down the cafeteria line, I see only dignity—no matter how fragile—in all the faces lined up with me, all of them adults, none with children, some who look like they're working like me, others who are definitely unemployed.

You never felt like you were less after going there to eat. You were in line with men, women, blacks, whites, Latinos, Chinese, like the United Nations, many at different stages of some kind of issue: drugs, alcohol, violence, poverty, or borderline crazy, on medication, on hard times. But we were just there to eat.

There were no questions, no interrogations or credentials required for being needy. It didn't feel like a handout. It was more like someone's mother wanting to feed you—*Boy, you sit down and get something to eat.* And when we got to the food, it was an ample serving, not skimpy, but hearty and tasty. American fare. More manna.

In later years I would have to tell everyone at Glide to warn folks what can happen to children when you start them off eating at Moe's Kitchen. In fact, Christopher later shot up to six-foot-eight, 260 pounds. He could really eat at Moe's, even as a toddler. When you left, you were never hungry, and it wasn't just that you weren't hungry, you felt better. You felt better because you couldn't wear out your welcome at Glide. You couldn't wear out your welcome at Moe's Kitchen.

The Reverend's sermons fed my soul too, reminding me of what I kept forgetting—that the baby steps counted, even if it wasn't happening as fast as I desired. After church service, without fail, the Reverend stood outside the sanctuary in the hallway or on the steps outside, hugging every single person as they left. Anybody who wanted a hug got a hug. First time I went to get a hug, it felt like Cecil Williams knew me even before he knew me. With what looked to be a smile permanently etched on his wise, round, ageless, handsome face, and with his larger-than-life stature that convinced me he was much taller than he really was, his arms were outstretched as he bear-hugged me and said: "Walk that walk."

I hugged him back, blessing him with my thanks, telling him I was going to walk that walk, not just talk the talk, that I was going forward.

Later, the Reverend admitted that I came to his attention because it was so unusual to see a man standing in a food line with a baby. There wasn't anything I had to explain about my situation. He seemed to know. Not just that he could see I was a single father, but that he could see who I was, my degree from God, as Moms would have said, my good, my soul, my potential. Maybe that was why, when I found out about the homeless hotel he had started down the street, he agreed that I could stay there.

Kindness personified. The first homeless hotel in the country, housed in the Concord Plaza at O'Farrell and Powell, started by Cecil with the ambitious idea of giving women and children without homes a place in which to transition, to start over, to be empowered. Many eventually went on to work at the hotel, at the restaurant, or in one of the many different expanding programs that Glide offered. Though rooms were free for the night, for reasons of safety, fairness, and efficiency, there were rules of conduct that had to be followed explicitly.

When I talked to the Reverend, I acknowledged that obviously I wasn't a woman, but I was homeless and I did have a child. Most importantly, I had a job. I just needed someplace to live until I could put together the money to get an apartment.

"Fine," he said, not thinking twice. He had been watching me with Christopher. He trusted me. "Go on down there," he reassured me, letting me know who to see and what to say.

When I stepped inside the first time, I was swept up in a sea of fading pea green—pea green carpet and peeling pea green wallpaper. Looking pretty much like any skid row Tenderloin hotel, it had been taken over by Glide and just needed work—just as all of us in many of the programs at Glide needed some work, some TLC, some time. But it was beautiful to me all the same. The deal was this. No one was admitted into the hotel before 6:00 P.M., and everyone had to be out by 8:00 A.M. No one received a key. No going out once you were in for the night, and no leaving your things in the room because they'd be gone when you returned. When you left the room, you took everything you owned with you. No one was assigned the same room two nights in a row.

It was catch-as-catch-can. And if you didn't get there early, before the hotel filled up, you were out of luck. There were no reservations, no one giving you special treatment and saying, "We knew you were coming so we held you a spot."

The rooms were all different, most of them with just the basics—a bed and a bathroom. Some rooms had televisions. Really, Christopher and I cared more about getting fed at Glide and checking in at night, knowing we were set until tomorrow, than about what was on television.

For the rest of my life, there will never be enough I can do for Cecil Williams and Glide. He was so beautiful to me, to my son, and to generations of San Franciscans from all corners of the community. Every Sunday morning in church, as I prayed to find my way out of the problems of this period, I just knew that if I could hold on, everything would be so fine I'd never have a care in the world after that.

Well, of course, as I later would learn, it doesn't work like that. Anyone who believes that money saves all has never had any money—like me back then. The late great rapper Notorious BIG put it best when he said, "Mo' Money Mo' Problems." What I would discover was that while money is better to have than not to have, it not only doesn't fix all problems but brings with it problems that Chris Gardner circa the early 1980s couldn't have imagined. The only glimmer of the future that I had that was correct was the idea that whatever success I was able to achieve, I was going to share some with Glide, to put it back into Cecil's hands, even if I didn't yet know how.

Did I ever in my wildest, most confident visions imagine that I would help bankroll a $50 million project that Cecil Williams and Glide would undertake twenty-five years later to purchase a square block of real estate in order to create affordable housing for lower-income families and a complex of businesses and retail shops to create employment opportunity—right there in the Tenderloin where I used to count the cracks in the sidewalk, a block away from Union Square and $500-a-night hotels, not to mention the most expensive stores in the city like Neiman Marcus and Gucci? Not for a minute.

All I knew was that if the Reverend had not been there, my dreams might never have come to pass. Maybe something else would've happened or someone else would have stepped forward. It's hard, though, to conceive of having the same incredible good fortune of being able to walk alongside greatness like his. Later married to the renowned Japanese American poet Janice Murikatani, Cecil was already a prominent social leader, someone who seemed tuned in at a higher level than most human beings. The important thing is that he was there, and he would be there long after I was blessed to have had his help, not just talking the talk with brilliant oratory but walking the walk—feeding, teaching, helping, sparking miracles daily.

An instant miracle took place for me once Cecil took us in. Without having to spend $300 to $600 a month on somewhere to sleep, I was able to get Christopher back into the San Francisco day care center in Hayes Valley, now at a cost of $500, but it was a place where I knew he was getting great care. Every morning, long before 8:00 A.M., I had us packed up with all our gear as I performed my poor impression of a man pretending to have eight arms, somehow holding the umbrella over my head after setting up the tent over the stroller and Christopher from the sheets of dry-cleaner plastic as we took off.

To get on the bus wasn't even worth it because unbalancing my hanging bag, the umbrella, the briefcase, the duffel bag, and the box of Pampers and then trying to fold up the stroller was more trouble than just walking the extra fifteen minutes. Even in the rain. That was, as long as I could avoid the hills. The good news was that I could park our car (the stroller) at day care, stash our stuff in it, and then hop on the bus downtown to the office.

On the weekends we had to be out of Concord Plaza during the day. These rules were stringent. There was no just laying up. You either went to work or to look for work. Christopher and I already had a routine of pursuing every free bit of entertainment in the city. We went to the park, the museum, the park, the museum, park, museum, then maybe we'd go see friends, or if we had a couple of extra bucks, we'd ride the train over to Oakland, go visiting and get something to eat, and head back in time to make sure we got into a room.

As long as I could stay in the light, figuratively speaking, by keeping my focus on what I could control, worry and fear were kept at bay. That's why I pinned my concentration to tasks in front of me, not letting myself agonize about the grade of the hill I was pushing our unwieldy ride up, but studying every crack and crevice in the concrete sidewalk, studying the sounds of the stroller wheels, noticing that I could move to that syncopated beat. Sometimes the effort made me happy, it let me dance, when some might have said that I didn't have anything to dance about. It made me happy to put money away, in small $100 or $50 increments, to just deposit it and not touch it, to not even think about it but to know I was doing something to move us closer to the goal of having our own place.

In order not to touch my stash, there were occasions when I sold blood, each time swearing I'd never do it again. It wasn't the shame of having to go there that ate at me, although I wasn't proud that I was choosing between the lesser of two evils—whether to sell blood so as to be able to afford a room if we missed the cutoff at the shelter or sleep in the park. What haunted me were some of the down-and-outers I saw at the clinic; some had made some bad choices, and some had gotten there through no choices of their own.

One rainy evening after I tore out of the Dean Witter office fifteen minutes late, raced across town on the bus and sprinted up the several steps to Christopher's room at the day care center, packed us up and then hauled ass at top speed over to the Tenderloin, we missed check-in at Concord Plaza by ten minutes.

Pissed, tired, wet, I head toward Union Square, walking Christopher under the awnings of the hotels and stores. With payday a week away, I have enough money for us to eat dinner and ride the train, which I've done before, just riding through the night until we've both had a little sleep and the morning comes. Aw, man, I realize, five more bucks and I could get us over to the trucker hotel for the night. Tense and tired, I get this whiff of cigarette smoke that smells so good. Of all the things that I'm not going to spend money on, it's cigarettes. But a Kool menthol cigarette right about now would definitely take the edge off.

"Poppa," Christopher says as we pass by the entryway to the Hyatt Embarcadero, "I gotta go to the bathroom."

"You do?" I say excitedly, since we've been working to get him out of Pampers. "Okay, now, you hold on, we'll get a bathroom," and I roll us right into the Hyatt lobby and follow signs to the back and down the steps to the men's room. After he does his thing, most successfully, we exit the bathroom and I notice a hotel guest, suit-and-tie guy, at the cigarette machine, putting in his quarters— ten of them—but having no luck getting the machine to give him his pack of cigarettes. Not about to walk away, he starts pounding the machine, rocking and humping it so that the cigarettes will fall down, apparently.

"Sir," says a bellman who comes to see what the ruckus is about, "that's okay, it must be broken. Just go to the front desk and tell them you lost your money. They'll give you a refund."

The hotel patron heads upstairs, and I follow, watching him weave through the crowd in the lobby and approach the front desk, soon pocketing the refund.

Two bucks fifty cents just like that. It's so easy, I have to give it a try. But instead of jumping on it immediately, Christopher and I mill about, acting *as if* we're patrons. Then I approach the young lady at the front desk and tell her about losing my change in the cigarette machine.

"So sorry," she nods, opening up a cash drawer, "somebody else lost their money earlier. We've got to put a note on that machine."

"Good idea," I say, graciously accepting my "refund" of two dollars and fifty cents.

That little hustle worked so well, I gave it a shot at the St. Francis, at the Hyatt Union Square, and at a couple of other hotels that same evening. With twenty-five or so hotels in the vicinity, in the days that followed I scored at as many as ten hotels at a time, making twenty-five extra dollars a day. Being really slick about it, I made sure that I slid in after a shift change, just so that nobody would recognize me from a previous time.

After two weeks of this, I called it quits before my luck ran out. Later, when I did pick up my cigarette habit again and could afford it, I figured that I paid back the tobacco companies big-time. As for the hotels, in years to come I would repay my debts to many of them many times over, although in early 1983, not long after Christopher's second birthday, that was not a future I could see.

While that million dollars and that red Ferrari I was going to drive one day still existed in the abstract of the future, there came a point when it wasn't like I could reach out and almost grab on to them anymore. My feet hurt, my body ached. A darkness began to seep into the days, not just outside in the weather, but in my head. At the office, no, that was where the sun was shining, where the brightness of my potential buoyed my spirits, where the crops I'd been planting were starting to bud all over the place. But the second I left work, my spirits dipped—because always in the back of my mind I knew that if the bus ran late, or if Christopher wasn't zipped into his cold-weather clothes fast enough, or if we got to the shelter late, or if I didn't have time to pick something up to eat before we went up to the room and locked ourselves in, I had to come up with a plan B right away.

Having to compartmentalize and organize all our stuff to keep it contained, like in the military, was beating me down. Everything had to be rolled up and ready to go at a moment's notice, everything had to be able to be located at all times, what you needed when you needed it—a sock, a Pamper, a shirt, a toothbrush, Christopher's clothes, a hairbrush, a book that someone left on the train that I was reading, a favorite toy. It started getting heavy, all that shit I was carrying and the weight of the stress and fear.

Weekends, when I tried to do fun things for Christopher and give him a sense of normalcy, I still had to carry the stuff. At the parks, the museums. At church.

The worst of this period takes place in approximately March, right when I know things are really about to bloom at work, and this one night I roll in to the front desk at the shelter, where they all know me, and I hear, "Well, Chris, we're all full, sorry."

What can I do? Out on the street, I head to the BART station, asking Christopher, "You want to go look at the airplanes at the Oakland airport?"

We've done this drill before, taking public transportation out to one of the two airports and finding a waiting area with semicomfortable benches—where we look like we're travelers anyway. As we ride over to Oakland and approach the MacArthur BART station, Christopher tells me he has to go to the bathroom, and I roll us off the train and head to an individual bathroom I've used there before—where I recall it being possible to lock the door from inside. As soon as we're in there I realize that we don't have to leave immediately. We can rest, wash up, take our time, even sleep.

"We're gonna wait," I explain to Christopher, " 'cause it's rush hour right now. So we're gonna wait in here and be quiet, all right?" I make up a game called "Shhh"—I tell him that no matter how loud someone knocks on the door, the object is not to say a word. No matter what.

MacArthur, a major transfer point in Oakland, is probably the largest station in the BART system, with every subway train coming through. With so much activity, they keep the bathrooms pretty clean, but they're much in demand. In no time, the pounding on the door starts—people obviously don't want to wait. But eventually we can hear the train coming and that wave leaves as those travelers probably realize they can use the bathroom in their own home. As it gets later the knocking becomes much more sporadic.

With no windows, no ventilation, no natural light, the bathroom was tiled from floor to ceiling and wasn't more than ten-by-five, with one toilet and one small wash basin and a mirror made out of reflective stainless steel. By turning off the light, it was completely dark—dark enough that if I was really tired I could sleep. Christopher had a gift for sleeping everywhere and anywhere. I couldn't bring myself to stay in there for too long, only once or twice staying the night, but for a short period, maybe a little more than two weeks, the blessed mercy of BART's public facilities gave me needed shelter during the darkest part of homelessness.

Maybe the reason I was able to see it that way came from the dual life I was living. At night, on weekends, and after hours, it was the dark side of California dreamin': being kept out, sneaking into fancy hotel lobbies to get out of the rain, wishing to be anywhere else but in that BART-station bathroom. By day redemption came from the fact that I was living the great American dream, pursuing opportunity, pushing myself to the limits of my abilities and loving every minute of it. My intimate knowledge of BART became a blessing in other ways. Many years later my firm was selected to be the senior manager on hundreds of millions of dollars in bond issues for BART. I do believe that my honestly being able to say to the BART board of directors, "Look, I know this system better than any of these guys from Merrill Lynch or Solomon Brothers because I used to live on BART," made the difference.

Though Glide was my saving grace back then, I did set a time limit for myself in terms of how long I would let myself stay there, knowing that I had some savings built up and that the time for my commissions to start adding up was just around the corner. Nobody was standing over me with a stopwatch or a calendar, of course. Still, I believed that if I could grab a few hours of rest during rush hour or stop in at that BART bathroom after sleeping at the airport or on the train, at least in time to wash up for work, then someone else could have a room at Concord Plaza that night. Or so I rationalized.

The one advantage to the BART station bathroom was that nobody else apparently ever thought of it, so there was no line to get in, not to mention that I didn't have to rush insanely at the end of the day to make sure we got there on time and there were no rules to follow other than my own. If I made it to Glide and got a room at the hotel, great. If I could get a locker at the San Francisco BART station and not have to haul gear for a night, even better.

A question now pulsed maniacally in my brain. Why was I putting myself and my kid through this? Why couldn't I slow down, take longer to get out of the rut, dig into my savings, and put us up back at The Palms? Why did I refuse to break the $20 bill that could have bought us a night at the trucker hotel? I followed my gut, which told me that breaking that $20 bill meant we might not eat. Twenty dollars was and is some real money, but when it's fifteen, twelve, seven, four, it goes fast. Having a pristine, unbroken twenty in my wallet gave me peace of mind, a sense of security.

But it wasn't just the internal struggle over each and every expenditure that was raging inside me. There was also a fight of a much bigger and different magnitude, a battle royal between me and the forces that would control my destiny. These were the same forces that robbed my mother of her dreams, everything from her father and stepmother not helping her go to college, to my own father for giving her a child to raise on her own, to Freddie for beating her physically and psychologically, to a justice system that locked her up when she tried to break out of her bondage. Over the six, seven, eight months that I'd been without a home, a taunting voice that had lurked in the back of my mind now seemed to suddenly gather strength—right at a time when I could see the finish line. The voice mocked me, sounding a hell of a lot like Freddie, just telling me, *You slick motherfucker, think you so smart 'cause you can read and pass that test, but that don't make you shit, you big-eared motherfucker, WHO DO YOU THINK YOU ARE?* Sometimes it sounded like a damn sociologist, quoting statistics, telling me, *Unfortunately, your socioeconomic upbringing has predetermined that breaking out of the cycle of poverty and single-parenting is highly unlikely given the fact that you are among the 12 to 15 percent of homeless people who are actually working yet still can't manage a living wage.*

The voice made me angry and made me fight harder. Who did I think I was? I was Chris Gardner, father of a son who deserved better than what my daddy could do for me, son of Bettye Jean Gardner, who said that if I wanted to win, I could win. I had to win, however I was going to do it. Whatever more I had to do, whatever burden I had to carry, I was going to rise up and overcome. But the quicker my pace and the harder I pushed, the louder the self-doubting voice became. *Are you crazy? You're deluding yourself!* At my lowest point of wanting to finally give up, throw in the towel, call it quits, spend whatever money I'd accumulated, and hitchhike to somewhere else, I caught a second wind—a burst of confidence—as a feeling of grace found me. *Hold on,* that feeling said, *hold on.* And I do.

Early spring arrives, bringing more rains, but it's warmer outside, my paychecks are starting to grow, and my savings account balance tells me that I've got enough to afford a cheap rent. San

Francisco apartments are way too expensive, so that leaves Oak-land, where I start my hunt on weekends. There are hurdles of questions:"Well, how long you been on your job? You're not mar-ried? You've got a baby? What's going on? What's a man doing with a baby?"

Some of the questions are overt, some not. But the process does become somewhat discouraging as I keep stepping down, notch by notch, both in the neighborhoods where I'm looking and in my expectations. In fact, as a last resort, one Saturday when the weath-er's taking a break—no rain, even some patches of sunshine break-ing through the fog—I decide to go check in the vicinity of The Palms, back in the "Ho"-stroll.

As I'm passing by a place on Twenty-third and West, my atten-tion is grabbed by the sight of an old man sweeping down a front yard—or really, more a patch of what could be called a front yard, now covered in concrete, with blades of rebellious grass still poking up from the cracks. It's not the grass that amazes me but what I see just in front of the little house—a rosebush. Of all the times I might have walked by this spot, I never saw this house, and certainly not that rosebush. Come to think of it, I never saw a rosebush any-where in a rough urban part of town like this. I'm fascinated. How do you get roses in the ghetto?

I strike up a conversation with the old man, whose name is Jackson. By the count of wrinkles on his brown leathery face, ei-ther he is really up there in years or he has seen some rough living. After some friendly chitchat about the weather and my good-looking son, just as I get ready to keep on rolling, I notice that the front windows of the house are papered over.

"Anybody living in here?" I ask Mr. Jackson, nodding at the house.

"No, ain't nobody living in there," he says, explaining that he and his family own the building but live in an upper unit. They've been using it for storage for almost three years.

"Is it for rent?"

"It could be," he shrugs, then offers to show me the unit and the work that would be involved.

The minute we walk in, right as I'm drowned in a funky, musty smell of a place that hasn't had any light or air in a long, long time, I see this whole downstairs space, covering the entire length of the building, and the smell is suddenly minimal. It's so beautiful, even in the dim lighting, I'm speechless. There's a front room, then a big-ass bedroom perfect for Christopher, a bathroom, over here a kitchen, next to it a dining area, and there's a little doorway to another room that could be my bedroom.

Now comes the test. "Can I rent it?" I say, right at the top, and before he can say no or start the qualifying questions, I let him know from the get-go, "Look, I'm fairly new on my job. I have my baby here, and there's no wife in the picture but—"

"Son," he says, "you can stop right there. You done told me everything I need to know. Y'all can move in here."

For a few moments I don't trust that it's over, that the long night of homelessness is over, that I've won. Mr. Jackson confirms it by saying that all I need to give him is the first month's rent and a $100 cleaning deposit.

"What if I clean it up myself and save the hundred?" I counter.

As he studies me for a beat or two, my heart races as I worry that he'll change his mind. Then he says, "Okay, son."

This was it. This was the most beautiful spot in the world to me, somewhere to call home for me and my son. There is no feeling in the entire emotional spectrum of happiness that can ever come close to the feeling I felt in those moments and on that fine spring day and in every day that followed whenever I returned in my mind to seeing that rosebush in the ghetto and having it lead me to our first home off the road of homelessness.

Appropriately, it was not long before Easter, a celebration of rebirth and resurrection, a time of new beginnings, new roads. To remember this time, from these days on I made it a point of trying to get back to Glide for Easter Sunday each and every year—no matter how far away or busy I was—not to relive the painful memories of where I'd been before but to celebrate the miracles that happened next.

Part Three

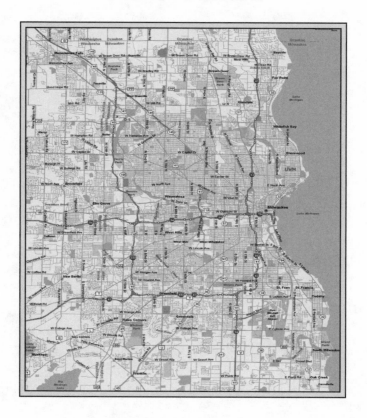

CHAPTER 11

Roses in the Ghetto

Everyone wanted to help as we began life in our new home—in our Oakland, California, inner-city version of Kansas. The minute I called friends who hadn't heard from me in a while, the offers started pouring in. There was the card table one friend had in his basement that we could have, a real bed and a mattress that someone else offered, sets of towels and dishes that weren't being used. As long as I could find a way to go pick the stuff up, it was ours.

My good friend Latrell Hammond insisted that I come get the five pounds of neck bones she had just bought that day. What the hell, I'd never cooked neck bones, but I went and got them just the same, figuring that I'd have some OJT in the kitchen, and then I went out to buy a secondhand freezer. At the grocery store, where the butcher, Ms. Tookie, had the hots for me, I got some helpful hints on the basics. And when the prospect of having to take on another domestic chore got me overwhelmed, I was set straight by the sight of a single mom with bags of groceries and two kids, plus a briefcase. If she could do it, so could I.

Friends from the different neighborhoods and stations in my Bay Area journey came over to help me get rid of the junk in the house and to clean the place, which was immediately improved simply from air and sunlight, which eradicated most of the musty smell. The place looked cool. Hell, it was the Taj Mahal compared to where we'd been staying.

Christopher was my number-one helper, not only with the mammoth undertaking of cleaning the place but also in helping organize our tasks and reminding me of what we had to do. "Poppa," he asked me before we moved in, "can we fix the backyard?"

I went to check out the three years of jungle growth back there and told him, "Not yet, son. We have to have a machete back here, and I don't have that yet." Step by step, though, inside, the place came together quickly.

After our first night in the new place, as we prepared to leave early that next morning so that I could get Christopher to day care and then get myself back on the train in order to get to the office on time, he became very concerned that we didn't have all our gear with us.

"It's okay," I explained and pulled out the single house key to show him why we didn't have to take everything with us. "We got a key, Christopher, see."

He looked at the one unassuming key in my opened palm and didn't get it. "Pop," he said, pointing to the duffel bag with all our stuff and my hanging bag with my second suit, "we have to carry this."

"No, son," I told him, "you don't have to carry nothing. We got a key. Let's leave all of this here, all right, and we can just go."

With a puzzled smile, he made sure that he understood. "We can leave it here?"

Bending down, bringing my face close to his, smiling with my own sense of wonder and relief, I repeated what I'd said. "Yes, we can leave all this stuff here."

Together we used the key to lock up, almost giggling, and then turned to go to the BART station, practically skipping all the way there.

It was still bizarre to me that we had journeyed in a full circle from the time I first found us a room at The Palms. Why had I never seen this place? The world had changed for us since then, and yet our four-hour round-trip commute every day took us right by the working women around the corner who remembered us from before.

"Hey, little player," they still called to Christopher, even though he was no longer in the blue stroller, which he'd outgrown, but walking hand in hand with me or playing a little game that the two of us liked to play to pass the time as we went to the BART station and back—taking turns kicking an empty plastic orange juice bottle. "Hey, little pimp," they'd call and sometimes hand him a $5 bill, just like before.

That was still manna to us. For one thing, it was usually nine o'clock at night when we returned from the city, so cooking wasn't the first thing I was dying to do, not to mention it wasn't my expertise yet. For another thing, the money was still tight, even with the modest rent I was paying. So $5 was dinner around the corner at Mossell's where the jukebox played Christopher's favorite song, "Rocket Love" by Stevie Wonder. Every time we walked in, somehow it was always playing, cause for Christopher to alert me, "Pop, it's Stevie. Stevie!" He already had great taste in music and in food.

After I ordered, he got to dig in first, and then I'd eat what was left over. As he and his appetite grew, I made sure to order whatever they served that would stretch the furthest—like red beans and rice with cornbread. We became such regulars that after a while the owners let me go on a payment plan, running us a tab that I'd pay off every two weeks when I got paid. We stuck with ordering the one plate, even then. Survival habits were hard to break, and I continued to look for every opportunity to save money.

But when the rice and beans came, I had to splurge on the jukebox so Little Chris could hear "Rocket Love" again. What a joyful image—my son chowing down as he grooved to his song, singing along and nodding his head. The hunger pangs and the salivating weren't necessarily joyful, especially one night when I watched him really go to town on that one dinner. He saw me watching, put down his fork, and said, "Why aren't you eating?"

"Naw, you go ahead and eat, son," was what I said, but frankly, I was thinking, *Damn, you're going to eat all of the food?* At almost two and a half, he could already eat like a little horse. Apparently he had learned at his young age that you eat it when you can get it.

This was also the case during the pizza party seminars hosted by Dean Witter at the recommendation of a consultant named Bill Goode, whose expertise was qualifying individuals as prospective investors on the telephone. I'd gotten pretty good but was always open to learning from the big guys. The concept was that after work a group of six or so of us would stay late and all call every single person in our book and let them know, for example, that there was a new stock offering coming out from companies like Pacific Gas & Electric. Amid the smiling and dialing, we could enjoy pizza on Dean Witter. I was able to go to day care, get Little Chris, and bring him back. As long as he could have some pizza, I was sure that he would be nice and quiet.

"Here, son," I told him at the first pizza party as I got back to work just in time for pizza to arrive and the dialing to begin, "you sit right here with your pizza. Poppa's got to talk on the telephone, all right?"

"Poppa, you're going to talk on the telephone again?"

"Yeah, I'm gonna talk on the telephone again."

"Pop, you're going to still talk?"

"Yeah, I'm still talking."

"Pop, you like to talk?"

"Yeah, son. I like to talk. Have some more of this pizza."

Pretty soon I was laughing and dialing, and so was the rest of the office.

Since Christopher was so eager to help, no matter what the

undertaking was, it occurred to me that I should enlist his assistance in getting him admitted to the Oakland day care center where they had the misspelled "happyness" sign. If we could do that, our long days of leaving at five in the morning and not returning until nine at night would be so much more manageable. The only hitch was potty training. He occasionally told me when he had to go to the john but wouldn't bother most of the time.

On the train headed back after the pizza party, I made my proposal. "Son, look, you want to help Poppa?"

"Yes!"

"The way to help Poppa," I said, "is when you think you might want to go to the bathroom, just raise your hand one time. When you think you might want to boo-boo, just raise your hand twice, okay?"

"Okay," he said, beaming, as though he was happy to have a job that was just his.

We made it a game. Sure enough, he was potty-trained in two weeks and enrolled at the day care center right next to the BART station. Our new routine was about as close as I could imagine at that point to a vacation. In the morning at 7:00 A.M., I dropped him off at day care, grabbed my train, and arrived at work early. In the evening I was back in time to pick him up at 6:00 P.M. so we could get to our soul-food greasy spoon for dinner, and afterward we stopped in to visit TV Joe—who owned a store by the same name that sold and repaired televisions.

A friendly, smart guy, Joe didn't mind if we just stopped to chat or if we sat down to watch television for a while. Most likely he figured out that we didn't have a TV set, but he never mentioned it. In fact, when there was a major sporting event being televised, like a Muhammad Ali fight I watched there once, we timed it right so that we happened along to catch whatever broadcast it was.

After dinner, a little television, and a visit with TV Joe, our last stop before heading home was to cruise by The Palms as the ladies of the evening gathered at their posts, several calling to me and my son, "Hey, Chris! Hey, little pimp!"

To Christopher, they were like family now. "Hey!" he waved back, knowing that even if we already had dinner, he might be lucky enough to be given one of those $5 bills he was used to getting.

Then we'd roll on down the street and come up to our house. A block away I had my hand in my pocket, making sure that key was still there. It reminded me of how nervous I was when I flew cross-country with the diamond ring in my pocket for Sherry. But the key was worth ten times the Hope Diamond to me. What I loved about it so much, I don't know. It wasn't attached to a key chain or key ring. It was just this bare little key. But it was ours.

And the feeling of elation I got every time I saw the roses blooming in the ghetto in front of our place and when I put my foot on that step, that first step, never diminished. What it meant, every time, to put my foot on the step with the key in my hand and to unlock the door and finally step into the house, is impossible to explain. It was the opposite of powerlessness; it was the antidote to the fear of not knowing what was happening that night, where we would go, how we would manage. The key was like the key to the kingdom, a symbol of having made it this far, all the way from where I had been, at the absolute bottom of the hole, to where I was now—an incredible transition.

Were things still rough? Sure they were. But they were manageable. Now that I could cover us having this home base, day care, transportation, and food, I felt that I could air my head out, just like the house, and then really kick into a higher gear at work. It wasn't that our worries were all behind us, a reality I faced early on in the new place when I missed a couple of electric bills and the electricity was turned off.

I set up candles, telling Christopher, "C'mon, you get to take a bath by candlelight," trying not to let him see that I was upset or overly frustrated about what was really only a minor setback in the scheme of things.

Even so, as I scrubbed Little Chris in the tub, I couldn't help fretting about how I could really accomplish the big vision if I continued to be dragged down by so much daily minutiae. Yes, of course, I saw the progress, but where I wanted to be still seemed too far in the distance. My most distinct thought was, *I ain't superman!*

At that very moment, out of nowhere, my son stood up in the bathtub and said to me, with a very serious look on his face, which was illuminated by the light of the candle, "Poppa, you know what? You're a good poppa."

Aw, man, I melted, forgot the worries, the minutiae, and knew that I was going to be fine. Coming from that little boy, those words were all I needed. Christopher could always cheer me up or give me whatever spark was missing at the time.

A photograph taken of the two of us not long after he made that comment summed up what this period was all about. I called it the "Picture of Two Lions." In it, Christopher and I are sitting side by side in front of our house, right on that top step, and I'm looking above the camera lens, as if off into the horizon, with a proud, determined Poppa Lion face and a king-of-the-pride expression that says, *Where's the next meal coming from?* And on the face of my son, the lion cub, is a look that says: *I'm hungry. I'm hungry.*

That framed everything, that Picture of Two Lions, erasing all doubt in my mind that I was doing the right thing. We weren't looking back. Never. My focus was on that horizon. What was next? How did I pursue it? What did I need to know to make it happen?

———

My learning curve became activated again when Dean Witter brought in one of the company's top producers, a super-smart, no-bullshit powerhouse by the name of Gary Abraham from Las Vegas, Nevada. Tasked with visiting different branch offices and helping the greener guys build their business, Gary clicked with me right away.

In person or on the phone, whenever I called up for advice or to touch base, he was down to earth and available, asking, "Hey, how you doing? What's happening?"

In spite of Gary's easygoing demeanor, he was razor-sharp, a wizard, chockful of insights about what he was doing and how he had built his business. One of the concepts he helped me begin to understand—something I wouldn't really master until later—was the idea that rather than telling someone what they should buy and why they should buy it, a much more strategic, productive approach was to find out what my customer wanted to buy. In my understanding of supply and demand, this approach made a lot of sense, although applying it practically was going to take time.

When Gary was starting out in Vegas, where there's always an influx of new money, always booming, instead of doing the phone thing, he went out to scout locations for new developments, where they were building million-dollar homes in various states of construction.

"You called on them in person?" I asked, trying to see myself doing something like that.

Gary recalled, "You bet. I put on my best blue suit and went and rang the doorbell on each and every one of those houses, without an appointment, and introduced myself."

Man, I wanted his script, his formula. What he had done and how he had done it.

There was nothing brilliant about it, he insisted. "I just said, 'Hi, I'm Gary Abraham, I'm with Dean Witter here in Las Vegas, and I'd like to know if there is anything we can do to help you settle in here, and by the way are you involved in the stock market?'"

That kind of maverick approach was exactly what had made me take the long road by building my own book rather than sticking to the company program like most of the guys working around me. I looked at Gary and knew that's what I wanted to do, how I wanted to play the game.

At the age of twenty-nine, I came to the realization that I was inordinately fortunate to have been mentored—either directly or indirectly—by extraordinary individuals, true role models. What a cast of individuals I had pulling me forward, whether it was the early inspiration of Miles Davis, who first made me want to reach for greatness, or the determination to be on the cutting edge of whatever I did that Dr. Robert Ellis instilled in me, or the ambition to hit the numbers like Bob Russell back when I got my feet wet in business, or the belief and passion for making it on Wall Street that Bob Bridges and his red Ferrari first ignited, or the different styles of Dean Witter stars like Andy Cooper, Dave Terrace, and now Gary Abraham.

There was never a sense in my gut that these role models helped me more or less because I was black or expected more or less because I was black. If they did, I didn't pick up on it. Later I read a quote from Berry Gordy about how he achieved the big crossover appeal of Motown, why he was certain his records would sell to white kids as well as black kids. His point—that his music business success wasn't a black thing or a white thing but rather a green thing—resonated with me. In the financial arena that I was in, my mentors and the examples that I was learning from could have come from any background. It happened that most of them were white, but they were Italians, Jews, foreigners, WASPS, from all up and down the socioeconomic ladder. Success in this field wasn't a white thing or a black thing, it was a green thing. That was the measure—how much green you were moving and how much you were making.

Maybe without trying consciously, Gary Abraham helped me

identify which of my strengths were going to help take me to the next level. At the top of that list was probably the ability to handle volatility—experience plucked right out of my life. This fact about myself struck me one day at work when the Dow started going crazy and went over 1,000, sending thrilling shock waves through the market. But one of the older brokers was beside himself. "You see that, son?" he said to one of the new guys. "It's all over. Sell everything."

We had been watching it inch up, around 850, then 900, in that vicinity. And when it broke 1,000 that day, he really thought it was the end of the world—which to a stockbroker translates as "Sell everything."

Volatility and change had been the watchwords of my life. If I had learned anything it was that it's never the end of the world, no matter how bleak things can be. What this also showed at that time was that hardly anybody around me truly knew anything. Shocking. They had the talk down, as if they knew everything, but ultimately nobody had a clue as to what the market was really going to do. As a matter of fact, very few in the brokerage business have that gift. That wasn't my gift either, although I was going to be damn sure I knew the best analysts and paid attention to what they were saying. But predicting the market's ups and downs and permutations wasn't what I cared about.

What I did know was that the market was going to open. Then it was going to do one of two things: it was going to go up or go down. You could bet money on that. That awareness allowed me to stay steady, to offer assurances to customers that weren't bogus. Of everything I took away with me from this initiation period in Wall Street, where it was all about writing tickets, the most important principle I adopted was the commitment that if I was going to write a ticket, it had to be an honest ticket.

Gary Abraham said it this way: "Write a ticket that's going to set up your next ticket. Don't put somebody into something just to get a piece of business. Because that'll be the last piece of business you get from them."

Gary was a phenomenal resource whose advice I not only tried to follow but also never forgot and who never seemed at a loss for information or wisdom when I sought him out. In time I'd look back and was able to see that it was in San Francisco that I learned to sell, while it was New York that would really teach me the business. Little did I know until later that knowing the business and selling are two very different things. Gary Abraham sold the way great singers seem to hit those notes effortlessly. People wanted to work with him, yet he never pushed, he let them sell themselves.

He introduced me to the effectiveness of not trying to sell you what I got but to find out what you want to buy, or what you will buy, what you already own. Boiled down, the question was: *What can I show you that is similar to what you already own, that's going to meet your current objectives?*

That was the direction I wanted to pursue, a departure from *I've got this product and this stuff that I have to move, and I don't care what you want or already own.* Unfortunately, Dean Witter was a wire house like other, similar wire houses—a huge corporation with an agenda that was not always the same as that of its clients.

Nonetheless, even as my paycheck improved somewhat and as Little Chris and I ventured out for more of a social life on weekends, I began to wonder if I should scope out some options.

The thought was on my mind when we hung out in a blues club in our neighborhood where the band, led by Troyce Key, an itty-bitty white boy who went with the finest sister you ever saw, was hot. The food, cooked up for five bucks a plate by Shep, was hotter. Christopher lucked into a musical and culinary education as we sat there all night long, listening to the blues, eventually trying everything on the menu. Shep fried up catfish with rice, beans, greens, and sweet potatoes, did ribs on the barbecue, smothered pork chops and steaks, both drenched with gravy and served with piles of hot-water cornbread. Chicken came every way it could come: fried, smothered, stuffed, barbecued. And I had to break the ban against sugar so Little Chris and I could both have sweetened ice tea. The best.

Afterward, we made our now-familiar stroll past the whore stroll—or the "ho"-stroll—and we waved at the same girls, had our same exchange, and usually headed home.

During the weekend days, when summer came, I'd sit out on the front stoop and bring Little Chris out on our concrete patch of a front yard, letting him know it was fine to play with the other neighborhood kids who came around but to stay close to the house and especially to stay away from the street. With two lanes going each way, it was a very busy thoroughfare, with parking and lots of streets intersecting the main drag. Days passed quickly outside watching the comings and goings.

In one part of my brain I was figuring how could I do more of the Gary Abraham kind of selling, and in the other part of my brain I was here on a summer day in the ghetto, all kinds of music blaring from cars and stereos and boom boxes. Straight-up ghetto with a palm tree down on the corner and one rosebush that happened to be in my front yard.

One of my favorite things to do if we felt like an outing was to put Little Chris in the shopping cart that had come to replace his blue stroller. Since I was nowhere near being able to afford an actual automobile and never would retrieve the one that I shared with Jackie, the cart became our only wheels. Christopher referred to it fondly as our car, inquiring, if we went inside anywhere, "Poppa, where'd you park the car?"

On good weather days, we'd roll on through the neighborhood, straight down Telegraph all the way to Berkeley—one hell of a long walk. Walking along, I'd forget everything and relax into the Zen of it all, feeling the vibrations and the bumps coming up through the wheels of the cart and into my hands. Making totally different sounds from the stroller, the cart made its own ghetto music with a *cluclack, cluclack, cluclack* as it rolled along the sidewalk. In Berkeley we sometimes stopped by my girl Latrell's mother's house, grabbed a bite from off the barbecue, and turned around to walk the long way home.

We were returning from one such excursion in our "car" when the sunny day all of a sudden went cold and blustery, with rain that began to fall in heavy slats.

"Poppa," Chris said, looking up at me and blinking through the raindrops, "when we gonna get a car with a top on it?"

I must have laughed as loud as thunder. Of all the things he could have asked to improve on our shopping cart, it wasn't doors, or an engine, or leather seats. No, he wanted a top.

On another summer day I'm pushing the car over to a park in West Oakland and spot an elderly black couple loading food and supplies into a little wagon to take to a family reunion picnic. With all the space in our shopping cart, it's only right that I offer to help.

Little Chris immediately starts to check out the contents of their bags and serving containers.

"Christopher," I try to stop him.

The elderly couple think this is so cute and funny, they don't mind at all. When we arrive at the reunion, I'm helping them take the stuff out of the cart when someone hollers, "That's Willie's boy!" I turn around slowly and notice everyone is looking at me.

What can I do? Explain to everyone that I'm not Willie's boy, or just go along with it and have a bite to eat with all my kin? The smell of the barbecue's awful good. Taking my best shot, I turn to the guy who's just hollered and say, "What's going on? What's up with you?"

Instantly, we are seated and food is heaped on our plates. Treated as if we're royalty, we eat like absolute kings as all the while I'm being deluged with questions.

"Well, how Willie doin'?" "He still in jail?" "When he supposed to get out?"

Of course, I don't know anything about Willie, what he's done or how long he's been gone, so all I say is, "Well, you know, Willie, he's doing all right."

"That's right, baby," says a matronly woman, "now you want some more of this?" as she serves us our third helpings, adding, "You get you some of that 'tato salad over there."

Please! This is no manna, it's milk and honey, overflowing. It gets better as the party comes to an end and they start divvying up the food, telling us, "Y'all take some of this, now, and some of this over here, and that cake, just take it." I'm biting my lip to keep from grinning. We have a week's worth of food packed up in our shopping cart. Glory be.

Just as we're starting to say our good-byes, with everybody telling us to give their best to Willie, I find myself standing face-to-face with a pretty young sister and it is on.

For much of the time that my son and I have been on our own, the last thing on my mind is the sexual and romantic void in my life. Not that I quite qualified for the monastery, or that there wasn't potential around the office or with friends of friends, but until recently, even if there had been a will, there was no way to put it together.

There had been an awkward visit from Jackie once we settled into the new home, when she showed up to visit Christopher. Interestingly enough, even though Little Chris had asked about her on occasion, he didn't cling to her or react like I had during and after separations from my own momma. Maybe it was because he didn't know her that well anymore. Or maybe it was just how she related to her child. In any event, my feelings were much more complicated, in part because of the mixed signals she sent me, but mainly because of so much residual anger I'd never expressed to her. Well, she sho nuff got an earful from me this time around. And then we fucked. That's what it was, not even a sport fuck, for the release of it, but more, from my point of view, a literal fuck-you. If she had any intention of getting back together now that I was moving up—not there yet, but beyond the gates she had been so sure I couldn't enter—she saw that wasn't going to happen and split for Los Angeles as suddenly as she had arrived.

Little Chris asked where she'd gone, and I explained, "She's moving to Los Angeles. You'll see her again soon." That was all he needed to know.

Now the slate's clean, and here I am trying to hook up with this fine beauty at an Oakland park family reunion where I'm fronting that I'm related to someone named Willie.

Just as I'm getting ready to get her phone number, one of the older gentlemen steps over and says, "You know, that's your cousin."

I'm nearly busted. Thinking fast, I say, "Oh, wow, I haven't seen her for so long, I didn't recognize her."

His hand on my shoulder, kind of eying me, he nods, saying, "Yeah, I can understand. Plus she got real good-looking, so you probably hoped she wasn't no kin to you, didn't you?"

"You got that right, she sure did grow up to be fine!"

"Yeah," he echoes me and looks at the young sister, who rolls her eyes and turns to walk away. "She sho did grow up to be a pretty little thing."

A close call. It's too late to volunteer my true identity to prove that I'm not really related after all. Instead, I turn to him and say, "Thanks for telling me."

"Don't mention it," he says, waving good-bye to me and Little Chris as I hurry us on out of there.

While I was delighted to be pushing a cart heavy from all the leftovers, and amused by how well a case of mistaken identity had turned out, that day marked another turning point for me. We were through the storms, and we had found a place in the ghetto in which to lay anchor long enough for me to get my bearings. And I was inching up toward a couple thousand a month. My next move, whatever it was going to be, was to double that, at least. With that, I could afford to move us back to San Francisco, which was, without a doubt, the Paris of the Pacific.

For the first time in a long time, maybe ever, I didn't feel like it was all on me, slugging it, pushing against the odds. Still a dreamer, yet more of a realist than ever before, I knew this was my time to sail. On the horizon I saw the shining future, as before. The difference now was that I felt the wind at my back. I was ready.

CHAPTER 12

Sphere of Influence

Every day as lunchtime approached, a skinny little middle-aged guy showed up and took a seat in the cubicle next to mine in the bullpen on the trading floor at Dean Witter. Just doing my thing on the phone in the midst of fifty other brokers talking and trading, I barely noticed him or took into account that the reason he was there probably was to see Suzy, the beautiful blond broker whose cubicle it was.

When I did pick up on him, I figured he was a devoted client, stopping in to see his broker. In her late twenties or early thirties, Suzy was bright, energetic, and appealing in her miniskirts and high heels, with a bustline she either bought or was just very proud to have. Good at what she did, she was always going to do well in the game.

Whether or not he was a client wasn't any of my business anyway, so I had no idea that he'd been sitting there listening to me. It came as quite a shock then when he spoke to me out of the blue one day, saying, "What are you doing here? You don't belong here. Here's my card. Call me and come over. Let's have coffee."

Turned out this was not some guy coming to see his broker, but rather she was his girlfriend. It also turned out that this wiry Jewish guy who looked and talked like a white Sammy Davis Jr. was Gary Shemano, the managing general partner for Bear Stearns in San Francisco.

What was Bear Stearns? That was exactly what I wanted to know when I looked at his card. I asked around. The answer came back that Bear Stearns was, at this time, one of the most profitable private partnerships in the history of Wall Street. I knew the big wire houses like Dean Witter, Merrill Lynch, E. F. Hutton, and Paine Webber. These wire houses might have ten, twelve, fifteen thousand brokers, with all transactions and communications done on the wire. Bear Stearns had only six to seven hundred brokers, and instead of being mass-market—the mom-and-pop investors, folks wanting IRAs and utilities, meat-and-potatoes—this smaller partnership was going after bigger fish in the institutional investment business: banks, pension funds, insurance companies, money managers, bigger businesses.

Selling directly to individual investors, you can tell clients about a new product that might be a great idea and let them know about a new stock offering. You'll move some shares. That's because, at least back in the day, they weren't savvy about the markets and what was out there to buy. They were relying on you, the broker, to tell them. But the large institutions really know the markets, and that's not what they need a broker for. They're investing humongous sums and don't want a little this or a little that; they want a broker to put together a lot of this and a lot of that, in the most profitable way possible. Down in the basement of mass-market selling, it's that numbers game of hitting X amount of calls that eventually become X amount of accounts and X amount of growth. You don't play that with big business. Instead of making two hundred calls to two hundred prospects, you might make one hundred calls to one prospect before you ever meet.

Up there it was then—and is now—about building relationships. Up there, in the Bear Stearns way of doing business, it's about the sphere of influence, something I would come to understand infinitely better in the months and years ahead.

Still not that hip about this company, I stop in to see my branch manager about getting more money, not long after Gary Shemano gives me his card. It's basically a no-brainer as far as I'm concerned. The attitude in the past whenever I've asked for more money than the smaller commissions I'm eking out has been: "Don't worry about the gross commission dollars. They'll come after you open the accounts."

Now I go in to ask for more money because I've earned it—I'm opening new accounts and doing the Dean Witter program, meaning I'm selling what the company wants me to be selling and producing all the way, and feeling confident about it. While I'm there, I casually run the question by him because I'm planning on meeting with Gary Shemano. "Who is Bear Stearns?"

Eyes narrowing, my branch manager says, "Why are you asking me that?"

"This guy named Gary Shemano just gave me his card. Can we do some business over there?" I'm naive perhaps, thinking it's a new business contact I've scored, because I don't see this as a conflict.

The branch manager does. He also knows a lot more about Bear Stearns than I do. Apparently, he knows that Bear Stearns has no training program for brokers and because they're building up their retail operation, Bear Stearns is making a practice of scouting talent at other firms, pulling out brokers who've already been trained and licensed by other firms, and luring them to their side of the street. That's what my branch manager knows.

But I don't. All I'm doing is asking for more money.

"No," he answers, without any room for discussion. "You haven't done enough to deserve more money."

That was a shove out the door. I resented his attitude as much as I did when I was constantly being made Broker of the Day only to set up business that was promptly given to a white broker because the client wanted "someone with more experience."

But the deal was really sealed the instant I walked into the offices of Bear Stearns to have coffee with Gary Shemano. It was the same jolt of juice that hit me the first time I stepped inside a brokerage house, only harder, and my instinctual reaction, just like before, was: *Oh yeah, this is where I'm supposed to be.*

At Dean Witter, I was the only guy topping the charts with two hundred calls a day. Here everybody was on my wavelength, making those many calls in pursuit of a couple of high-echelon prospects. Major VIPs on the institutional level or individuals with significant net worth, portfolio managers, investment advisers, corporations, bankers, insurance-company executives, the chief investment officer for the State of California, the City of San Francisco, or the City of Los Angeles. They didn't have to take calls from anybody. So to get them to call you back, you had to have it going on.

These Bear Stearns guys did. That first time I was stunned by the intensity of what they were doing. I thought I was the only guy who could focus like that. Once again, I felt like I was coming home to a place where I belonged, at the same time that I was moving into a whole mind-boggling new dimension. You could feel the energy, like these guys at Bear Stearns were on steroids or something. At Dean Witter, the environment seemed composed, very officious, almost formal. Guys sat at their desks, often with their coats on, especially if a client was coming in. At Bear Stearns, the guys had their sleeves rolled up, their ties loosened, some of them with a cigar in their mouth or between their fingers, everyone connected, on the phone, hammering out a deal, trying to get a better price for their client, hunting down information about a security that nobody else had. The adrenaline was flowing. You could feel it, taste it, and touch it. You couldn't miss it. Even Stevie Wonder could've seen this shit!

The timing could not have been more perfect. As it so happened, Bear Stearns wanted to build on the growth the company had already achieved in the institutional business by doing more business with high-net-worth individuals who were now starting to show up as Silicon Valley was set to explode. Even though the mega-boom of the nineties was still to come, there were some rocket-scientist types already striking oil in the high-tech world, and Bear Stearns was gunning for a big piece of the action. This was the start of the halcyon days of restricted stock sales, promising IPOs, and new clients who yesterday were engineers making fifty grand a year but today had a couple million all of a sudden.

Bear Stearns wanted to be out in front to ask these new millionaires relevant questions: "Do you want to put your money in one thing or spread it out? Do you want to think about putting some away for your kid's college? Do you want to buy some tax-free bonds?"

Gary Shemano, not a shy, easygoing type of dude by any stretch, invites me for coffee and tells me that he thinks I'm the perfect guy to help Bear Stearns get a foothold in this end of the business—based on observing me at Dean Witter.

A descendant of many generations of San Francisco Shemanos, Gary is hooked up every which way all over town, besides being a scratch golfer. Passionate and excitable, he's a table pounder too, and that's what he's doing as he tells me, "You're wasting your time over there, you know? You need to be over here. Here's where you need to be. Here!"

Pounding the table myself, I say, "Yeah! I want to be over here."

"Okay," Gary says without batting an eye, "what do you need to get going? How much draw?"

Going for the honest truth, I ask for what I need for me and Christopher to get a nice place in San Francisco: "Five thousand." That's five times the draw I've been getting at Dean Witter.

"Fine," he says, no eye batted yet again. "And I'll throw in a fifty percent payout. Be over here in two weeks, let's go to work."

Whoa! For a second I wonder if I should have asked for more. But what I am offered is the ideal structure—guaranteed six months of drawing five grand per month, with a requirement for the next six months to make twice that for the company, in order to maintain it, with a 50 percent commission on every dollar earned over and above that. It's security, pressure, and incentive. Oh baby.

Leaving Dean Witter wasn't hard on either side. If I felt like I owed them anything for giving me my shot, my debt was repaid when I was informed that they were taking over all my accounts. All my detailed notes about what stocks my clients owned, where they worked, what their family histories were, names of pets and secretaries. All those accounts and the priceless information that I'd cultivated for months and months, handed out willy-nilly to the yokels who'd never called anybody.

My first day on the job at Bear, I have to work up the guts to admit that I've arrived without any of my former accounts. When I do, Gary sneers, "Don't worry about that. We don't want any of those people anyway."

The Bear philosophy is, "No trade is too big. No trade is too small. We want a shot at all of them." But I come to find out that they really want the former rather than the latter. This is good news to me. I'm in.

The first day I also get a chance to meet some of the guys who'll be working with me in the new retail room that Bear is starting up. One's a fellow named Jerry Donnelly who has his own cold-call specialist named John Asher, affectionately known as "Asher the Basher." Then there's Bob Edgar, a poker player who's not calling anybody, but his phone is ringing all the time. In a group of eight guys to spearhead this new business, I'm coming in at a top tier. Again, I'm the only black broker at the firm, which is no big deal for me or my new colleagues, from what I can tell.

With a combination of nerves and excitement, I'm arranging my new desk, trying to put away my pencils, when I hear a receptionist calling from the next room, "Chris, you've got a phone call, pick up."

Clueless as to who it is, since nobody knows I'm here, I pick up and ask, "Who is it?"

The receptionist tells me, "It's Ace Greenberg."

To myself I say, *Ace Greenberg?* Out loud to her, I say, "Ace Greenberg?"

I don't know any Ace Greenberg, but in unison everybody in the room with me says, "Take the call, take the call!"

The call is put through. "Hello?" I say, oblivious to the fact that Ace Greenberg is the senior partner and CEO of Bear Stearns, responsible for building the firm up to where it is at this point in time.

His call is to welcome me to Bear Stearns, to which he adds, "We want you to know something, Chris Gardner. Bear Stearns was not built by people who have MBAs. Bear Stearns was built by people with PSDs!"

PSDs? I'm stumped.

But before I can ask, Ace Greenberg explains, "PSDs are people who are Poor, Smart, with a deep Desire to become wealthy. We call them PDSs. Welcome to the firm, Chris."

Then the phone goes click. I have died and gone to heaven! Poor, Smart, with a deep Desire to become wealthy. That's me, to a tee, a PSD.

That phone call kicked it all off. It was *on*.

——

Over the next year, as my star rose at Bear Stearns, I found myself making another full circle when I moved myself and Christopher back into the city, to a beautiful second-floor apartment in a large corner Victorian building on Mason and Hays in Hays Valley. We were back in the 'hood, within walking distance of our regular day care center, living the San Francisco life, not lavishly, but with security and stability.

Filled with rented furniture, the apartment had hard-wood floors, two bedrooms, a big living room, and a fireplace. One of its most quirky assets was the bus stop right outside the front door: if our windows or blinds were open, whenever the bus stopped and people stepped off, it was as though they were going to walk into our living room for a visit.

This was the American dream, 1980s San Francisco style. We could make choices. If we needed something, we could buy it. We could stay home and I'd cook, make a sandwich or warm up some soup, or we'd go out to eat. The difference in not having that commute anymore was staggering. My biggest indulgence was taking a cab to work every day. Now, that was a luxury. It was six dollars, plus a buck and a half for tip, and I'd sit in the back and appreciate every second, like sitting in the back of a limousine in a slightly later era.

Having noticed that every time he saw me I was wearing the same suits—either the blue one or the gray one, with my white shirt and one of two ties—Gary Shemano had even given me an advance so I could get a new suit.

Gary was always sharp. He was partial to Brioni suits, alligator shoes, loafers, cuff links, beautiful ties, and an ever-present pocket square. Money didn't change me on the inside, but it definitely allowed me to give in to my clothes habit. As the months went on and my buying power rose, I had the resources not only to wear the kind of sharp suits I'd always loved but to add subtle touches of color and style that other guys might not be able to pull off. One of the senior guys at Bear Stearns, Dave "Socks" Cranston, with his distinctive accessorizing, was extremely impressed later on when I took to wearing fire red socks with whatever I was wearing. A sharp blue suit with a crisp white shirt and fire red socks. Subtle but strong. My first real splurge was one I could barely believe I'd gone and done: buying my first anaconda belt at Neiman Marcus. Four hundred bucks for a belt? It took me many months to feel okay about indulging like that.

But there was no splurge big enough for Little Chris as far as I was concerned. At two and a half, three, three and a half, even he understood what it meant to have new things. A new bed, new clothes, new toys. He was excited. What was more, he and I were so connected emotionally, he could feel my peace of mind. We could go do fun things in San Francisco, not because we had nowhere to live, but because we wanted to go to Golden Gate Park and fly a kite or try to ride a skateboard together that I'd made instead of buying—because I could. Now, unlike the days when he and I had to find shelter where we could sleep or escape from the rain, we spent rainy weekends going to the movies, sometimes seeing as many as three or four in a day, sometimes the same movie.

We went to see *Ghostbusters,* during which Christopher freaked out at the sight of the monster Pillsbury Doughboy thundering down the street. "Poppa," he whispered to me, "I want my seat belt on."

During one of our many trips to see Prince's *Purple Rain,* Christopher had an accident and peed himself, probably because we had stayed inside the movie house too long, but I snapped and said, "All you have to do is say, 'I gotta pee'!"

We marched up to the bathroom so I could wash him off, and he saw that I was still annoyed, just wanting things to always be easier, and he said very seriously, "Poppa, I don't want to make you mad. I want to make you happy."

There weren't enough times that I could tell him after that, "You make me happy, Little Chris, you make me the happiest!"

If I had learned anything about being a parent, that right there was the most important lesson, just as my son said it—kids don't want to make us mad, they want to make us happy.

It was unbelievable how many times we went to see *Purple Rain*—not just because it was entertaining but because it kept us out of the damn rain. We saw it so often that it was inevitable that we'd run into someone we knew, and indeed, not long after I'd started at Bear Stearns, I found myself sitting next to another new guy at one of the showings.

His name was Mike Connors, one of the smartest guys at the firm, and he was destined to be one of my best friends, and someone with whom I could launch a business one day. In Wall Street terms, even though he was white and I was black and we came from very different backgrounds, we were homies.

The atmosphere at Bear Stearns, leading up to the era of the avalanche of the eighties' mega-mergers, was conducive to everyone finding their own niche—that product or segment of the market you really know inside and out, your own little special group of institutions to pursue. One guy covered nothing but thrifts. Someone else handled bank trust departments. Another guy only talked to insurance companies. As I searched for what my specialty might be, just as I had been a complete sponge in the medical field, learning from Rip Jackson and Gary Campagna, I wanted to learn everything I could from the very best and master it, but right away.

Pretty soon that's what I was doing, learning not just how to get my calls returned but how to cultivate those relationships based on my command of information that my competitors might not have. So if Bill Anderson called, I could easily say, "I understand you've got a broker. Now, we're not interested in interfering with that relationship. However, we would like to be able to complement that relationship by showing you one or two special situations here."

A smart investor was almost always open to that.

"Great. The next time the partners at Bear Stearns are doing something, we'd like to just give you a call. Is that fair enough?"

The answer was almost always yes, because who would want to miss out on the chance at least to hear what the special offering might be? Another yes almost always followed that one in response to the question of whether I could send some materials out, along with my card. Thus, a relationship was established, so that when I followed up, it was not to waste his time but to build a rapport and a dialogue, to find out what Bill Anderson wanted to buy, what he had been buying, whether he liked or understood technology stock. Was he looking for some opportunities for capital appreciation? If he was older, was he looking for ways to supplement his income when he retired? What about his pension-fund assets if he was close to retirement?

Borrowing perhaps from my background in medicine and health care, I approached these conversations exactly in the same way we might have discussed something as vital and personal as his personal health—his personal financial health. In my own way, I was becoming Dr. Chris Gardner after all.

Thankfully, from the start the Bear Stearns brass liked what they were seeing me accomplish. Gary was a fan right out of the gate, but Marshall Geller was *the* guy, and the jury stayed out for a while with him. Gary ran the office, Marshall ran Gary. In fact, Marshall simultaneously ran offices for Bear Stearns in San Francisco, Los Angeles, and Hong Kong. Marshall—or "the Screaming Skull," as he was popularly known behind his back—was six feet tall, wore glasses, had thinning white hair that he managed to maintain in what I called the Jewish Afro style, and had a small overbite on his front two teeth that made him look almost cute. Indeed, much of the time he was the most charming, nicest, sweetest guy. But just like that, in a blink of an eye, he would lash out, "Do you ever fucking think? Do you people ever fucking think?!"

If Marshall was on your case, you could be in his office with the door closed and everybody on the floor knew he was chewing your ass out. I definitely tried to stay on his best side or avoid him altogether.

Eventually, however, when he saw me going over my call list one day and arranging the contact cards for the two hundred calls I had to make, Marshall decided it was time for a lecture.

"Hey, Gardnerberg," he said, using the nickname that made me part of the almost-all-Jewish club at the firm, "come here." I followed him into the conference room, where he pointed at the stack of contact cards still in my hand. "That's not how the big guys do it," he said, letting me know that the numbers volume game that I'd been trained to work didn't impress him.

I thought—*Well what do the big guys do?* But I said nothing.

"Let me show you how we do it here at Bear Stearns. Big guys do it through a sphere of influence." Seeing that I had no idea what he meant, he beckoned to me once more. "Come with me."

Down the hall we stopped in to observe Phil Schaeffer, a guy who supposedly could not tie his shoes, so he wore loafers. His sphere of influence included Walter Mondale, the soon-to-be Democratic presidential candidate. Phil's top client was the State of Minnesota's pension fund. Oh, simple, right? Great, but how could I get there?

"Sphere of influence," Marshall repeated, pointing me back to my desk, without one practical suggestion as to how I could develop that. The implication was that I would know it when I found it.

That would take me another twenty years, but in the interim, in order to build relationships, I still had to hit the numbers. I still had to work my magic to get past the gatekeepers, the secretaries who liked my Barry White crooning voice, and the proverbial alligators who would bite my head off if they even suspected I was calling their boss about an investment opportunity. Every now and then, I struck gold and the prospect actually picked up the phone. That was exactly what happened one day after I decided to pursue some Texas oil millionaires by cold-calling.

One of these cowboys who has a nickname like J.R. not only answers his phone but then hears me out.

"J.R.," I begin, "this is Chris Gardner out at Bear Stearns, San Francisco."

"Yeah, I know y'all, what you want?"

"Well, I just wanted to tell you about . . ."

"Well, look here, before you tell me anything, let me tell you something." Then he proceeds to tell me every nigger joke, every Jew joke, every spic joke in the world. Not knowing whether I should hang up or get on a plane to kick his racist ass, I get real still and just listen. Then, taking a breath, I return to right where I was before, pitching him on me and the firm.

That's all he needs to hear. "Okay, now," he says, "buy me fifty thousand shares of whatever you called me about and let's see how that works."

Fifty thousand shares at 50¢ a share was a commission of $25,000! For that much money, hell, yeah, I can put up with a nigger joke. And I do. I start calling him, and he throws me bigger business every time, always telling me all the most racist, demeaning jokes he's accumulated since the last time we talked, without repeating himself. To further my sphere of influence, I go on, laughing myself silly—"Hilarious!"—sometimes even finding a joke or two funny. Every now and then I do stop to think, *If only he knew that I was black.* Obviously, he has no clue.

Much to my chagrin, he calls me to say, "Hey, this is J.R. My wife is going to China. I'm going to bring my girlfriend up to Lake Tahoe, and we're going to stop in San Francisco so I can see this broker named Chris Gardner who has been making me all this money."

Oh boy, here we go. In a panic, flashbacking to the Broker of the Day era when all the clients had an issue with the "more experienced" thing, I'm seeing all his business go away when he realizes he's been telling all those nigger jokes to a "nigger." Trying to stay calm, I remind myself that only one of two things is going to happen. In scenario A, he'll close his account with me, and that'll be the end of our relationship. In scenario B, if I play it right, he'll close the accounts he has at all those other places and let me handle all of his business. What can I do to play it right?

As it so happens, Marshall "the Screaming Skull" Geller is out of the office on the day J.R. and his girlfriend are coming. There's no one to say that I can't temporarily move into Marshall's huge executive office. Nor is there any harm in replacing his name with mine on the door. Thinking fast, I also take all those pictures of his cute white family off his desk and put them in his drawer.

My secretary and colleagues agree to go along with this temporary setup, saying nothing. When J.R. and his woman companion arrive, they are welcomed by my secretary, and she leads them back to come see me. When J.R. walks in, I'm sitting in Marshall's big chair, looking out his window at the spectacular view of San Francisco, and pretending like I'm talking on the telephone, just reaming somebody's ass out in unedited, colorful vernacular. As if just noticing my Texas visitors, I hang up, whip around in my chair, and say, "Hey, J.R., how you doing? Have a seat. How about a cup of coffee?"

Literally, I can see blood draining away from J.R.'s face. He is in fucking shock. It's not just the nigger jokes and the color of my skin, although that's enough to give him a coronary. It's also that he's a short, little, wide cowboy—clean-shaven, in his midsixties, with a crew cut, gleaming aviator glasses, jeans, some kind of boots made out of the hide of an endangered species, and a big-ass buckle, like he's just won some rodeo—who has to look up to me to shake my hand. His girlfriend—not a spring chicken, though younger than J.R., also taller than him, with the big blond hair and the big chest—just looks on, not sure what's happening but apparently happy to be anywhere other than where she's usually tucked away.

So here I go, spreading out paperwork on the close to half a million he has invested with Bear Stearns, in a full report: every position, every recommendation, every stock we ever put in his portfolio, where we bought it, where we sold it, and the percentage gained. Showing him how much money I've made him so far, the numbers look good: between a 34 and 35 percent return. This is my shot to go for double or nothing. Straight out I say, "Based on these numbers and what you've let me know about the other accounts you've got, we need to be doing more of your business here, J.R. What do you think?"

What he thought, it turned out, was that I was right. It seemed that he had undergone an epiphany and seen the light: it wasn't a white thing or a black thing, it was a green thing. He closed his accounts at Goldman, Lehman and Morgan and at wherever else he had his money invested so that I and Bear Stearns could oversee all his business. From then on, with his account alone, I probably made $200,000 a year. Interestingly enough, after that visit he stopped the nigger jokes. In all our contact that followed, he never uttered the "n" word again. He still told me a couple Jewish jokes and a couple spic jokes, but by all indications he was henceforth down with his black brethren.

Because I did *all* his business and he was my biggest account, he was the first phone call I made every day, financially more than compensating for all those nigger jokes I had endured at the start.

Every day our morning pow-wow began with my report on what the market looked like for that day and my recommendations on whether we should sit tight or trade. Because of the vast amounts of money I was making for him, his answer was always, "Whatever you think, Chris."

This went on for over two years, starting there in San Francisco and continuing after I made the inevitable move to New York City—to work at the Bear Stearns office there on the real Wall Street, the mother ship.

While not all brokers have to go to New York to hit the big time, from the moment I had fantasized about being in this business, that was always part of the dream. It was embedded in my DNA, part of being a PSD, just as it was inevitable that I had to buy that Ferrari one day—which I did, by the way, after I moved to Chicago in the late 1980s to establish my own company. Then again, dreams do change. While my first Ferrari was red, the second one I bought was black. In fact, I bought Michael Jordan's black Ferrari, and as a symbolic gesture that only Moms and I could truly appreciate, my personalized license plate read NOT MJ.

When I was seventeen, my mother had set me on the path, letting me know, in effect, that I didn't have to be a basketball player to make a million dollars. Seventeen years later, I proved her right when I made my first million for that year alone. To get to that point, once I started to make a living as a stockbroker in San Francisco, it was always in my mind that I had to go live in New York. That was to be the ultimate proving ground: like the song said, if you could make it there, you could make it anywhere.

Lots of folks in the San Francisco office weren't happy with my decision. My buddy Dave "Socks" Cranston warned me the minute he heard that I was leaving the West Coast: "Are you fucking crazy? Do you know to live like a fucking dog in New York you're going to have to make three hundred thousand fucking dollars your first year?"

"Yeah, I know," I lied.

I didn't know, and damn if he wasn't right. Plus, what he didn't know was that besides having to support myself like a dog, my income now had to cover not one but two kids.

Yep, surprising as that might sound, by 1985 I was the proud father of a gorgeous, brilliant, amazing baby girl named Jacintha Gardner. Her mother was Christopher's mother, Jackie, my ex. Conceived during a visit that Jackie made to see Little Chris, Jacintha, like her brother, was always going to have me in her life, and I was always going to be there for her. This was despite whatever issues I had with her mother. For twelve hours that one night when I gave in yet again to the sexual temptation that Jackie had always been for me, I actually convinced myself that we were supposed to get back together. Even with everything that had happened before, there was a part of me that thought, *Well, for Christopher's sake.* Maybe now that the money wasn't so tight and I had established myself in the business, she'd have the chance to pursue her goals. God knows what I was thinking. Sometimes, it seemed, I had to just put myself in the fire in order to find out that's how you get burned. It took me less than twenty-four hours to come to my senses.

When I decided to move to New York, Jackie, now pregnant, was busy campaigning to get back together. While I was adamant that the possibility was out of the question, I did propose that, with my financial help, she should have Christopher come live with her and our new daughter in Los Angeles. This was a practical choice, considering that I would most likely be working even longer hours and making Little Chris adjust to a whole new day care system. She eventually agreed, and ultimately getting to spend some time with his mother was the best thing for him, even though I went through horrible separation pains those first few weeks apart.

Going in, New York was as daunting as everyone had told me it would be. Fortunately, I had just scored a new account that helped set the stage for me to make a splash in the New York office. Again, just like with J.R., this was the result of a cold call.

The guy I contact while dialing numbers in Las Vegas is a fellow named Ed Doumani, who says in response to my introduction, "No, I don't buy too much stock, but I might want to sell some stock."

Not sure where this is headed, I'm polite and say, "Well, what stock is that?"

Ed casually notes, "I own a piece of a little company down here in Las Vegas, and I'm thinking about selling some shares."

"Oh, yeah? What company is that, Mr. Doumani?"

"The Golden Nugget," he says.

"Great," I say, then ask, "how much of it do you own?"

"About six million shares."

Not skipping a beat, I let Ed know that Bear Stearns specializes in restricted stock sales. "So let us know if there's a way we can help, and if there's a way we can help you to minimize the tax bite."

"Yeah, I'd be interested in that."

After I hang up the phone, somewhat in a daze, I have to figure out how I'm going to play this out. It takes me a while to put the pieces together that Ed and his brother Fred are the producers of the scandal-ridden movie *The Cotton Club*, along with Bob Evans and some other cats, not to mention that the Doumani brothers are having some issues with the New Jersey gaming commission.

Rather than trying to pull off the trade for six million shares of stock myself, I put Ed and Fred together with the right people at Bear Stearns—which turned me into an overnight star by the time I arrived in New York. Bringing in six million shares, or about 6 percent of the ownership of the Golden Nugget, gave me instantaneous credibility with the heavyweights at the New York Bear Stearns office. The buzz was: "Who is this fucking guy in San Francisco? How did he get this? Who does he know?"

It wasn't only that I was handing their office what was potentially a ten-million-share trade, it was also that Ed Doumani would only talk to me and he wouldn't talk to nobody out of New York without me on the telephone with him.

So even though I had a lot to learn to hold my own with these guys, I came in with a few arrows in my quiver. What I came to see right away was that Bear Stearns, east or west, was kind of like the Oakland Raiders of Wall Street. Everybody there on both coasts was tough and talented, many were PSDs, and many didn't necessarily go to Harvard. There were plenty of colorful characters, but the bottom line was that in spite of the competition, everybody cared about each other, and everybody at some point and time was there for the other. The difference between the Bear offices in San Francisco and New York was a lot like the difference between those two cities. Bear Stearns in San Francisco had energy, drive, creativity, opportunity, and super-bright people. The New York office of Bear Stearns was all that, but on steroids! Everything was done to the nth degree. The added intensity suited me and I suited it. Plus, there was a whole new level of challenge. Where I was coming from, we were writing tickets, taking commissions on every trade we made. In New York a lot of the cats were talking about establishing a fee-based business that would eliminate the need for writing tickets—setting up a revenue stream of, say, $3 million a year.

That was the business I wanted to be in. But how? Same as I always had done, by asking questions: "How do you do that?" The answer was to get into the asset management business for clients. One of the guys broke it down for me, and I was frankly flabbergasted.

"Let me see if I got this right. So somebody gives you one hundred million dollars a year to manage. They pay you fifty basis points, so you make five million dollars a year?"

That was the sphere of influence Marshall Geller had been talking about. In the meantime, between the Doumani brothers, a couple of other meaty accounts, and J.R., I didn't start my New York Bear Stearns adventure empty-handed. But then, early in 1986, J.R.'s secretary called me to say, "Chris, I've got bad news. J.R. died in his sleep last night at home."

It was really bad news. My biggest account was gone! This wasn't going to kick in down the road, this was immediate pain. That was because, when an account dies, trading is halted by the estate, which then comes in and divvies everything up between a whole host of vultures and beneficiaries. Ironically, over the last few days J.R. had been worried about the market and telling me that we should sell everything and just go to cash. So to honor his last order, I picked up the phone and sold every last share in his portfolio, taking my $60,000 commission as a repayment for all the nigger jokes. The estate had nothing to say about it, not after all the money I'd made for him and his heirs.

But with good old J.R. gone, I wasn't looking to replace him with a similar type of account. My idea was to give the fee-based asset management business a shot. On a cold call, yet again, I connected with Bob, an executive who was in charged of a fixed-income portfolio for an Ohio company called the Great American Insurance Company. We hit it off, and he was interested in working with me, but there was a problem, as it turned out, in that the company was supposed to already be covered by Bear Stearns. To be on the safe side, I called Ace Greenberg, the CEO and senior partner who had first introduced me to the meaning of PSDs. Asking for his okay on my covering Great American Insurance, I was fine when Ace checked out the situation and told me, "Here's the story, Chris. You can cover the account, but I want to hear from you once a week. I want to hear how you're doing." Click.

Two weeks go by, and I'm working with Bob, showing him ideas, bonds, all kinds of things, and he likes what he's seeing and gives me my first order for starters. And it's a $25,000 ticket. Not bad, and I'm in the institutional arena. Thrilled, I call Ace and tell him, "We just made $25,000."

Dead silence. After a pause, he says, "Gardner, you're fired." On the spot, this is it. His reasoning? "You've been talking to this guy for two weeks and all you got out of him was twenty-five grand?"

For about the second time in my life I know what it means to have a sphincter muscle engage that prevents me from shitting myself. Being fired by Ace Greenberg is the end of my career. There is no higher appeal, no higher court.

Before I can think of what to say, the biggest belly laugh you ever heard comes booming over the phone line. Ace says, "Nice going, Chris. Have a good day."

That was a definite rite of passage into the world of institutional investment, and an example of Ace Greenberg's perverse sense of humor. The experience also opened my eyes to the intense competition for the institutional market. To have that cutting edge, to be able to offer something unique, I developed an innovative strategy in the months that followed for going after that asset management and fee-based business the other New York guys were talking about. But my approach was strictly my own. It was a multi-step process that involved first contacting the number-two person in the management hierarchy and offering some special investment opportunities and then, when there wasn't interest right away, tracking in real dollars what they had turned down. Three months later I would place a call to the number-one person at the company and note that I had called before, saying, "I would have been calling you to send you a check for one hundred thousand dollars, but you didn't feel that it was of interest at the time. Here's what I'm calling you about now. . . ." Almost across the board immediate interest and some subsequent trading followed.

As I was mastering this strategy, it finally dawned on me what business I really wanted to be in, the market that was being grossly ignored by Wall Street, the niche that I would be allowed to develop in New York and that would soon become a key part of my own business when I opened up shop in Chicago.

My idea was to go after this untouched market and offer prospects the scope of the products and services provided by Bear Stearns—one of the most profitable firms in the history of Wall Street. What was this untouched market? Well, I wanted to start calling on African Americans. I wanted to manage money for individuals in the sphere of influence shared by Quincy Jones, Stevie Wonder, Oprah, Michael Jordan. I wanted to invest not only for famous entertainers and athletes but on behalf of black institutions, black banks, black insurance companies, black entrepreneurs and executives, black foundations. That's what I wanted to do. Besides the fact that nobody else was pursuing this market, I liked the idea of promoting minority ownership and prosperity.

With the support of Ace Greenberg and my other bosses at Bear, I went to town, sometimes hitting, sometimes missing. But at the end of the day, which took place in early 1987 when things really started to roll, I was doing so much business that no one questioned my decision to take the next leap and set up shop under my own auspices.

This was a huge risk, maybe the biggest of my life, and would require that I start pretty much from scratch. It also required some financial assistance and someone who believed in the ambitious vision I had for my enterprise. The person who stepped forward with a willingness to invest in my dream was a gentleman by the name of W. J. Kennedy III, chairman of the North Carolina Mutual Life Insurance Company, the largest minority owned insurance company in the country.

I was going forward. The vision kept expanding. In addition to the minority business, I wanted to honor my hardworking uncles and manage money for the labor market. I wanted to invest for educators and proponents of public education and literacy. To create the rainbow coalition of expertise that I envisioned, I wanted to hire PSDs, maybe not exactly like me, but with similar abilities to dream big; I wanted to take the same kind of chance on cultivating potential that Dean Witter and Bear Stearns had taken with me. To grow my business, I wanted to explore some ideas I had about what I eventually began to call "conscious capitalism"—both as a personal philanthropic interest in returning a percentage of my business profits back into public sectors in the areas where I made the money and as a way for investment to encourage potential and opportunity on a global level. Some of these ideas had been shaped by the Reverend Cecil Williams and Glide Memorial Church, and others had come from some reading I had been doing in advanced economics; I'd stopped by public libraries whenever I could, just to reassure Moms that I hadn't forgotten all of her advice.

By picking Chicago as the town in which to plant Gardner Rich & Company, as I dubbed my enterprise, I had once again made a round trip, returning to a spot not far from Milwaukee and

Moms, as well as a town where I had plenty of relatives. This move made sense because Chicago was a city where six-year-old Christopher and two-year-old Jacintha—both of whom moved from Los Angeles to Chicago—could grow up and have a place to call home. So in a sense, I had circled back around. But I was breaking new ground as well, by raising my kids, I had broken the cycle of fatherless children that my own father had started.

As my company grew and my dreams materialized, giving me the opportunity to work for institutional pension funds and assets to the tune of several billion dollars and to nurture the growth and financial health of organizations like my top client, the National Education Association, with its millions of members, I lived out that other dream of getting to travel and see the world. The women were everything Uncle Henry had described and more.

All that travel is inevitably exhausting, but it never gets old. Arriving in the next city for the next opportunity is always a thrill. As busy as I am, wherever I am, I try to get out and walk the streets, to check out the sidewalks for cracks, to remember how far I've come and appreciate every baby step of the way, to stand in amazement and joy that the pursuit never ends.

Blessed Beyond the Dreams of a Thousand Men

April 2004

Nothing can prepare you for the stark beauty that is Johannesburg, South Africa, as you descend through the clouds and behold the southern outline of Africa spreading out below you. It is indeed a living map.

No matter how many times I've visited South Africa, each time I return I experience an emotional intensity unlike anything else I've known. Those feelings are made even more intense as my plane touches down for this visit, in April 2004, after I received an invitation from the leadership of COSATU (Congress of South African Trade Unions) to be one of two hundred observers from around the world to observe the 2004 elections—a monumental event that will coincide with the celebration of the tenth year of democracy and freedom for the people of South Africa.

While I had accepted this invitation—this honor—with great pride, I threw in a caveat, saying, "I will not leave South Africa without having a one-on-one meeting with Nelson Mandela." Fine, I was told; if I could be patient, they would make it happen.

Excited about the total experience, upon my arrival I do something that I've never done in my life—I go out and buy a camera, intent on capturing the reality of what I am about to witness, the culmination of ten years of democracy and freedom. I, like so many millions of South Africans and people all around the world, am in a state of awe. Who knew this would ever come to pass?

During my first visit to South Africa, I was accompanied by a man I've come to regard as a father, Bill Lucy of AFSCME (American Federation of State County and Municipal Employees) and CBTU (Coalition of Black Trade Unionists), and he introduced me to Mr. Mandela. Mr. Mandela shook my hand firmly and said words to me that I'd never heard from a man in my life. "Welcome home, son," Mr. Mandela said to me.

I broke down and cried like a baby. At that time, to be forty-six years old and have Nelson Mandela be the first man to ever say these words to me was worth every day of the no-daddy blues.

Now, four years later, I am back. On April 14, election day, all international observers have been placed in small groups after receiving credentials and instructions the previous day. I am placed with two black South African women, both of whom are experienced observers and veterans of the struggle against apartheid that has been going on their entire lives. My camera at the ready, we begin our rounds in East Rand, then journey on to Alexandra, Orlando, and finally Soweto. Seeing the unbelievably long queues— or lines, as we call them in the USA—of black South Africans, all standing with such grace, dignity, humility, and patience, I do not take the camera out of my pocket one time. To do so would have been as disrespectful as taking pictures in church.

The faces strike old and familiar chords in me, as if they might be folks I know from back in Chicago, New York, Oakland, Milwaukee, or down home in Louisiana. These folks, however, seem to know that I'm not from South Africa. I later mention this and ask Jan Mahlangu of COSATU how everyone knows that I'm not South African. With a smile, Jan says, "It's the way that you walk. You walk in like you own the space. Must be all the time on Wall Street."

I can't help but laugh.

Election night finds me in a polling place converted into a fortress. Our tent is in a parking lot in downtown Johannesburg, not far from the Nelson Mandela Bridge. Our instructions are simple: among others, "no one in and no one out" until we've all agreed on a final count. My first thought is, *No more coffee or fluids.* There is no restroom in our tent. Finally, after some very long, tense, and sometimes anxious hours, we are done. As expected, the ANC has captured 86 percent of the vote in our count alone.

For me it is very interesting to observe not just the count but also the interaction between the blacks, coloreds, and Indians. The chains of apartheid, while physically broken, are evidently still psychically functional.

Continuing to digest much of what has transpired during my visit so far, on April 15, 2004, my wait for my appointment with Mr. Mandela officially begins. As I was made aware, the anniversary of South Africa's democracy and freedom is being celebrated around the world with seemingly every country on the planet sending representatives, ambassadors, and heads of state. My place in line, while secure, seems to be very fluid. No problem, I'll wait.

During my waiting period, the inauguration of Thabo Mbeki to his second five-year term is another unprecedented experience in my life. Black folks have never looked so good, so beautiful, so royal. It is almost life imitating art—in a scene right out of Eddie Murphy's film *Coming to America,* a procession and ceremony take place at the Union Building, the South African White House, and on its enclosed lawn, equivalent to our Rose Garden. Cheers erupt while leader after leader makes an entrance. The Jumbotron monitors show the crowd across from us, numbering over 100,000 folks awaiting the inauguration and subsequent party. Finally, there is a roar like nothing I've ever heard. It can only mean one thing: Mandela has arrived!

At this stage in my life, I have had the pleasure of sitting courtside at NBA playoff games, ringside at boxing matches, and in front-row seats at concerts, but I have never in my life experienced a sound like 100,000 souls crying out, "Mandela!" Again I cry, and others around me ask why. They can't understand, but as I approach nearly fifty years of life, this is the first time that I've ever seen a black president!

My sobs are drowned out only by the sounds of three 747s from South African Airlines that fly over our heads in a salute to the president.

In the days that follow I use my time awaiting my meeting with Mr. Mandela to prepare. Nelson Mandela was trained as the first black attorney in South Africa and went on to found the firm of Tambo and Mandela with ANC leader Oliver Tambo, his dear friend. I keep this in mind in preparing to make a case—a clear, concise, compelling case.

I also find the company that manufactures the beautiful silk shirts that Nelson Mandela always wears. "I have a meeting with Mr. Mandela," I announce as I enter their main offices. "You must make me a shirt. I want to be appropriately attired."

While continuing to wait, I explore Johannesburg, Soweto, and Cape Town, and my eyes are opened in ways they have not been before. I used to think that I knew something about poverty. You have not seen poverty until you've seen it in Africa. My heart aches as I see and learn more about the conditions that human beings are forced to live in. Yet in spite of this abject poverty, there is a sense of hope everywhere I go. The sense among South Africans is that, yes, things are difficult, yes, we need jobs, yes, we need housing, yes, we must address HIV/AIDS, but yes, also for the first time in all of our lives we can dream. The impossible is now simply possible.

The waiting is not stressful at all. The sense of what is possible eases the passing days. I also find the exact place where I will one day live. The property is not for sale, but, yes, it is possible.

Again preparation consumes me. I have two pages of notes to discuss, which I condense to two envelopes front and back, then to one envelope front and back, and finally the phone rings. "Mr. Mandela will see you tomorrow at 11:00 A.M.," I am told.

I'm ready. I've waited twenty-seven days, but I figure Mr. Mandela waited twenty-seven years in prison, and I stayed in a much nicer place than he was in. When the morning arrives, the only decision that remains is which of the fabulous silk shirts I will wear to the meeting. Hazel, my favorite employee at the Park Hyatt, looks at them all and selects the most regal shirt of all, explaining, "That's the one—you look like Madiba!" She is using Mandela's clan name to describe the shirt and why I must wear it.

I'm accompanied to the meeting by one of the leading businessmen in South Africa, Eric Molobi, who at one point was also imprisoned on Robben Island with Mr. Mandela.

I have never been so positively tense in my life. I've been in a few big meetings with what I'm sure are very important people, but this is mythical, beyond the realm of anything that has happened to me before or since. Only a few true heroes have mattered to me—my mother, Miles Davis, Muhammad Ali. The fact that I'm about to meet Nelson Mandela, a hero personified, makes me realize what it is to have an out-of-body experience.

Finally, Mr. Mandela's personal assistant, Zelda, comes to escort me in, informing me that I've been scheduled for fifteen minutes with Madiba.

I walk through the door, and there he stands, ramrod straight, looking nothing less than royal wearing a fabulous "Madiba" shirt. Sensing the tension in me, he proclaims in a most majestic voice, "Chris, why are you wearing my shirt?"

I totally relax and sit across from him as directed. Eighty-six years old, he moves purposefully but gingerly. The eyes, however, are scanning me. These are the eyes of an eighty-six-year-old freedom fighter who for most of those years had to look at someone and make an instant decision: *Can I trust this person? Is this information correct? Is this worth my time?*

I begin to make my case. U.S. public funds have increased their allocations to emerging markets around the world but have not returned to South Africa. A very significant number of the "young Turks" in the U.S. labor movement who led the movement to divest American companies of South African investments are now presidents, secretary-treasurers, and trustees of their pension funds. As such, they are in a position to influence, control, or direct billions of dollars of capital. On a comparative basis, South Africa has outperformed all other emerging markets. South Africa has recently celebrated ten years of democracy and freedom. Just as capital was once used as a tool to help create change in South Africa, capital can again be used as a tool to help sustain the growth and development of South Africa.

Zelda comes in and gives the international hand signal for "time's up" and says, "Mr. Mandela, the ambassador is here for his appointment."

Mr. Mandela speaks again in his rich, majestic voice. "Tell the ambassador he can wait."

Now I'm really pumped. I conclude my pitch with a comment that I clearly see touches a nerve. "Sometimes the stars just line up," I remark. "This is our time. This is my time. This is my opportunity to use everything that I've learned in twenty-five years of working Wall Street and capital markets to help make a difference in the world for people that look like me." It's an opportunity, I tell him, to make economic freedom as available as political freedom. Mr. Mandela asks a few questions after I'm done and finally says, "How can I help you?" I mention specifics, and we agree to see where my idea takes us.

At long last I am able to use the camera I purchased for the election, asking Zelda to take a shot of Madiba and me, sitting side by side. It remains my most valued possession to this day.

We shake hands, and I lean down to kiss his forehead. He smiles. He knows what our time has meant to me. I am prepared to go forward, prepared to pursue.

Ironically, as I leave the meeting and pass by the ambassador who has been kept waiting for forty-five minutes, he and his entourage look at me, all appearing to wonder, *Who the hell is this guy?*

In this same time frame, continuing with the pursuit of my concept of conscious capitalism, I flew from South Africa to San Francisco where I met with Rev. Cecil Williams in order to discuss his vision for the economic development of the Tenderloin (my old 'hood). Cecil's basic idea was to purchase an entire square block in the 'Loin to be developed into a complex large enough to include a small convention center, retail stores, and restaurants, even parking, but most importantly affordable housing for working people in downtown San Francisco. The meeting concluded with the decision that our original plan be scaled down from purchasing the entire square block for approximately $250 million to select sites and properties at a cost of close to $50 million. It was never the size of this undertaking that motivated me. It was truly about coming full circle. It's not business, it's personal.

What is the American dream if it isn't about the possibility that someone, anyone, can go from walking the streets of the Tenderloin and wondering how to take the next step to being able to help provide safe affordable housing in that same neighborhood for working folks? After all, studies have shown that approximately 12 percent of all the homeless people in America have jobs and go to work everyday. More and more Americans are seeing the dream slip away from them and that's wrong. And, by the way, the attainment of wealth that we all want to strive for shouldn't be about the attainment of money. In fact, I've often been asked how much money equates to real wealth. My answer is always the same. By my definition, money is the least significant part of wealth. My net worth is not among the Forbes 400, nor is it my ambition to be so listed, but I am healthy, have raised two children as a single parent (blessed with a village of support) that have become outstanding young people, and I'm in a position to do work that reflects my values. That's my definition of wealth.

Wealth can also be that attitude of gratitude with which we remind ourselves everyday to count our blessings. It has been a blessing for me to have been able to break the cycle that prevented me from having a relationship with my father—one of the reasons I was so intent to be there for my kids. And they have been there for me. My son, Christopher, and my daughter, Jacintha, are two remarkable young adults, and really some of my favorite people in the world—so much so that I hired them to work for my company, not just because I love them but also because they're hard working and capable. They have always made me proud to be their father and have always given me true happiness.

Being happy, for a workaholic like me, can also mean taking some time off from the pursuit of this, that, and the other to have some fun. June 26, 2005, presented me with such an opportunity. Our firm hosted a party for the National Education Association in Los Angeles. My partner, Ndaba Nstele, flew in all the way from South Africa. Sydney Kai Inis, our special-events coordinator, once again outdid herself by producing Grammy-award-winning artists such as Dave Koz, Jonathan Butler, and Waymon Tisdale for the event. To raise funds for the NEA Black Caucus, we arranged a raffle. First prize was two round-trip business-class tickets to South Africa, including a ground tour package. The total value of the trip was over $30,000 while the price of a raffle ticket was only $10 and we sold a lot of them.

The celebratory atmosphere and coming together of wonderful friends and clients was unforgettable while the true highlight of the evening for me personally was an opportunity to pay thanks to so many who have been part of my journey—all of our NEA family, and a special acknowledgment of my old boss, Marshall Geller.

It was Marshall Gellar who gave the final nod to my being hired at Bear Stearns and who taught me the value of the sphere of influence. To this day, Marshall never knew how I used his office as a prop when J.R., my racist joke-telling client, decided to visit me in person that first time. But Marshall did know my heart. He saw me, day in and day out, attempt to make a quota of two hundred phone calls a day, often while he stood over my desk, and ultimately commented, "That's not how big guys do it, big guys do it through a sphere of influence." It took me the next twenty years to develop that sphere. Recently, I think that I've gotten the hang of it. I've got to tell you that it is amazing who you can get on the phone when you can honestly say that Mr. Mandela suggested I call.

In addition to fund-raising for the NEA's Black Caucus, our party in Los Angeles was to honor dear friends and educational powerhouses, Anne Davis of the Illinois Education Association and Linda Poindexter-Chesterfield of the Arkansas Education Association—both of whom were retiring after decades of representing public school teachers and school support personnel. The event, which attracted close to eight hundred representatives of the NEA, was a perfect venue to publicly say thank you to Marshall. My mom always taught me that the most important words in the English language are *please* and *thank you*.

For many kids growing up, I reminded the crowd, sometimes there is only one person in their life, often a teacher or employer, who is willing to give them that chance, that vote of confidence, that needed break. Marshall Geller, I explained, was someone who'd given a break to a young stockbroker named Chris Gardner.

Marshall followed up my comments by telling the crowd he was in the business of making lots of decisions, some good ones and some bad. "Chris Gardner turned out to be a good decision we made," he said with feigned modesty, even though he couldn't hide his almost paternal pride.

The one person who was missing from this unforgettable night was Moms. Had I never been able to share my success with my mother, it would have broken my heart. Thankfully, before she passed away ten years ago, she had a chance not only to see me prosper but also to share in it. For some time, Moms didn't understand what the hell it was that I did for a living. After numerous explanations and attempted analogies, I finally put it this way: "Let's say all these companies that I represent are at the casino and I'm the house." That clicked for her.

Toward the end of her days Bettye Jean wasn't at all well. What her body and her psyche had been put through over the years had taken their toll. If money could have given her back her health, I would have spent every dime I had to give that to her. But that wasn't possible, and when I got the news that we had lost her, I and my sisters were fairly certain that Moms, that pretty lady who first came to make candy for me so very long ago, had hastened her own death by drinking when her doctors had forbidden it.

Losing Moms did break my heart, creating a void in the world where once her smile had been—the sight of which I will miss until the day I die. There was so much more to come that I still wanted to share with her, to make her happy.

That was what I told my Aunt Dicey Bell when I got caught up with her back in Chicago to let her know about all of the exciting happenings, not only the NEA party but the unfolding projects with Glide and my partnership with Pamodzi Investment Holdings in South Africa. I had grown up right and had graduated to become a citizen of the world, credit due to many who took those chances on me, but no one more so than Moms. It was so important to me that she know how far I had been able to come, thanks to her.

Aunt Dicey Bell assured me that my mother was exulting in every single glorious second of all my adventures. "Chris," she said to me, and it was all I needed to know, "right now your momma is in heaven dancing with her wings on."

That was so perfect; just the way she said it, I had to believe that it was true. She was dancing with her wings on and making sure that I continued to be blessed beyond the dreams of a thousand men. Absolutely.